JOURNEY
TO
TRIUMPH

JOURNEY ✶ TO ✶ TRIUMPH

110 Dallas Cowboys Tell Their Stories

CARLTON STOWERS

tpc

TAYLOR PUBLISHING COMPANY
Dallas, Texas

Book design by Kathleen Ferguson

Copyright © 1982, Taylor Publishing Company
1150 West Mockingbird Lane, Dallas, Texas 75221

Library of Congress Cataloging in Publication Data

Stowers, Carlton.
    Journey to triumph.

    1. Dallas Cowboys — History. 2. Football players
— United States — Biography. I. Title.
GV956.D3S76 1982 796.332'64'097642812 82-60136
ISBN 0-87833-330-4

Printed in the United States of America

For Pat,
who makes the journey a joy

The author wishes to thank the *Dallas Cowboys Official Weekly* for permitting in this book materials which appeared earlier under his byline in its pages, though sometimes in slightly different form. Too, a special thanks is due *Weekly* editor Steve Perkins who first originated the idea of seeking out former Cowboys players for their reflections of playing days gone by. And there is the Cowboys organization which so generously provided use of the photographs included in this tome.

★ CONTENTS ★

THE CHAMPIONSHIP YEARS

✯ INTRODUCTION ✯

When I took the job of coaching the Dallas Cowboys, I thought it would be something I would do for a few years, maybe four or five. . . . You see what happened to those plans.

Looking over the list of players in this book makes me glad I decided to stay around. I really don't think I had any idea what I was getting into. Since we were the first expansion franchise in the league's history, we had no guidelines, no yardstick to measure our progress. For whatever reason, though, I was always confident that we would eventually build a solid team. Quite honestly, I was never aware that there were a lot of people in Dallas in those early years who would have liked to see me get on to some other profession even earlier than I had originally planned. It just never occurred to me that I might be fired. I felt secure and confident — probably to a point of being naive — that things would work out.

The players, of course, had much to do with that feeling. I think players like Eddie LeBaron and Dick Nolan, who you'll read about, helped set the pattern for the kind of players we would eventually have on the Cowboys. They were the kind of individuals I wanted to begin building a team with; players who were intelligent, competitive and good, solid citizens.

And their grasp of what we were trying to do in those early years helped me a great deal. Then, eventually, we got more and more quality players like Bob Lilly and Lee Roy Jordan, and confidence began to build.

I suppose if I were forced to point to one aspect of coaching that has been the most enjoyable over the years, it has been watching various players develop and reach high levels of performance: A guy like Jethro Pugh, who came to us from a small school like Elizabeth City College and developed into a solid NFL player; Dave Edwards, who advanced from the taxi squad to become the kind of player you could count on for a steady, high quality performance every week; Rayfield Wright, who played safety at Fort Valley State before becoming a great pro tackle; Cornell Green, who made the transition from college basketball player to All-Pro cornerback; and Walt Garrison, who performed to the full limit of his capabilities every time he stepped on the field. Those are the things you remember.

As you read the following pages, I think you'll see there has been a consistency in the quality of players we've had. Players who have come to us have quickly realized that our philosophy is to develop our own, that there is some measure of security to be enjoyed with the Cowboys. We don't do a lot of trading and we've always given a player a chance. If he comes in and proves himself, he's got a job with us.

It has also been interesting to watch the changes in players over the years. There was a time when you coached everyone the same, as a group. You didn't really deal with players individually. Then, however, some changes began to take place. The players we were getting were products of the post-war affluent society. They were more independent — which was good — and they wanted to be treated more as individuals than as just one of the group. The coaches who weren't adjusting to that social change didn't stay around long. Today, coaches deal with the individual athlete far more than when I was playing or even in the early days of my coaching career.

Still, it is my belief that players like discipline. They want to know the rules and the boundaries. I think they realize that in a team sport discipline is the key if you are to ever succeed. Discipline is one of the methods a coach uses to gain the respect of his players.

I hope that the players included in this book have left with some measure of respect for me as a coach. That's what you strive for in this business. When it is all over, you hope they have a good feeling about what you tried to do for them, that they benefited from having been a part of it all.

Tom Landry

⭐ PREFACE ⭐

He was, the records indicate, a halfback of modest talents during his prep school days and later wrestled in the 126-pound division while an undergraduate at the Massachusetts Institute of Technology. The fact that he graduated Phi Beta Kappa, however, far overshadowed any athletic legacy he might have left.

Still, Clint Murchison was and is a sportsman in the truest sense of the word. A man who oversees a myriad of corporations and business interests, he has still found time in days gone by to serve as coach of a YMCA Little League football team in Dallas. Among his numerous holdings are golf courses, tennis clubs, ski lodges, automobile speedways, an air rifle company and an outdoor magazine.

And the Dallas Cowboys.

Acquiring the latter was a dream of long standing. As early as 1952 he tried with no success to purchase the struggling Dallas Texans and keep them in Dallas but the franchise had already been promised to Baltimore where it would come to be known as the Baltimore Colts. In 1954 he had all but completed the financial arrangements to purchase the San Francisco 49ers when the deal fell through. In '56 and '57 he tried unsuccessfully to acquire the Washington Redskins franchise and spoke on more than one occasion with the owners of the Chicago Cardinals (who would later make their home in St. Louis).

By 1958 he'd been encouraged by word that the NFL would announce expansion plans for the 1960 season and, due to his longtime interest in securing a franchise, he likely would head a list of potential new owners.

His motive for campaigning so earnestly, he insists, was not so much financial as it was basic fan interest. "I've always been interested in pro football," he says, "and have always loved watching it. I just wanted to have it here in Dallas."

Even before his dream would become reality he was mentally laying the groundwork for his new team. It would operate first class, with the best front office personnel available and the best possible man to head the best coaching staff. He would call his team the Dallas Rangers.

On the advice of Chicago Bears owner/coach George Halas, one of the pioneers of modern day professional football, Murchison hired a young man

1

with the unlikely name of Texas E. Schramm away from his job as assistant sports director at CBS-TV to serve as his general manager. Though the franchise was not yet in hand, Schramm was advised to begin seeking out players who could be signed as free agents to supplement the players Dallas would receive from the rosters of the existing franchises.

The franchise, which Murchison would later rename the Dallas Cowboys, was awarded on January 28, 1960, to Murchison, his brother, and longtime business associate Bedford Wynne. They paid $50,000 for the franchise and $550,000 for the players they would eventually draw from the other twelve NFL teams.

Even before fielding a team, they had competition for the local entertainment dollar and fan support. Another millionaire businessman in Dallas, Lamar Hunt, who had tried unsuccessfully to gain an NFL franchise, had bought into another league and brought his American Football League Dallas Texans to do battle.

The initial Cowboys team, composed of woefully unprepared players, staggered through their first season without a single win while the AFL Texans, drawing (and initially playing) better, finished with an 8-6 record. Neither team, however, turned a profit. The Cowboys, suffering the worst of it, lost $700,000.

Now, however, the Texans are gone; off to Kansas City. And the Cowboys have developed into one of professional sports' most traditional winners. They have come farther faster than anyone dared to expect.

This is the story of the Dallas Cowboys climb to "America's Team" as told by over a hundred players who saw things from an inside vantage point. It is, in a sense, a history of the Cowboys, told by those who were the most important participants in its making — the players.

It is a story told with the insight of men who were there, through good times and bad. Those who heard the locker room gossip, were in attendance at the weekly team meetings and stood on the sidelines on Sunday experiencing the feelings of victory and defeat. They played the game, they earned their honors and they contributed mightily to the legend the Cowboys have become. And they had their fun along the way, slipping out after training camp curfew, sending head coach Tom Landry's young son on a late night snipe hunt, and pulling all manner of practical jokes on one another.

The tome now in your hand tells more than the history of a team that climbed from the depths of its inaugural, winless season in 1960 to travel to the Super Bowl five times. It is more than a reflection on memorable triumphs and All-Pro performances. This is as much the story of the Tom Franckhausers (the first Cowboys player ever to carry the ball in a NFL game) as it is the story of Bob Lilly (the team's first Hall of Fame inductee). The reflections of a zany kicker named Sam Baker play as much a part in the complete story of the Cowboys as do the remembrances of Roger Staubach, the team's most productive quarterback.

It is also a story of success beyond professional football glories. Former Cowboys have gone on to become college professors, bank executives, lawyers, television personalities, authors, high school teachers, general managers and coaches at the pro and college level, heads of multi-million dollar corporations, priests, ministers, golf professionals and stockbrokers. Without exception they point to their days in a Cowboys' uniform as a valued step toward the careers they've established.

It is unlikely that even a man with Murchison's foresight could have imagined what his team has become or predicted the status it would demand in the world of professional sports.

"Frankly," he admits, "pro football was not a big money sport when I entered the league. We lost something in the neighborhood of $3 million before we finally began making a profit in 1965. And since 1966 the profits of the Cowboys have not increased. They've been up one year and down the next. That, I realize, is hard for some people to comprehend, particularly in view of the fact that television revenue has gone up dramatically and attendance is so good. There are just so many expenses of which people aren't aware. The truth of the matter is that football is not a highly profitable venture because it isn't really a growth business. There are only so many tickets you can sell. The only real growth you have is the TV revenue and much of that filters down to players' salaries, as it should."

Why, then, would a man regarded as one of the world's shrewdest businessmen wish to own an NFL franchise?

"The reason is very simple," Murchison says. "It is the same now as it was back in 1960. I love pro football and wanted to see it played in my home town."

Carlton Stowers

★ THE ★ PIONEER YEARS

They began as a band of castoffs, has-beens and never-wases. A roguish collection of characters Damon Runyon wouldn't have dreamed of creating. They were the Dallas Cowboys, a team in search of identity and respectability.

For the first time in National Football League history a team was fielded without benefit of the player stockpiling a draft affords. Instead, the twelve existing teams in the league were advised to "freeze" twenty-five players on their respective rosters and Dallas was told to pick three from each team. Needless to say, there were no All-Pros to be found in the marketplace. Instead, the first Cowboys team was built with players in the twilights of their careers, players with no real futures in the game and players who had, for whatever reason, become thorns in the sides of other managements.

Dallas had twenty-four hours to select the thirty-six veterans who would provide the backbone of their first squad. That accomplished, they brought in busloads of free agents, hoping to find talented athletes. "There was," recalls one player, "one bus leaving and one arriving daily. It was a real revolving door operation."

For every Don Meredith and Eddie LeBaron that reported to that 1960 training camp in Forest Grove, Oregon, there were half a dozen Bobby Lunas and Duane Putnams and John Gonzagas. The younger players, making their first attempts at pro ball, were baffled by the complex system head coach Tom Landry was bound and determined to install. The veterans who had seen their better days in other NFL outposts, bucked it, collectively pleading they were too old to learn new tricks.

From the confusion and frustration was molded a team which went through the first season without so much as a single win. For five years the Dallas Cowboys were light years removed from dazzling, in fact, never coming close to a .500 season.

Fan attendance was poor and many of those who spent their hard-earned dollars in support of the rag-tag band began to shout to management for Landry's dismissal. Dallas lost no love on its loser.

The Cowboys did, however, get a good laugh now and then. It was in the 1962 season that they made their first mark in the NFL history books, losing points to a penalty. Quarterback Eddie LeBaron had thrown a 99-yard touchdown pass to Frank Clarke in a game against the Pittsburgh Steelers but officials threw a flag on guard Andy Cvercko who had been caught holding in the endzone. Thus instead of a touchdown, Dallas was penalized and the Steelers were awarded a two-point safety.

Such were the difficulties in the pioneer days.

TOM FRANCKHAUSER

★

The Ultimate Trivia Test

Casting modesty to the wind, Tom Franckhauser says he may one day be recognized as the all-time trivia leader of the Dallas Cowboys. Not that he is one of those who clutters his mind with an endless list of little-known facts. Franckhauser, for that matter, could care less about trivia. He's not, you see, one who asks such questions. Tom Franckhauser is the answer.

On opening day of 1960, the official birthdate of the franchise, Franckhauser received the opening kickoff against the Pittsburgh Steelers. By doing so, Tom assured himself a spot in the trivia annals. He would forever be remembered as the very first Dallas Cowboys player to touch the football in a regular season game. Take that to your next cocktail party.

"I wasn't aware that it was such a favorite trivia question," the Dallas resident says, "until a few years ago when Norm Hitzges was doing some kind of magazine story, using a lot of Cowboys trivia. He called my secretary, Laurie Garrett, whose husband Tony is a radio personality. Norm wanted to get in touch with Tony to ask him a question about the Cowboys.

"Laurie told him that her boss was once with the Cowboys, suggesting that maybe I could help him. Norm asked her who her boss was and when she told him it was me, he broke out laughing. 'He's the answer to the question!' Norm said.

"I had never really thought about it," the former Purdue wide receiver-turned-defensive back says, "but it had to have been either Bill Butler or myself since we were the ones returning kicks in those days."

Both players should have been paid overtime in that 12-game 1960 season. Franckhauser returned 26 kickoffs for 526 yards (a 20.2 yard average) and Butler fielded an equally large share of returns. Such are the memories of that 0-11-1 season. "We had some talented players," Franckhauser says, "but just not enough of them. We were a lot like an oil slick; we came from everywhere but we just weren't very deep."

Franckhauser came to Dallas from the Los Angeles Rams where he spent his rookie year making the transition from receiver to the defensive backfield. Once a member of the Cowboys, he was tried briefly again at end but soon asked to be moved to the secondary. He quickly became a starter at cornerback and played the position for two season before being traded to yet another expansion team, the Minnesota Vikings.

"That move," he recalls, "made me aware of just how much groundwork the Cowboys had laid to get things going. They were the first expansion team,

7

and went through some rocky times and a lot of trial and error. Everyone else, the Minnesota Vikings included, went to school on what Dallas did and got their business in order a lot quicker than they would have otherwise."

Franckhauser's contributions to the Dallas cause were far from being limited to kick returning. In his first year he also tied Butler for the interception lead with three. A knee operation forced him to miss the first three games of the 1961 season but when he returned he regained his starting job.

"It was an enjoyable experience back then," he says, "even if we weren't winning and players were coming and going like it was a bus station. I'll never forget cornerback Don Bishop's arrival. He came to us from the Steelers after playing in an exhibition game for them on a Friday night and started for us on Saturday."

And while head coach Tom Landry was then forming the foundation of his unique offensive and defensive attacks, it was still, says Franckhauser, a simpler time.

"There were no specialty team coaches or specialty team captains back then," he says. "I don't remember that phase of the game being approached with the same intensity that it is today. About all we had then was 'return right' and 'return left' and let the offense get on the field. Soon thereafter, though, you could see that coaches throughout the league were beginning to realize that the specialty teams were an important part of the game."

Although he never scored on either a kick or punt return, Franckhauser had his moments. "I guess the longest one I ever returned," he says, "was against Baltimore. Lenny Moore had just scored for them and I took the kickoff at the five and returned it to the Colts 45 and we went on to get the touchdown right back."

After three later years with the Vikings and a frightening incident in which he suffered a broken blood vessel in his brain, Franckhauser retired and returned to Dallas.

JOHN HOUSER
★
A Fine Price to Pay

To most of those who endured the early days of Dallas Cowboys football, the memories give little cause to smile. The 1960 version of the team was a combination of aging veterans, wide-eyed rookies, contents and mal-contents; everyone running everywhere and getting nowhere. Eleven losses, one tie. Practices at Burnet Field where there was seldom any hot water for showers and the rats gnawed the tongues out of shoes and the padding from helmets.

Crowds in the Cotton Bowl consisted of little more than close friends and relatives.

"Yes," says former center-guard John Houser, "that's about how I remember it. Looking back, I'm not sure anything went right that first year." The onetime Los Angeles Ram who came to the Cowboys in that initial season has examples:

"Well," he says from his Colorado home, "there was the time our plane was 45 minutes late leaving because a rookie named Bob Lilly was late. Seems he had left the house in plenty of time and stopped at a drug store along the way to pick something up. He dashes in, dashes out — and his car is gone.

"Since he had left the keys in it, his first thought was that it was stolen. What had actually happened, he later found out, was that he had parked on an incline and had failed to put on the emergency brake. His car had rolled out into the street, gone down about a block and collided with another parked car. Before all was said and done, Abner — that was the nickname we had for him — got a ticket and was then fined for being late to the airport. It wasn't the greatest way in the world to start a road trip."

But then, Houser had already become aware of Tom Landry's fining system.

"When we traveled," he said, "you had the option of studying your playbook on the plane or putting it into a locker for safe keeping. If you lost it, the fine was $1,500. We were going to Cleveland and I chose to keep mine to look over. About halfway through the flight I was confident I knew my assignments so I put the playbook under the seat and went to sleep. The next time I thought about it we were on the bus, nearing the hotel where we were to stay.

"I don't want to get into salaries, but suffice it to say I couldn't afford to pay a $1,500 fine, so as soon as the bus stopped I jumped off, ran into the hotel lobby and called the airport control tower. The tower got me in touch with the pilot by radio, patched me in, and I told him my problem. He went back to my seat and found it. The problem was he was just fixing to take off for South Bend, Indiana, where he was to pick up the University of Oklahoma football team which had been playing Notre Dame. All I could think to do was tell him to hang onto the playbook and not say anything about it to anyone.

"But in a team meeting later that afternoon Coach Landry asked if anyone was missing his playbook. Someone had snitched. I told him I was but knew where it was. 'I'm sorry, John, but that'll cost you $1,500,' Landry said.

"Back then we had a player's grievance committee made up of people like Eddie LeBaron, Bob Fry, Don McIlhenny and Nate Borden, so I appealed. LeBaron was a lawyer, so I went to him. I pointed out that there was a very fine line between losing something and knowing where it is but not having it. He finally agreed. Besides, I pointed out, someone had finked on me. Eddie took my case to Landry and I got off with a $500 fine."

9

Then, there was one of the most memorable moments in Cowboys playing history, an infamous moment which has become a legend. And John Houser was not only there; he played a major role.

It was that '60 season and the quarterback was a young rookie named Don Meredith. At times things got a bit confusing for him. "I think everyone in the world has heard this story," Houser says, "but it's still fun to tell:

Of course, Landry's offensive scheme was pretty complicated with all kinds of colors and numbers and check-offs. Well, Don calls a play and we go up to the line of scrimmage. He starts calling the play: 'Blue . . . 42 . . .' and stops and pulls his hands away. The defense shifted, so Don checked off to another play. Halfway through calling it, the defense anticipated him again and he starts still another play. Finally, he just stepped back and said, 'Aw, hell, ref, time out.' The defense just broke up. It wasn't one of our finer moments."

Neither, for that matter, was the kickoff on a windy afternoon in the Cotton Bowl when Houser and other members of the kickoff team raced downfield and were a bit taken aback by the fact the receiving team was standing motionless, craning their necks to see what was happening downfield.

"It was a weird sensation going down full-speed-ahead and realizing that the opposing team was doing nothing to set up a return. They were all just standing around, looking downfield. Finally, I looked back to see what was going on and saw that the wind had blown the kickoff back behind our kicker. The 3,000 or so in the Cotton Bowl for that one really loved it."

Such were the early days, the struggling times.

"One of the biggest problems we had in the early going," says the former Redlands collegian who was with Dallas in 1960-61, "was our lack of leadership. No one — and I'm as much to blame as the next guy — wanted to step forward and take the role. There was an unstated atmosphere of being unwanted. A lot of the older guys were just wondering how long they could last and how much they could get before their time was over.

"And because Landry's system was so complex, there were times when he had difficulties communicating with us. Looking back, I wish I had tried harder to comprehend it all. To my way of thinking there is no coach who knows the science of football as well as he does."

Houser's career with the Cowboys came to an end with a knee injury in an exhibition game in '62. He sat that season out and tried to return the following year but suffered a second knee injury in a Portland, Oregon pre-season game.

It was a career as unusual as it was enjoyable. He had come to the Rams as a free agent after a Los Angeles scout, viewing a Redlands versus a George Allen-coached Whittier College game film, noticed his defensive abilities. He made the Rams team along with his rookie roommate, Jack (Gabby) Pardee, as a wedge-busting member of the specialty teams.

"You know," Houser says, "I called my own shot in a way. One summer I was in school there at Redlands, taking a few additional courses, while the Rams were training. One afternoon I was hitchhiking into Los Angeles and this fella gave me a lift. It was Tex Schramm who was then with the Rams front office. He didn't have a lot to say to me, me being a college kid and all, but I remember telling him, 'Mr. Schramm, I'm going to play for your Rams one of these days.' "

By the time Houser made the prediction come true, Schramm had moved, working as assistant director of sports for CBS Television. The next time he would see his hitchhiker was when, acting in the capacity of general manager of the NFL's newest franchise, he signed him to a Cowboys contract.

EDDIE LeBARON
⭐
Clubhouse Lawyer

In a world heavily populated by clubhouse lawyers, Eddie LeBaron was one who knew his business. While other professional football players in the '50s and '60s, concerned with contract negotiations and management procedures, spoke the jargon of the law loosely and with flaws, the former Dallas Cowboys quarterback had a degree upon which to base his arguments. "The only thing," says the man who owns the distinction of being the first starting quarterback in Cowboys history, "is I could never convince them to let me negotiate my own contract." And for good reason. His ability as an attorney rivaled his talent as a quarterback.

"If we'd let him get involved in that aspect of it," laughs president and general manager Tex Schramm, "I might be looking for a job today." Indeed, the man still looked upon as the finest ball handler in Dallas history, is himself a general manager today, overseeing the operation of the Atlanta Falcons and is regarded as one of the top business minds in the game. In fact, throughout most of his adult life LeBaron has enjoyed football more than the preparation of briefs.

In 1952, following a brilliant quarterbacking career at College of Pacific, he went to the Washington Redskins but stayed only two seasons. Then Redskins coach Curly Lambeau was convinced that a 5-7 quarterback had no business in pro ball. Miffed by that attitude, LeBaron called it quits after the '53 season and went to Canada where his former college coach Larry Siemeering was working for Calgary. "I knew my talents and was convinced I could be a professional quarterback," LeBaron says.

It would be Joe Kuharich who would successfully talk Eddie into returning to the Redskins in 1955, convincing him that he would build the Redskins offense around him. "Nobody I've ever seen," Kuharich said, "has the ball-handling ability and know-how of Eddie LeBaron." It would be a happy relationship until the quarterback's retirement after the '59 season. His retire-

ment would be brief, however, as a new franchise in Dallas made a trade with the Redskins for the rights to negotiate with him. The Cowboys paid dearly, giving up a No. 1 draft choice in the first draft they would ever be involved in. To make a move to Dallas more attractive, Dallas even offered the young quarterback, who had earned his law degree at George Washington University while playing for the Redskins, a position with the firm of Wynne and Wynne. (Bedford Wynne was, at the time, a minority stockholder in the Cowboys.)

"But my chief desire, deep down," LeBaron says today, "was to play for Tom Landry. For several years I had played against those great (New York) Giants teams, which were winning with their defense. I figured any time you had a good enough defense to stop the other club, you could score enough points to win. My feeling was that we could have a great defense at Dallas and despite a rather motley crew on offense we could score enough points to win. I never had played on a team that had a really good defense. I liked the idea of playing with a team which could stop somebody.

"What it boiled down to was I was a big fan of Tom Landry and he was a great friend. We didn't win too many back in those days, but I could see that his system was going to work. He would change up the offense a great deal from week to week, always trying to find some way to exploit the weakness of whatever team we were going to be playing. It was Tom's theory that you set your offensive attack up to beat the quality teams, the Clevelands of that time. We had our moments, but there just wasn't enough overall Cowboy talent. We couldn't execute the kind of run at people we would liked to have made.

"In fact, I suppose you always think you can accomplish things quicker than your ability allows. After the first couple of years it became obvious that it wasn't going to happen overnight. It was going to take a while, but we were making headway.

"We didn't win much, but I enjoyed those days. I felt I was helping something along that was going to develop into a team of which people were going to take notice." Indeed, in those first three seasons, Eddie LeBaron was one of the stabilizing factors.

Following his three-year stay with the Cowboys, he entered the legal profession on a full-time basis, working first in a Reno, Nevada firm with the father of Dallas quarterback Glenn Carano. Even then, however, he stayed in touch with the game, doing TV color commentary on pro games. He then worked for a time in a Las Vegas firm before the Falcons called him back into the NFL.

"One of the really amazing things to me," he says, "is that I was out of football for 13 years and when I came back and started looking around the league, there were the same people running the Dallas club who had been there in 1960 when I was with them. Tex Schramm, Tom, Gil Brandt. That says a lot for the way they've run their business."

Things have not changed in some respects for LeBaron. Even today no mention of his outstanding professional career is made without reference to his size.

"It still gets a little old," he admits. "I'm never referred to as a quarterback; it's always a 5-7 quarterback. But I learned to live with it a long time ago.

"I'll never forget a time when I was still with the Redskins and was invited to be the guest of honor at a father-and-son night for parishioners of a Washington church. I was sitting quietly there on the dais as ladies hurried around, serving the food. This one woman with a very distinct brogue set a plate in front of me and waved her finger at me. 'Don't ye be leavin' anything on yer plate, sonny,' she said.

"I didn't know what to say. Then I looked down at my plate and saw that she'd served me a child's portion."

Despite it all, Eddie LeBaron has grown to great stature in the NFL.

BOB FRY
★
Learning Left from Right All Over

It was not a time of great celebration in his career. The year was 1960 and suddenly offensive tackle Bob Fry was starting over. And certainly it was not a situation he could have anticipated inasmuch as there wasn't even the suggestion of an NFL franchise in Dallas when he was winding up an outstanding career at the University of Kentucky under the legendary Paul (Bear) Bryant.

He had been a third round draft choice of the Los Angeles Rams in 1952 and would spend six seasons on the West Coast. A man named Sid Gillman, who had been hired to replace Hamp Pool, was responsible for the constant advancement of the Rams' offense, Texas E. Schramm was the assistant general manager and his public relations director was an energetic young man named Pete Rozelle. It wasn't all bad, says Fry, currently the offensive line coach for the New York Jets.

When the Dallas Cowboys opened for business in 1960, Fry and Schramm were reunited. Schramm had advanced to general managership and Fry had become one of many veteran players selected by the league's newest franchise in the expansion draft.

"That first year," he says, "was unbelievable. I'd never seen so many football players. We were staying at the Ramada Inn before the '60 season got underway and everything was done in shifts. We had two groups at meals, the veteran players and the new ones that seemed to come in daily. We even had two workouts. It went on like that right up until the season started. Because we were the thirteenth team in the league, we were dealt a bye that first week and I remember Mike Connelly, who was a guard with the Rams, coming to Dallas on a Tuesday and starting at center the following Sunday.

"To this day I strongly feel we went out on the field that first season doing everything we could do to win, but it was hard for many of the older players to deal with finding themselves in the first year of a building program. Everyone knew that the day would come when the Cowboys would be a respectable and representative team, but there were a lot of the players who knew full well they wouldn't be around that long, that they wouldn't have enough years left on their careers to reap any of the good things that Tom Landry and the Cowboys were building toward."

And, yes, Fry says, there were numerous teams in the league those first couple of seasons which delighted in fattening their statistics against the struggling Cowboys. "There were teams, generally the ones who were struggling a little themselves, who looked forward to playing someone they could really bury. On the other hand, the really top teams would generally build up a comfortable lead and then ease off and let some of their younger players get some experience.

"The Dallas Cowboys built a lot of confidence in other people in those days."

By his third year with the franchise, however, Fry could see definite improvement. "We were even picked to win the Eastern Division before the season got underway. With new people like Bob Lilly, George Andrie and Chuck Howley coming in, the turnaround began."

Fry remembers Landry as a very thorough person, but one who was a little lacking in offensive knowledge in his early years as a head coach. "When he took the Dallas job he was determined to run it all and he admits today that he tried to spread himself a little too thin back then. But, we were all learning."

And it wasn't easy. "I know this is going to make me sound like the stereotype dumb offensive lineman, but the biggest problem for me after I moved from Los Angeles was to remember that in the Cowboys system the left side of the line was even and the right side was odd. In LA, it had been just the opposite and you become a creature of habit and reflex; you condition yourself to do things certain ways to a point where you no longer think about them. It took me two years to relearn which was my right and which was my left."

One of the greatest misfortunes of his career with the Cowboys, he says, came as a result of a decision made by the defensive coaches of the Pittsburgh Steelers. "Through most of my career they played Ernie Stautner on the inside where I didn't have to deal with him. After I moved to Dallas, though, they moved him outside where he became my responsibility. The man was incredible. He came at you just as hard on the last play of the game as he did on the first one. When you played against him you could just get ready for a real physical beating.

"I remember one afternoon, in particular. On a pass play I took a step back to get into position and lost my balance even before Ernie began his charge. As he was coming in low I just jumped on top of him and rode him to the ground. He got up spitting dirt and yelling like crazy. He told me he was really going to get me on the next play. To my good fortune Landry took me out after that play for some reason and sent someone else in. I don't remember who it was, but Stautner knocked him five yards deep into the backfield."

In 1965, his playing days over, Fry joined the Atlanta Falcons as a scout and later served as offensive line coach in 1967-68. He then went to the Pittsburgh Steelers where he worked as an assistant coach for five years before joining the Jets staff.

TOM BRAATZ
★
Fond Farewell to Burnet Field

Tom Braatz, a man who has seen the dark side of the NFL, no longer even tries to hide his satisfaction with the state of things these days. At age 48 he has, though personally hesitant to admit it, arrived.

Oh, he's not as well-known or highly publicized as Dallas' baby photographer-turned-scouting wizard Gil Brandt, but he's working on it. As player personnel director of the Atlanta Falcons, he is one of those to whom credit for his club's recent success is justifiably due. It is his scouting department that has, in recent years, acquired the personnel which has turned Atlanta from a NFL pitstop into a championship contender.

The bush league days of the franchise are now nothing more than fodder for the historians. And, Lordy, is Braatz glad to have them behind him. No more bus rides to broken down practice facilities. No more also-ran label on the organization for which he works.

There were times, however, after he had come to Atlanta that he was convinced he was living his former pro football life all over again. When he rode a bus to an outlying golf course to watch the Falcons practice for yet another defeat, it brought to mind that time twenty years ago when he was wearing a Dallas Cowboys uniform; struggling along with a team that appeared to be going nowhere fast.

He had come to Dallas with Eddie LeBaron and Doyle Nix from Washington in the 1960 expansion draft to help the Cowboys through their inaugural season. Nix, he recalls, failed to make the squad. There is even today a school of thought which suggests that Doyle might have been the luckiest of the three

LeBaron, now Braatz's boss as general manager of the Falcons, was the

Cowboys quarterback. It would be twenty years before his record of twenty-five interceptions would be equaled. Braatz, meanwhile, labored at right linebacker for the team that stumbled and staggered its way through a 0-11-1 season.

"Highlights? Shoot, I can't remember any," Braatz says. "Things were pretty dismal. In fact, when I think about my time as a member of the Cowboys, the first thing that comes to mind is a game we played in the Cotton Bowl. I don't even recall who we were playing against, but it was one of the coldest days we had had in a long time. What few people that had come out for the game were all huddled up beneath the pressbox overhang on the home side of the field. It honestly looked like we were playing in an empty stadium."

He tells of his early days as the Falcons' player personnel director when the practice facilities were "pretty backward for the NFL." Prior to the 1977 season, when Atlanta built its own practice field, the Falcons bused to an open field adjacent to the Snapfinger Golf Club for practice during the couple of months the baseball Braves were still playing in the stadium. It was, he admits, almost as bad as old Burnet Field where the infant Dallas Cowboys used to work out. Or the city parks they occasionally bused to when the bottomland baseball field was too wet to plow or play on.

"That old baseball field was something," he says. "There were rats that would eat the tongues out of shoes left on the floor overnight and there were the scorpions which more than one player stepped on enroute to cold water showers. I'm frankly glad those days are over."

So, too, are the Falcons, a club which Braatz says follows the Dallas philosophy in many areas. The comparisons, which are bound to come, don't bother him in the least. "Dallas is an organization that has done things right," he says. "By operating through the draft, Dallas has built a solid club, and that's what we're trying to do here. The Cowboys organization is first class and that's what we like to think we are."

"You aren't going to find a better coaching mind than Landry's anywhere. My impression of him when I was with the Cowboys was that he had a computer-type mind. He thought of everything in terms of numbers and statistics. He's very bright and, I guess, the best sideline coach I've ever seen. I thought Norm Van Brocklin was outstanding on the sidelines, but Landry's the best."

Braatz was still living in Dallas, working for an antique arms dealer, when criticism of Tom Landry began to echo through the city. "That's when (Clint) Murchison came up with the ten-year contract. That's where the stability really began."

And, yes, he admits, Landry was never one to take his business lightly. Good times and practical jokes were for the off-season. "Once when we were at training camp Tom brought his son, Tom, Jr., with him and this player named Bob Cross decided to take the kid on a snipe hunt one night. Now little Tom wasn't but 12 or 13 years old at the time and Cross does the whole bit.

He gave him a pan and a wooden spoon and a gunny sack and told him to go out there and beat on the pan with the spoon and pretty soon he'd have a sackful of snipe. Well, you know how it works. Tom, Jr. spent most of the night in the woods, holding that sack and beating on his pan with that wooden spoon.

"A couple of days later Coach Landry got wind of what had happened and Bob Cross got his release."

Braatz, however, left of his own accord. In his second season with the Cowboys he suffered a back injury and was admitted to Baylor Hospital. Doctors gave him two options. "They told me I could give up the game and get up and walk out of the hospital right then or I could stay and they would operate and chances were I would be able to play again.

"I got up and walked out of the hospital."

L.G. DUPRE
★
A Dramatic Case of Culture Shock

He had come out of Texas City as one of the state's most celebrated schoolboy running backs, casting his collegiate lot with the Baylor Bears. There, in Waco, where his name quickly became a household word, he gained the nickname which he carries even today.

It was the late Kern Tips, a broadcasting legend in the Southwest, who determined that the young man who was regularly scoring on weaving, long-distance jaunts should not go through his college career known simply as L. G. Dupre. The initials begged for explanation. Kern thus dubbed him "Long Gone" Dupre. The nickname followed him to the Baltimore Colts where he played on some of the greatest teams in the club's history. In that legendary 1958 overtime championship it was not just Alan (The Horse) Ameche running through the New York Giants. Long Gone was there too.

In 1960 he returned to his native state, the best days of his storied career supposedly behind him, to become one of the charter members of a new expansion franchise in Dallas. Looking back on it all, Dupre remembers it as a dramatic case of culture shock.

"When I learned I was coming to the Cowboys," he says, "I had mixed emotions. The idea of coming back to Texas was exciting. The idea of going from a team which had won the World Championship to a team which had never even won a game wasn't.

"As soon as Weeb (Eubank) told me I was going to Dallas," he says, "I spent several days trying to figure out whether I should do it or call it a career."

Dupre decided to report to the Cowboys, but spent the remainder of the off-season in Baltimore wrapping up various business deals. There was, for instance, the bowling alley he owned with quarterback Johnny Unitas and Carroll Rosenbloom which he gave up. "I had made up my mind to come to Dallas so I just sold them my part of the partnership."

The move to the Cowboys, he readily admits, took a great deal of adjusting. "It was no different, though, for a lot of the veteran players who came here. Frankly, it was tough — and more than a little discouraging. I can't remember the number of times I thought about giving it up.

"I had been doing things a certain way for six years and had seen some success. But those of us who came to Dallas were suddenly rookies again, trying to learn a lot of things all over again.

"Of course we went through the entire first year without a victory (0-11-1) and it was a little disheartening at times to look up in the stands of the Cotton Bowl and see maybe 5,000-6,000 people, after playing before sellout crowds in Baltimore."

It was, however, primarily through the efforts of the displaced and discouraged Colt that the original Dallas Cowboys were able to manage that lone tie, the one thing which kept the initial Dallas season from being a totally negative beginning. In the 31-31 deadlock with the New York Giants in Yankee Stadium, Dupre scored three touchdowns.

"That was a great feeling," he remembers. "We had gone through so much that year that even that tie looked good to us. Shoot, I felt like a hero and we didn't even win the game."

The truth of the matter is there were precious few highlights in those early days — particularly when measured by the moments of greatness Dupre had shared in as a member of the Colts.

"But, in its own way, it was a great experience. I could understand why Landry had to do a lot of the things he did — shifting people from position to position, constantly bring in new players, teaching a bunch of old dogs a lot of new tricks.

"After three years, though, I knew it was time to call it quits. I had been looking around for quite a while, trying to get myself set for retirement from football. I was fortunate that General Electric offered me a job in contract sales which I worked at for five years after I retired following the '62 season."

DON McILHENNY

From Box Lunches to Steak

It was a homecoming of sorts; one mixed with enthusiasm which would be tempered with frustration during his two-year tenure in a Dallas Cowboys uniform.

For Don McIlhenny, news that he was leaving Green Bay and joining the NFL's newest franchise prior to the 1960 season was exciting.

For the transplanted Texan who had been born in Cleveland, played his high school ball in Nashville and spent his college days as a running back for SMU, it was an opportunity to live in Dallas the year round. During his four years of pro ball (one with Detroit, three with the Packers), it had always been Dallas to which he returned once the season was over.

"There were a lot of guys who weren't too happy when they went to the Cowboys in that expansion draft," says McIlhenny, "but I wasn't one of them. I thought it was the greatest thing in the world. I had never dreamed of such an opportunity."

The early winless seasons when the Cowboys were struggling to build a foundation were not all pleasant, however. "Being in Dallas was enjoyable and playing for Tom Landry was exciting," he says, "but it was frustrating to go out every Sunday and bang your head against defensive linemen all day and maybe pick up just 30 or 40 yards. The simple fact was we just didn't have the manpower to compete in those early days. I guess the thing that I had the greatest amount of trouble accepting was that I had left a team that was on the move. Vince Lombardi had come to the Packers my last year there and he had put in that power sweep and flatly said it would work, and believe me, it did. It doesn't take a great running back to make yardage when everyone else is lying on the ground, out of his way. That's how it worked up there. We didn't get too many people on the ground in Dallas."

For the team's first exhibition game, he remembers, there were but two running backs on the roster when they faced the San Francisco 49ers in Seattle. "L.G. Dupre and I did it all," he says. "That made for a long day."

Yet despite the lack of depth and overall talent, McIlhenny resents the manner in which players on those original Cowboys teams have been pictured by the press. "Just about everything you read makes it sound like we were a bunch of no-talent pirates. That's unfair. There were some outstanding football players on the team in 1960 and '61, and some outstanding people who went on to be quite successful once their football careers were over."

But as with most, the seemingly endless string of defeats wore on McIlhenny. It was a drastic contrast from playing with the likes of Bobby Layne in Detroit and under Lombardi at Green Bay.

There were, however, a few high spots. "Late in that first season we went up to Chicago to play the Bears in Wrigley Field," Don recalls, "and came very close to putting it all together. We played what I felt was our best game by far despite the fact we lost (17-7). And I had had a pretty good day, scoring on a 60-yard screen pass. Afterwards, I went up to Landry and told him that it had been the first time I had really felt we were an NFL-caliber team. Evidently he agreed with me because the next week he quoted me in a team meeting."

It would, for that matter, prove to be a game which provided the foundation for Dallas' finest moment in that otherwise dismal season. The next weekend they battled the powerful New York Giants to a 31-all tie, escaping defeat for the only time all year.

Despite the fact Dallas won but four of the 26 games it played during his two-year stay (before he went to San Francisco to finish out his career), McIlhenny saw something special in the making.

"It was obvious from the first that there was a strong commitment to building a first class organization," he says. "There were a lot of little things: in Green Bay, for instance, we were still eating box lunches after the game. At Dallas we ate steak and all the trimmings on the plane trips home.

"And anyone with any football sense at all had to know that Tom Landry was going to be a winner just as soon as he was able to get the right people to carry out his plan. It's ironic, really," he says. "I had long admired Tom and even visited with him a time or two in the off-season when I came back to Dallas. He was selling insurance then, working in the Hartford Building. It never entered my mind that one day I would be playing for him. Looking back, having had the opportunity to play for Landry and Lombardi is something I'll always cherish. Both were strong believers in hard work, and they made what you were doing have a purpose."

Then, of course, there were the tribulations; the rides on city busses out to a park near the Brook Hollow Country Club for practice when rain made it impossible to work at Burnet Field. "We would go out there and practice and no one would even bother to stop and watch us," he recalls. "There we were, out there with the swings and teetertotters and nobody seemed to give a hoot."

And there was the dressing room at Burnet Field; cramped, cold and seemingly always without hot water in the showers. "I remember one really cold day as we were dressing, Ray Matthews, a wide receiver on the squad, decided to do something about the cold and went over and dropped a match into this barrel where trash and used tape were thrown. It blazed for a bit and then died out and we went on out to practice. Later it really began to smoke and soon it looked as if the whole dressing room was on fire. The coaches halted practice and began running toward it, ready to fight the fire. Ol' Ray just stood there with the rest of us, hoping that maybe the place would burn down. But, no such luck. It did accomplish one thing, though: it smoked the rats out for the next couple of weeks."

In those days, clearly, good fortune was wherever you could find it.

JACK PATERA

★

The First Middle Linebacker

In the history of the Dallas Cowboys, only four players can claim the honor of starting at middle linebacker, the job now occupied by Bob Breunig. Before him there was Lee Roy Jordan. Prior to Jordan there was current linebacker coach Jerry Tubbs. And before Tubbs there was Jack Patera, now the head coach of the Seattle Seahawks.

While it was not a duty he labored at long, Patera, the record books will forever show, was the starting middle linebacker for the Dallas Cowboys the first time they ever stepped on the field in the expansion year of 1960.

He came to Dallas after spending three years with the Baltimore Colts (who had drafted him in the fourth round following an all-conference career at the University of Oregon) and two more with the Chicago Cardinals. He stayed with Dallas for two seasons but played sparingly because of a knee injury. Still, he had come to the Cowboys in that summer of '60 to be new coach Tom Landry's middle linebacker.

Tubbs, who had played the position for the San Francisco 49ers for a couple of years, started at one of the outside spots. Some people were predicting big things for a rookie kid named Wahoo McDaniels, but it was the professional experience of Patera and Tubbs that Landry was counting on. "Back then," Patera says, "Tom was looking for help anywhere he could find it. He was looking at everyone who even remotely looked like a football player.

"Even as we were getting ready to open that first season Tom was looking at people right up to the day of the game. I started that very first game and, for the life of me, I can't remember anything about it except for the fact we lost (to Pittsburgh 35-28). I'm relatively safe in saying that I didn't exactly set the woods on fire.

"Then in the second game I got hurt and was out until the fourth game. About all I did was limp around and try to get in the way of the ball carrier or knock down a receiver before he could get into a route. It wasn't one of those seasons you can do much bragging about." Its highlight, in fact, Patera points out, was being associated with Landry. "When I think back to the time I spent with the Cowboys," he says, "the first thing that comes to mind was Landry. I admired his knowledge of the game and the way he taught it to the players. About the only criticism I have of Landry as a coach back then was the fact he tried to do too much."

Told of the observation, Landry smiles and nods in agreement. "When you're desperate," he says, "you do some crazy things. Jack was not one of the flashy, big play linebackers, but he was a hard hitter and a dedicated worker, the kind of player we didn't have enough of in those early days. He was one who gave you everything he had, whether it was in a practice or in a game."

The season of 1961, Patera had hoped, would be one in which he could lend a better showing than he had in the Cowboys' initial year. A noteworthy pre-season camp was strong indication that he would. In the first pre-season game of '61 in Sioux Falls against the Minnesota Vikings he suffered additional injury to his knee and was to remain on the sidelines for all but the final two games of the regular season. By that time Tubbs had established himself in the middle.

But in that final game of '61, Landry again put Patera in as the starting middle linebacker, moving Tubbs to the outside. The result, Patera laughs, was virtually the same. "I didn't do anything memorable ... and we lost again (this time to Washington, 34-24). I knew the knee was never going to be solid again, so I called it a career after that second year."

He has since gone on to become one of the NFL's most celebrated coaches. After laboring as a defensive line coach for Los Angeles where he directed the original fearsome foursome, and at Minnesota where he coached the Purple People Eaters, he was named to coach the expansion Seahawks in 1976.

DON PERKINS
✪
Biscuit and Gravy Fullback

There was, in the formulative days of the Dallas Cowboys, a training camp ritual referred to as the Landry Mile. It was the first-order-of-business test of endurance, stamina and grit forced upon all who hoped to earn a spot on the team. Those unable to complete it in the prescribed time, word had it, could anticipate but small chance of gaining notice from head coach Tom Landry once practices formally began.

Don Perkins, a stocky running back with a superlative collegiate career at the University of New Mexico to his credit, was among the first to recognize the seriousness that Landry attached to the test. It was a hot July day in Forest Grove, Oregon during the inaugural Dallas training camp, when Perkins' professional career flashed before his eyes, and all but ended before it even began.

He had reported 20 pounds over his college playing weight, confident in the belief that in pro ball bigger was better. The added weight and what he would later describe as a "biscuit and gravy" off-season training program resulted in a Grade A disaster.

President and general manager Tex Schramm, an eyewitness that July day in 1960, remembers it well: "He looked absolutely awful. Trying to run the mile, he would fall down, get up, try to run some more, and fall down again. He never finished it. We didn't know what to think. Usually, when a guy pulls something like that it tells you right away that he doesn't have much of what you're looking for — pride, courage, determination."

With precious few bonafide players on hand, the Cowboys immediately had cause to doubt their own good judgement. Here was an athlete who had wrecked school rushing records in Albuquerque; a 5-10, 200-pound powerhouse who had been selected to play in the annual College All-Star game, unable to pass the first test of camp. Touted by U.S. Senator Clinton Anderson of New Mexico, Perkins, they felt, was one of the few "can't miss" players they had. Clint Murchison, so eager to have him, had signed him to a personal services contract even before the Cowboys formally existed. It was even necessary to deal away a ninth round draft choice to the Baltimore Colts to be assured that he would remain Dallas property.

And there he was, struggling through, and not even completing, the Landry Mile.

Now, 21 years later, Perkins still finds little humor in that failure. It is, on the other hand, a moment in his life he still vividly remembers. Now a staff member of the New Mexico Governor's office where he oversees a statewide incentive work program, Perkins admits that he spent several anxious years as a pro wondering if he had been forgiven for his miserable showing. "The fact that Tom Landry gave me a second chance after that mile," he says, "is probably the thing that stands out in my mind when I look back on my career with the Cowboys. Without his patience and fairness, nothing I eventually accomplished would have been possible. He gave me a break and in return I gave him my best shot."

Landry's patience, of course, would come to pay high dividends. During an eight-year professional career Don Perkins represented the backbone of the still developing Dallas offense. He gained 6,217 yards rushing, earned All-Pro recognition and participated in no less than five Pro Bowls. When the Cowboys initiated a Ring of Honor in Texas Stadium, Perkins and former quarterback Don Meredith were the second and third players selected after Hall of Famer Bob Lilly had become the original inductee.

And, he became the prototype of the Dallas Cowboys fullback. Though he lacked blazing speed, he could cover 10 yards faster than his Olympic sprinter teammate Bob Hayes. His blocking earned him remarkably high grades week in and week out, and, when short yardage was needed, he could deliver a blow that belied his size.

About the only man in Dallas who did not feel Don Perkins was among the best in the business was Don Perkins.

Even with the advantage of two decades of hindsight, he views his career with surprise and some measure of wonder. "The honest truth of the matter," he says from his Albuquerque office, "is that I never felt I was good enough to be playing at the professional level. I spent most of my career afraid someone would find me out, suddenly discover that I didn't have any business being where I was. I never even had aspirations of a pro career while I was in college. That was before the game was so much a part of the public consciousness, before the big money and overwhelming publicity. Even after I signed with the Cowboys it never occured to me that I might be around for a long career.

"My lack of confidence or negative feelings about myself — I don't really know what to call it — made every play of every game a maximum challenge for me. I never felt comfortable that I could have a bad game, an off-day, and come back and still have my job. Maybe I'm just one of those underachievers, but the fact was I was always looking over my shoulder. That's the way it was from that first rookie camp until the last couple of years of my career."

Indeed, the failure in the Landry Mile was not the only difficulty Perkins had to deal with in the early going. In that same rookie season he suffered a broken bone in his foot during practice for the College All-Star game and, following an operation, returned to Albuquerque to await a second chance when camp opened prior to the '61 season. "It was," he recalls, "a year of anxious waiting. I wasn't sure the failure in that mile run had really been forgiven. But, I had signed a two-year contract, so I felt obligated to go back and give it a better try."

Though he would earn himself a spot on the roster with relative ease, training camp was far from an enjoyable experience. "At one point in practice I thought I had broken my foot again. And I didn't really think I had been doing that well. Things had just sort of built up. The usual agony and loneliness of camp had begun to get to me so I decided to tell them I'd had it. I had a no-cut contract but was willing to let them keep their money. All I wanted to do was go home. But, eventually, they talked me out of it."

A year later Don Perkins would be selected to Associated Press and NEA All-Pro teams. And throughout his career the honors would come in a steady flow.

"Things like that," Perkins says, "didn't have the importance to me at the moment that they do now. Oh, I appreciated something like being named to the Pro Bowl, but it was really just another game. And, as I've said, I spent most of my time wondering why I was there with all those great players. Now, though, it means a lot more. It's a neat thing to look back on. In retrospect, you look back and it's almost hard to believe that things like that happened to you."

Perkins is not one of those who had difficulty severing his ties with the game. It was, in fact, only after great amounts of persuasion that he extended his career for two more Pro Bowl seasons in '67 and '68. "After five or six years," he says, "I felt I had had enough. I wasn't getting any younger or faster or learning any new moves, so I was ready to retire. But after talking

27

with Tex at great length, I agreed to sign another two-year contract. Looking back, I'm pleased to say those last two years were among my most productive."

And then, without fanfare, he called it quits after that '68 season. "It was a cut-and-dried matter when I walked away from it," he says. "I knew I was through and felt comfortable with the decision."

BYRON BRADFUTE

★

Signing with CBS Made More Sense

Another Cowboys Reunion was fast approaching when former offensive tackle Byron Bradfute received a call in 1980 from friend and former teammate Bill Herchman suggesting it was imperative that he be in attendance.

"Byron," he said, "they're really counting on you. Hey, there was even talk of retiring your old number . . . but no one could remember what number you wore."

For the record, the former Abilene Christian/Southern Mississippi lineman, who labored as one of the pioneering members of the Cowboys (1960-61), wore number 77.

It is a fact, to this day, some former classmates back at Southern Miss, where he played his final season of collegiate ball, do not know. For all they know Byron went off to record country and western songs.

"That's what I told everybody," the funloving New Braunfels resident says. "All my negotiations were with Tex Schramm when he was then still working with CBS-TV. I would get these calls while I was in class, and since they were originating from CBS, everyone was really curious about them. I just told people that they were trying to get me to come up there and cut a record."

His story certainly made more sense than signing with a non-existent football team whose contract came in a CBS envelope and had Dallas Rangers Football Team written across the top.

"I really didn't know what to think about it all," Byron says, "but it was something I wanted to try."

And once on the scene at the initial training camp of the team which had by then changed its name to the Dallas Cowboys, he did his best to see that he had a chance to make the team. Bradfute had his inside sources who kept him posted on his daily status.

"Even before I reported to camp I was driving through Fredricksburg (Texas) and stopped at a gas station I had used for years when driving home. I got to talking to the owner and he asked me what I was going to do since I was finally out of college. I told him I was going to go up to Dallas and try to make the new football team they were putting together. There was this skinny guy sitting in a chair in front of the station and when I mentioned the Cowboys he lifted his baseball cap and said he was going to be the trainer. Turned out he was Clint Houy who had been with the Pittsburgh Pirates.

"We struck up a friendship and he took an interest in me once we got to Forest Grove, Oregon (site of the first Dallas training camp). He encouraged me and let me in on what he was hearing from the coaches. Then there was this girl who was the secretary to the coaching staff who I started dating right away. She was good about letting me know anything that might help me out."

He made the team and quickly found the world of the NFL to be unlike any of his previous competitive spheres.

It was in an exhibition game with the Green Bay Packers that he first witnessed the violence the game had to offer. "I don't remember where the game was played but it was in one of those stadiums where both benches are on the same side of the field. Paul Hornung (Packers runningback) came around on a sweep and was tackled in the area between the benches. I don't recall who tackled him but I do recall that (linebacker) Jack Patera came up late and really plowed into Hornung.

"Vince Lombardi was absolutely livid. He ran onto the field, yelling at Jack, and Jack just made a little obscene gesture and walked away. The veins in Lombardi's neck were standing out and he yelled, 'Patera, we'll get you.' Four or five plays later they did, putting Jack out for the season. In fact, it pretty much ended his career."

That same Packers game would also have something to do with the short duration of Bradfute's stay with the Cowboys. As a rookie he had started five exhibition games before Green Bay's Willie Davis worked him over. "To put it mildly," Byron says, "I had a bad game against him. What he did was send me to the bench."

The starting assignment went to Bradfute's friend and roommate Bob Fry, and any chance of regaining it was lost the next season when a knee operation sidelined him following the first exhibition game of the season. Then, during his third training camp he went to head coach Tom Landry and informed him of his decision to call it a career.

"One of the things that really weighed on my mind during that time," he says, "was the need to establish myself in some career. Back then a lot of the players we had were guys in the twilight of their own careers who had come from other teams to try to stick in the league another season, maybe two. So many of them were guys who had been playing for ten years and didn't have anything but their names to show for it. The average salary of a lineman back then was something like $8,000 a year and it seemed to me there were a lot of guys who had no idea what they would do when football was finally over for them. That had a great impact on me."

So he went to Landry to advise him of his plan to retire. "It was a pretty emotional thing for me," Byron admits. "I had a hard time not crying. I told Tom that it was just no fun losing all the time and he tried to convince me that I hadn't really given it a chance. Anyway, I quit and went down to the dressing room where everyone was getting ready for practice. I went over to Bill Herchman, still feeling pretty low, and rather dramatically told him I had decided to hang 'em up.

"He looked up at me and said, 'Can I have your shoes?' "

DON MEREDITH

★

Fun and Games in the Frozen North

Winter had fallen on Detroit like a sledgehammer. Snow swirled, the temperature had long since dipped well below the freezing mark and a 17 mile-per-hour wind was coming off the icy lake. All in all, it was an almost poetic setting for the end of the Dallas Cowboys' initial season in the National Football League. Yet on that dismal day in 1960 a crowd of 43,272 had braved the elements, probably because they were virtually assured of seeing their hometown Lions win over Dallas. Everyone else had. They built fires in the stands to keep warm as their coffee froze in their cups.

It was, to be sure, not Don Meredith's kind of day. Yet even now, 17 years and a small fortune removed from his rookie season as a pro quarterback, he remembers it as if it were yesterday.

Sitting in the Baltimore Cross Keys Inn recently, preparing for his regular chores on ABC's Monday Night Football, he put aside his studies of the Washington Redskins and Baltimore Colts and began to laugh.

"There was," he remembers, "no way I was going to play against the Lions. Eddie (LeBaron) had been playing well and I was dead certain he would go all the way. So, the night before ol' Don decides to spend the entire evening introducing himself to the Motor City. That was the first time in my football career I had ever made a complete night of it. But, shoot, I wasn't worried. In fact, by the time the sun came up I wasn't even feeling the cold anymore."

If the truth were known, by the time he reported to the visitors dressing room and began preparation for the last hurrah of Dallas' 0-11-1 season — the worst in 18 years in the NFL — he was feeling very little of anything. Except for the need of eight or 10 hours of hard sleep. Only when coach Tom Landry informed him that he was going to be the starter that afternoon did the former SMU All-American begin to worry.

"I was sitting there," Meredith recalls, "with my pads on, my jersey, my socks and shoes, trying to figure how I was going to make it through the day when Nate Borden (the former Green Bay defensive end who had come to Dallas that first season) came up. He looked down at me and said, 'Boy, you

30

are gonna need a lot of help today.' I told him, 'Hey, man, I'm ready.' Well, he started laughing his head off and then said, 'Maybe it would be a good idea, then, to put your pants on before we go out. Which I understand we're going to do in just a very few minutes. It's a little cold today.' "

The cutting cold air in the stadium performed a minor miracle. Meredith quickly made a return to the living and, in fact, became more and more excited about the prospect of commanding the team. Then at the last minute Landry had a change of heart and informed his rookie field general that LeBaron would be starting. "But," the Cowboys coach said, "I want you to be warming up through the first quarter in case I decide to turn it over to you."

"I got tired of warming up," Don recalls, "and besides I was getting cold, so I went over to the bench and bundled up. I was sitting next to Don Heinrich (who had come to Dallas by way of the New York Giants) and he always carried a pack of cigarettes on the field with him in his socks. I bummed one from him and had me a smoke while Eddie kept on quarterbacking."

Another sinking spell plagued him when the team returned to the warmth of the dressing room during halftime yet Meredith, the man who would one day become the leader of some of the Cowboys' finest hours, the eventual winner of such honors as the Bert Bell Award and a man who would earn himself a place in the hallowed Ring of Honor when all was said and done, wearily made his way back onto the field.

"It was even colder and snowing harder," he recalls, "but Tom told me to warm up and be ready. I did. And Eddie opened the second half. He got his hand stepped on and for a few minutes they thought something might be broken. But he stayed in and I kept warming up until the third quarter ended. Then I went over and sat down on the bench again. Late in the fourth quarter Tom said warm up again. I couldn't believe it. I told him I wouldn't do it. I was worn out from warming up and didn't see any reason to do it again with the game almost over."

Thus it is that 23-14 loss at the hands of the Detroit Lions on that final day of the '60 season; a game in which he did not play so much as a single down, which Dandy Don Meredith, fun-loving, free-spirited, Emmy Award-winning man that he is, looks back on as one of his most memorable moments in a Dallas uniform.

"I didn't play any football that day," he says, "but I learned a couple of things. First, I found out that all-night partying is okay if you don't have to play a football game the next day.

"And, it was on that afternoon that I first began to realize that Tom and I were going to really have a lot of fun together."

DON HEINRICH

★

Dallas' First Quarterback — Almost

He had come to Dallas filled with anticipation, convinced the opportunity to emerge from a backup role and prove himself as a NFL quarterback was just around the corner. Never mind that the team he would be directing was preparing for its initial year in the league. The Cowboys, he felt, would be his team to direct and Don Heinrich made no attempt to hide his enthusiasm.

Owner of the NCAA pass completion percentage record after his senior year at the University of Washington, Heinrich was hailed as a "can't miss" professional. Twice he had set the pace for the nation's college passers — in 1950 and again in '52 — and had led Fort Ord to the service championship before joining the New York Giants in 1954. There, however, the headlines ended. For the next six years he would serve as the backup to Giants' veteran Charley Connerly.

Thus when New York owner Wellington Mira asked him following the '59 season if he would be interested in going to the new Dallas franchise, Heinrich jumped at the opportunity. The pluses were too numerous to turn down. He would be joining a team without an established quarterback, would be reunited with former Giants' teammate Tom Landry who was to coach the new team, and he would be working in the capacity of player-coach.

So eager was Heinrich to get this new phase of his career off and running that he spent the spring in Dallas with Landry and his staff, helping to design the Cowboys' offense. The only other quarterback in sight was a rookie kid from SMU named Don Meredith; gifted but lacking professional experience. He was, Heinrich knew, the man of the future. But for the present the job belonged to him.

Until a swift turn of events just prior to the opening of the first Cowboys' training camp. Little Eddie LeBaron, the retired Washington quarterback, had been lured into the Cowboys fold. "Right then," Heinrich says, "I began to wonder just where I was to fit in."

Already he had gone a few rounds with general manager Tex Schramm, asking for but not receiving an additional $2,000 for his services as a coach. It would be the first of a succession of squabbles with the front office. "I began to wonder if maybe I hadn't put the cart before the horse," Heinrich says. "I just assumed too much. In training camp the three of us got equal time and all of us saw considerable action in pre-season games. But I had a bad feeling about what was coming."

In a pre-season game against St. Louis, Heinrich was sharp, hitting rookie receiver Gary Wisener for a 67-yard touchdown in a 20-13 loss. But when the regular season opened, the 5-7 LeBaron was Landry's starter. Heinrich spent much of his time waiting, watching, and giving tips to the youthful Meredith. "In time Don and I were both pretty frustrated by our situations. We both felt we were not getting a fair chance to show what we could do."

Which is not to say Heinrich sat idle. "It seemed to me," he recalls, "that the tougher the opponent was, the more I was called on to play. In 1960 we didn't have too many All-Pro offensive linemen and the quarterback could expect to take a pretty good beating from anyone. The really good defensive teams were murder.

"We were playing the Chicago Bears in Wrigley Field one Sunday and Eddie went down with an injury in the first quarter so I went in. We were working out of the Shotgun that day — only we called it the spread formation — because the Bears' rush was so good. Still, I got killed. Then killed some more. Late in the game I remember Doug Atkins breaking through for about the hundredth time. Instead of really putting it to me as I threw the ball he just ran on by, laughing. 'Man,' he said, 'you've been down enough for one day.' "

His biggest disappointment in a Cowboys uniform, however, came a few weeks later when Dallas traveled to New York to play his old teammates. Throughout the week Landry had indicated that he would start. A 64-yard touchdown pass for the lone Dallas touchdown in the Chicago game had obviously caused his stock to rise and LeBaron was still suffering from torn rib cartilage. "As we were leaving the locker room to go onto the field," Heinrich remembers, "Landry said he had one lineup change to announce. He said LeBaron would start at quarterback. That killed me."

Thereafter, it was just a matter of making it through the season for the disappointed quarterback. When the winless campaign was finally done, he called it quits and returned to the Giants to coach.

"I just went to Dallas expecting too much," he says today. "I really didn't understand what they were trying to do there. At the time I was pretty upset, but, looking back, it makes more sense to me. The funny thing about it all is that even when I felt I was getting the short end of the stick I had a lot of respect for Landry and LeBaron. Both are good friends to this day.

"And Meredith, he was fun. I knew he was going to keep Tom guessing for a lot of years if Tom kept him around. I'll never forget one morning in a quarterback meeting when Tom was giving us certain situations and asking what play we'd call. He dealt a lot of attention to Meredith since he was the rookie and had so much to learn. So he asked Don, 'If we're on the opposition's 20 and it is second-and-three, what are you going to do?'

"Don stood up and said, 'Well, I think I'd go to my five iron and hope to hell I didn't hook it.' Landry turned red as a beet."

Heinrich would stay active in the NFL for seventeen years, coaching with the Los Angeles Rams, Pittsburgh Steelers, New Orleans Saints and San Francisco 49ers before ending his pro career. Even today he stays in close touch, commuting from his Saratoga, Calif., home to do color commentary on the Seattle Seahawks' radio broadcasts and publishes a pre-draft magazine called "Don Heinrich's Scout Report," as well as a pre-season preview.

"It beats having your brains knocked out by people like Doug Atkins," he says.

MIKE FALLS
☆
Straight Out of Abbott and Costello

Reverend Mike Falls, once a member of the Dallas Cowboys and now an Episcopal chaplain for the Stephen F. Austin College campus in Nacogdoches, is a man of understatement.

Looking back on the first two years of the Cowboys' existence, 1960 and 1961, the seasons in which he labored in great frustration as an offensive guard, he says, "Things were pretty strange."

He's not necessarily referring to the dismal won-lost records or the pioneer facilities or even the swinging door atmosphere which existed as new head coach Tom Landry searched from day to day for a bigger, better football player to fill one of the manholes then existing on his roster.

"Oh, that part of it was a little unusual, too," Rev. Falls admits. "For instance, I came to Dallas after being cut by Green Bay and at the airport I bumped into the guy I was replacing; a guy I had been playing behind only a few weeks earlier at Green Bay. He just glared at me."

The most unusual aspect of his two-year association with the Cowboys, however, was his off-season job which had him and then middle linebacker Jerry Tubbs doing publicity for the club.

"It was a real war back then between the Cowboys and the AFL Dallas Texans (later the Kansas City Chiefs)," he recalls. "They had Jerry and I doing all sorts of things to promote the team. For instance, in the summer we would drive around town in this old Model T that was a part of Clint Murchison's collection. It was painted up blue and white and had the Cowboys' insignia on the doors. We would drive around all day, going from one park to another, signing kids up to memberships in the Cowboys' Club. I'll never forget one afternoon when we were on McKinney and I made a turn and one of the wheels fell off. There were times when I felt like we were something straight out of an Abbott and Costello movie.

"We participated in donkey baseball games and were in a cow milking contest held at Dealey Plaza, matched against a couple of players from the Texans. Looking back, I'd have to say my greatest contribution as a member of the Cowboys came the day I convinced the local 7-11 Stores to sell our T-shirts."

34

But even an eager-to-please Mike Falls drew the line when, after letting it be known that he planned to marry an SMU coed named Sandy that summer, the Cowboys insisted a marriage ceremony conducted in the team offices would be great publicity. "I told them no deal," he says.

On the playing field things were not nearly as funny. During his two-year tenure with Dallas the team won four, lost 22 and tied two, and he's still trying to figure out how they won those four.

"There was very little feeling of team unity in those days," he points out. "Everyone here was literally fighting for his professional life so there was a lot of individuality, a lot of discord. We had all been more or less thrown together, many not of their own choosing. It was a difficult situation. More than once I saw players cut simply because of their attitude toward what was happening. They just weren't able to adjust to being a part of a team that everyone in the world knew was going to be a loser for a while.

"For some, however, the grimness of the situation brought a closeness. It just depended on the individual's frame of mind."

And through the turmoil there stood Tom Landry, patient and firm in his belief in the system he was attempting to install. "It amazed me to watch how the man operated," Rev. Falls remembers. "I really admired him. It takes a special kind of man to stick with a system, working on it, drilling it into the players, when nothing was really working. He just somehow knew that one day it would. He believed in it. He believed in himself."

Falls began his professional career in 1956 when, after graduating from the University of Minnesota, he played a season with Toronto in the Canadian League despite the fact he had been drafted by the New York Giants. After two years in the service he returned to football with the team that originally drafted him and found himself being coached by a new member of the Giants' staff, Vince Lombardi.

You will not find the name of Rev. Mike Falls on any All-Pro lists. "The fact is," he says, "when I try to think back on memorable performances I had, they're all negative. Like, for instance, a game we had with Cleveland. I was playing against Bob Gain and he was literally wearing me out, beating my brains out. I've never been so frustrated.

"Finally, there was this play where Eddie LeBaron was rolling out to pass. Gain was chasing him across the field and finally ran him out of bounds. The whistle had already blown, and there was Gain standing there out of bounds and I still had up a full head of steam. It was the best shot I had all day so I took it. Man, I creamed him. And, of course, got a 15-yard penalty for it. Which wasn't that big a deal, really, since we were always facing third-and-20 anyway."

Knee problems forced him out of the game after the '61 season and into the clergy. There are those who will tell you that his trials and tribulations as an early day member of the Cowboys provided him great preparation for his calling.

ALLEN GREEN

★

He Finally Turned the Boos to Cheers

They had endured an entire season without once tasting victory, thus it was high drama indeed when the score was deadlocked at 24-24 with just seconds remaining in the 1961 season opener. The Cowboys had marched deep into Pittsburgh Steelers' territory as time ticked away, but finally the drive stalled and head coach Tom Landry was faced with a major decision.

He called for a young Ol' Miss graduate named Allen Green to attempt a 30-yard field goal. It was not a decision held in high regard by the Cotton Bowl crowd who had spent a great deal of the afternoon booing Green's less than impressive efforts.

"I had definitely not had a good day," Green remembers. "Big Daddy Lipscomb had been putting tremendous pressure on me all afternoon, blocking one and forcing me to rush all afternoon. I was getting pretty roundly booed every time I came off the field."

The booing blossomed into enthusiastic cheers in those final seconds, however, as Green's field goal was good, lifting the Cowboys to a milestone 27-24 victory. "It was a great feeling," he says today, "to come off the field that day knowing I had made a contribution to the first regular season win in the team's history."

It had not, however, been the way he had hoped to contribute to the Cowboys' fortunes. A center and linebacker for coach Johnny Vaught at Ol' Miss, he had only seriously begun to kick midway through his senior season in college. At 210 pounds he considered himself a linebacker even after the New York Giants drafted him, making it clear they felt his professional future was as a kicker. He never got the opportunity to prove it in the Big Apple. Green was traded to Washington, then Dallas before ever putting on a practice jersey.

"Actually, I was delighted to wind up with the Cowboys," he says, "because they had been writing me all through my senior year and I had begun to follow them a little. I felt since it was a new team I had a chance to make it. But, I thought I could make it as a linebacker and a kicker.

"It was an idea which almost prevented making it as a kicker. I had too much competition at linebacker, people like Jerry Tubbs and Chuck Howley. But I spent far too much time trying to improve and I really didn't get my leg in shape for kicking the way I should have. By the time the season opened I still wasn't kicking really well, wasn't in a good groove."

It was, of course, long before the advent of kicking coaches and Green's

36

practice time was generally spent on the field following the regular practice. "Coach Landry would generally stay out and punt with me," he recalls. "I guess he recognized the fact that I really needed the work."

It was well into the season before Green began to kick in the manner he believed competent. In one game he got off a 53-yarder and felt he was on his way.

Then he met up with Pittsburgh and Big Daddy Lipscomb again. Not only did he play no part in a hoped-for victory (the Steelers won, 37-7), but he was clipped on one punting attempt and had a bone chipped in his ankle. For several weeks the punting chores fell to quarterback Eddie LeBaron while Green mended and tried to round back into form.

"It never fails," he says. "Going into that game I really felt I was in form. I was punting well and in warmups kicking field goals from the 50. And I was punting well in the game until that clip."

By year's end his punting average stood at only 36.7 for 61 attempts and in the off-season he was traded away to the Green Bay Packers. "I learned a lesson too late," Green says. "If I have any advice to pass on to a rookie it would be to not try to spread himself too thin, to concentrate on whatever it is he does best. I realize that things are even more specialized now than they were when I was playing, but they were even then and I didn't fully recognize the fact."

Still, he has his place in Cowboys history. Dallas may have had better field goal kickers since him, but none who can lay claim to the fact they kicked the one which provided the team's first ever victory.

DICK NOLAN
★
One Up on the Deacon

It seemed at the time like a good opportunity to call it a career as a player and move on into coaching to New York Giants cornerback Dick Nolan. He had been through the dynasty years with the Giants of the '50s and, at the end of the 1961 season, was thinking of searching new avenues even though there was time left on his contract.

Former Giants teammate and coach Tom Landry called from Dallas where he was attempting to build a team from a crop of expansion dealt players, asking if Nolan would be interested in becoming his secondary coach. Nolan accepted.

"I saw it as a good opportunity to learn a lot about the coaching business in a short period of time. I had seen how Tom worked, both when we were the Giant cornerbacks and later when he was just coaching. I had watched him so many times back in the Polo Grounds, playing and coaching, that I knew he was probably one of the most knowledgeable football men around, regardless of age or experience."

Thus, Nolan took the job that February following the '61 season, believing his playing days were behind him and that a coaching future loomed ahead. Never, he insists even today, did the urge to play again bite at him. Not through the summer months as he looked ahead to his new job, certainly not during the toil of training camp, and not even when the exhibition season began. Nolan gave no thought to coming out of retirement. Landry, on the other hand, quietly plotted.

On a Saturday before the next day's season opener, Nolan and several of the assistants were on the practice field throwing the ball around while waiting for the players to dress. Landry, saying nothing, took his stance next to Nolan, watched the impromptu game of pass for a few minutes, then said, "Dick, would you mind playing tomorrow?"

Aware that injuries had dealt a serious blow to the depth in the defensive backfield, Nolan said, "Coach, if you want me to, I'll give it a try. You know I haven't done any conditioning to speak of."

Landry smiled. "Dick, I know you. You'll do just fine. By the way, I activated you yesterday." What it had boiled down to was Landry's having already made the decision that Nolan would return to playing status but he allowed his friend and assistant the opportunity to think the decision was at least in part his own.

Now serving as receiver coach for the Cowboys, Nolan looks back on the incident with laughter. "We were really struggling in those days," he says. "The simple fact that I had to come back and play was a pretty good indication of how we were struggling. I never was able to get in shape.

"Think of it: One day you're just coaching and the next day you're suited out, standing out there in the Cotton Bowl where the temperature is 110 degrees on a mild day. The thing I most remember about the season of 1962 was that I started it weighing 195 pounds and ended it weighing 165."

That and the fact he dislocated his shoulder more times that season than he cares to remember. "I had had trouble with it in New York, in fact, and believe it or not, that very day we were throwing the ball around before Tom came up to me and asked me to play, I had dislocated it slightly when I tried to throw a long pass.

"Seems like every time I turned around I was dislocating it. They had this harness that I played in that was supposed to prevent my injuring it again. I could never tell that it did much good."

But, Ann Nolan, Dick's wife, tells the story better — as she did to Peter Finney in *Pro Football Weekly:*

"He hurt it in New York and in Dallas they rigged up a funny contraption to keep from hurting it again. It was a leather harness with a chain going from under one arm to the rib cage. The idea of the chain was to keep him from raising his arm over his head. But every time he played, he broke the chain. The shoulder kept popping out all season. Dick would go to the

38

sidelines and the doctors would just pop it back into place."

Shoulder pain aside, Dick says, there wasn't too much about that '62 season — Dallas went 5-8-1 — that he likes to think back on. "One of the best things," he says, laughing, "was the fact that when the season was over Tom assured me I would only be coaching the next season."

In '63, he became full-time coach of the defensive secondary. Three years later he was elevated to defensive coordinator. In 1968 he moved to San Francisco as head coach of the '49ers and in 1970-71-72 led his team to NFC Western Division titles. In '70, after a 10-3-1 season, he was cited as the National Conference Coach of the Year. Before returning to the Cowboys he would serve as head coach of the New Orleans Saints and worked as the defensive coordinator for the Houston Oilers.

And with his return to the Cowboys came a resurrection of Nolan stories. Dick, himself, is hardly bashful about telling them. Particularly the one about the time he finally took the measure of famed Los Angeles running back Deacon Dan Towler:

"We (the New York Giants) were really having a hard time with Towler one Sunday. He had been running over us all day. The Rams had moved to our six-yard line and they sent Deacon on a straight-ahead dive play. The hole opened for just an instant and he went through it like a shot, head down.

"The top of his helmet hit dead center on the upright of the goal post, bouncing him all the way back to the six. The ball went flying all the way back to about the 15-yard line where we recovered it.

"Now, Towler was just sitting there, stunned, with a dazed look on his face, trying to figure out what had happened. I couldn't resist. I ran over to him, bent down in his face and waved a finger at him. 'Deacon,' I said, 'I didn't really mean to hit you quite that hard. But, if you try coming through there again, I'm really going to have to let you have it'."

DICK MAEGLE

A Day Even Landry Celebrated

In the early, struggling years, when the Dallas Cowboys were a renegade band of athletes running everywhere and seemingly getting nowhere, there were no small victories. Each triumph was cherished, savored, held up as a sign that progress was indeed being made. And to defeat a quality team, one highly regarded throughout the professional football world, was an occasion for high celebration.

Such was the case one October day in 1961 in Yankee Stadium in New York as 60,254 slack-jawed fans watched the Cowboys, of all people, score a

17-16 victory over the powerful New York Giants. This, remember, was the Giants of Y.A. Tittle, Kyle Rote, Frank Gifford, Sam Huff vintage, by every measure a team that NFL history would deal kindly with. And the victor was a Dallas club which the year before had gone winless in its first test of the professional waters and would manage only four wins in its second campaign.

"I was involved in a lot of exciting, satisfying victories in my days as a football player," says Houston motel manager Dick Maegle, "but that day in New York was something else. Shoot, even (Tom) Landry was jumping around, yelling in the dressing room afterwards. To beat a great team like that and to do it in the last minute or so of the game on the other guy's home ground was like having one of your childhood fantasies come true."

For Maegle, the former Rice All-American who entered the pro ranks as the number one draft selection of the San Francisco 49ers, it would be one of the last memorable moments of his superlative dotted career. The talented safety led the 49ers in interceptions for each of his five years on the West Coast and was later traded to Pittsburgh where he worked in the Steelers secondary for a season before coming to Dallas as a player-coach for the 1961 season.

"We had some good athletes then," he is quick to point out, "but there was a problem of everyone not working together. It's the same problem all expansion teams have."

But on that aforementioned day in Yankee Stadium it had all come together. Eddie LeBaron would go all the way at quarterback because shuttle partner Don Meredith was sidelined with an elbow injury suffered the week before. He put the Cowboys into an early lead with a 12-yard touchdown pass to Frank Clarke. Defensive back Bob Bercich then intercepted a Tittle pass and returned it to the New York 20 to set up another Dallas score. (Bercich would, unfortunately, suffer a concussion later in the game.) LeBaron later hit tight end (and Pro Bowler) Dick Bielski on a 14-yard TD toss that upped the Cowboys' lead to 14-0 before the Giants' offense came alive.

Despite a tremendous defensive effort from Dallas, the Giants finally went ahead 16-14 early in the fourth period. But a Cowboys' rookie from Mississippi named Allen Green came on to kick a 32-yard field goal with 1:31 left in the game to give the Cowboys a one-point advantage.

"Even then," Maegle recalls, "it wasn't over. Tittle really cranked up his passing arm and was moving the ball on us. Finally it was left for a defensive tackle to kill the drive. I'm still not sure how or who he got back in the secondary, but Don Healy intercepted a pass at our 35 to stop the Giants. It was a pretty happy moment for a lot of us."

Maegle, who would be credited with one interception that day, recalls that road victories against quality teams were not a regular occurrence in those days. "That's back when travel was a lot harder," he says. "There were no jets and a trip to New York from Dallas was a six, seven hour proposition. You got there already tired."

While that game (as well as an earlier 28-0 shutout of Minnesota) are

pleasant memories of that '61 season, it was not a banner year for Dick Maegle. "I was excited about coming back to Texas to play," he says, "but the second day of training camp I tore some ligaments in my left knee and spent most of the exhibition season in a cast. And because of the fact we were a little thin in the secondary I rushed myself to get well.

"I got out of the cast, in fact, just before our last exhibition game which was to be against San Francisco. I had not intended to play but several people were injured and I wound up limping around out there, playing the whole game. I remember that it was 108 degrees at kickoff and 100 degrees when the game was over. I was staggering at the end because I wasn't yet in condition to go a whole game. My problems weren't helped by the fact we played on that concrete turf at the Cotton Bowl every week. They never watered that place and it was like playing on a parking lot. Things just went from bad to worse. I wound up playing the last five games of the year with a broken bone in my foot. You can imagine how effective I was."

His situation was indicative of the Cowboys that year. Following a promising start, injuries mounted — and so did the defeats.

"I considered trying to play again in '62," Maegle recalls. "I had to get ready for training camp. But when I reported I was still limping. I gave it a try for a few days and then went to Landry and told him it looked like time for me to get into the motel business on a full-time basis. We talked at length and he asked if I would be interested in staying strictly as a coach. I told him I didn't think so. They later went out and hired Dick Nolan, one of Tom's old Giant teammates.

"I enjoyed my stay with the Cowboys," he says, "but I can't help but be a little disappointed in the fact that, because of the injuries, I wasn't able to do what they had hoped I would be able to do for them."

Thus in his only year with Dallas, Dick Maegle, player-coach, had little time to explore the opportunities of the coaching side of his new job. He was always needed in the role of player.

AMOS MARSH
★
The First Long-Distance Cowboy

He is still, 15 years after his final season with the Dallas Cowboys, high on the club's all-time rushing list with 2,065 yards in 427 carries.

Yet it was difficult for Amos Marsh, a member of the Cowboys from 1961 to '64, to break away from his discussion of the talent and ability of the recent Dallas teams and instead focus on his own exploits during the club's building days. Now a loan broker in San Jose, Marsh remains an attentive Cowboys fan.

But long before All-Pro running back Tony Dorsett was priming himself for professional stardom, Marsh and Don Perkins were a highly respected pair of backs, on the growing and improving Cowboys team.

"My best year with the Cowboys," Marsh finally admits, "was 1962. We were finally beginning to understand coach (Tom) Landry's system then and were winning some games (Dallas went 5-8-1 that year). That year, in fact, Perkins and I both finished in the top 10 in rushing and I wound up leading the league in average yards per carry with 5.6. Wound up with 802 yards for the year."

A performance he had in Dallas' 41-19 victory over Philadelphia before 18,645 in the Cotton Bowl that season does not show up in his rushing statistics. "That day," he says, "was one of the greatest of my life. I ran a kickoff back 101 yards for a touchdown. And to really top things off it wasn't but a few minutes later that Mike Gaechter intercepted an Eagles pass and returned it 100 yards for another touchdown. I doubt that kind of thing has happened since. It's one of those things you find yourself thinking about every now and then for the rest of your life, I guess."

Much of the '62 season was a memory maker for the 225-pound fullback who had 9.7 speed. "It was of those years when I seemed to have a lot of things going for me," he says. "Against Los Angeles I scored on an 85-yard pass from Eddie LeBaron (a mark which still ranks as the third longest pass reception in Cowboys annals) and against Washington I went 70 yards (a step shy of his best of 71 against Chicago the year previous and fifth on Dallas' all-time scrimmage run list). It was just one of those years when the holes were there and I was able to break some big plays."

There were no long distance runs later in that memorable season when Marsh and the Cowboys stunned a Cotton Bowl crowd with a 45-21 victory over the heralded Cleveland Browns. With the Browns keying on Perkins, Marsh rushed past the 100-yard mark while the Dallas defense held the legendary Jim Brown to only 13 yards rushing for the day. "That was a game," Marsh recalls, "when we played like we could beat the world. I don't think we ever played a game better than that one during my career with the Cowboys."

"We had a better than average crop of backs then," Marsh remembers. "Of course, there was Perkins who was the fastest man I've ever seen for five yards, and Amos Bullocks and J.W. Lockett. We were all pretty big backs and had better than average speed. They were good days, and a lot of fun. I learned a lot of football with the Cowboys. In fact, I never really thought the Dallas offense was as complicated as a lot of people say. It was just that there were so many formations. Once you got the formations down, it was actually relatively simple. When I went to Detroit (where he played out the final three years of his career), it was a lot easier for me to learn the Lions' system because of the background I had from being with the Cowboys."

That he was with the Cowboys in the first place still is something of a surprise to Marsh. "After the football season my senior year at Oregon State, my brother and I had just returned to school from Christmas vacation and were settling in to watch the New Year's Day football games when this guy came into the dorm. He came up to me and shook my hand and said, 'I'm Gil Brandt and I've come here to sign you to play for the Dallas Cowboys.' I was a little surprised to say the least. Everything in town was closed that day but he insisted on taking us out to eat so we finally located this hamburger place.

"I had started my college career as a wingback in a single wing formation and later, as I gained some weight, had been moved to end. Brandt signed me as a wide receiver but when I got to training camp the coaches told me that since there weren't too many rookie running backs there they were going to work me at fullback until the veterans reported. I never even got to learn the plays for a wide receiver."

Which is just as well. Had he become a wide receiver, the Cowboys record books wouldn't show Amos Marsh to be the seventh leading rusher in the club's history behind only Dorsett, Perkins, Calvin Hill, Walt Garrison and Robert Newhouse. The recollection of his accomplishments as a rusher, Marsh says, is nice.

The best memory, though, is of that 101-yard kickoff return for a touchdown against Philadelphia on October 14, 1962. It still ranks atop the list, tied after nine years by Ike Thomas in a game against the New York Jets.

BUDDY HUMPHREY

★

No Records, But It Was Fun

In his senior year at Baylor, he had been regarded as one of the — if not *the* — most likely college quarterback to make the demanding transition into the professional ranks.

Buddy Humphrey, at 6-2, 200 pounds, had the physical requirements and the proper background, having spent his days as a schoolboy sensation at Temple High and then as a collegian setting records throwing the football. In his senior year on the Waco campus he led the nation in passing, had engaged in a couple of headline demanding shootouts with SMU quarterback, Don Meredith, and was selected to participate in such post season competition as the 1959 College All-Star Game and the Senior Bowl.

More importantly, when he became second round draft selection of the Los Angeles Rams, the headlines stopped.

Back home in Texas today, working as a purchasing agent for Kilgore

Junior College, Buddy Humphrey is wholesomely candid about his professional career which saw him spend two and a half years in a Rams uniform, a year and a half with the Dallas Cowboys, and three with the St. Louis Cardinals. "You're not going to find my name in any record books," he laughs, "but it was a lot of fun."

And, no doubt, a bit frustrating.

"When I got to the Rams," he remembers, "they had Billy Wade and Frank Ryan as their one and two quarterbacks. You can guess how much I played there." As time passed, Wade was traded to the Chicago Bears and proceeded to win a championship. Ryan was shipped to Cleveland where he accomplished the same. Humphrey's future would not hold such promise.

A struggling new franchise in Dallas was in need of an insurance quarterback, someone to back up Eddie LeBaron and Buddy's old Southwest Conference rival Meredith. Humphrey was traded to the Cowboys, returning to the site of collegiate glories. "It was good to get back to Texas and the Cotton Bowl," he says. "But, to be honest, I didn't spend much time on the playing side of the sidelines. Oh, I remember playing quite a bit against the Giants in the last game of the '62 season, but there wasn't much at stake." Indeed, it was the final loss (41-31) in a 5-8-1 season.

The following year he was traded off to St. Louis where for three years he backed up Charlie Johnson. "I could never get away from the really top notch NFL quarterbacks, it seemed," Humphrey says. "If, in fact, my pro career had a highlight, it would have to have been while I was with the Cardinals. I got to play quite a bit there and remember coming back to the Cotton Bowl and having a pretty good game against Dallas in the first game of the '63 season. (The Cardinals won it, 34-7.) No touchdown passes or anything like that, mind you, but a pretty solid game with which I was personally satisfied."

For Buddy Humphrey, the season and a half he spent doing his part in helping build a foundation for the then struggling Dallas Cowboys was not as frustrating as one might expect. In a time when a number of twilight heroes from around the league were being shipped to Dallas, grumbling all the way, Humphrey didn't mind.

"First of all, it was good to get back to this part of the world. And, the fact was I hadn't exactly been burning up the league in Los Angeles. I have some good memories of the time I was with the Cowboys.

"There was a feeling, I think, that we were a team whose time would eventually come. Everyone could see what Tom Landry was building toward. For those of us there at the time, it was just a matter of biding our time. It wasn't time yet for Dallas to enjoy success, but you could see it coming because the organization was going about things in the right way."

Even in those dog days, Buddy says, there were areas in which the Cowboys excelled above the more established clubs. "The quarterback meetings, for instance, were a lot different in Dallas than they were in LA and St. Louis. Landry went into far more depth, gave you more detailed reasoning for what he wanted you to do. Though he was calling the plays, he wanted you to know what was going on. He just demanded more of his quarterbacks than other coaches I played under."

And of the quarterbacks he worked alongside, who would he rank as the best?

"I'd have to say Meredith. Maybe he didn't ever win a championship like some of the others I've mentioned, but so far as being an outstanding leader and doing the things a quarterback has to do to help his team win, he was superior."

Today Humphrey still keeps close tabs on the Cowboys. "I made some good friends while I was on the team," he says. "When I came to Dallas in the middle of the season in '61 I didn't have a place to stay so Bob Lilly invited me to share his apartment with him. I don't believe I've ever been associated with an athlete who was as outstanding as he was and managed to remain such a modest, easy-going kind of person.

"He had a great deal of class. Just like the Cowboys organization."

JOE BOB ISBELL
⭐
The First Messenger Guard

Joe Bob Isbell, for one, sees no fault with Tom Landry's manner of sending in plays from the sideline. Once a messenger guard whose chore it was to carry plays from the bench to huddle, Isbell insists he can't recall a time when the Cowboys were ever called for delay of game because of Landry's system.

"Of course," says the Guaranty Bond State Bank security officer who now makes his home in Tomball, Texas, "back when I was playing for Dallas (1962-65) there wasn't quite as much shifting around and all that. But being one of those shuttling plays never really bothered me. If anything, it was to my benefit. Going from the sideline to the huddle with the play in mind gave me a chance to think about what I was going to have to do on it."

It was a chore he shared with fellow guard Dale Memmelaar in his first two seasons in a Cowboys' uniform. "The big criticism I always heard about being a lineman who shuttled plays," he says, "was that the constant running on and off the field would eventually tire you to a point where you wouldn't be as effective as you normally might be, particularly late in the game. I always thought that was a bunch of bull since you were supposed to be in pretty good shape to play professional football in the first place. It was a good, solid system so far as I was concerned."

In fact, during the six years he spent coaching schoolboy football in the Houston area before taking his banking position, Isbell followed Landry's pattern, always calling plays from the sidelines.

"I don't care how good your quarterback is or how smart he is," Isbell says, "he's got a tremendous responsibility out there on the field. There are a lot of things he's got to be constantly aware of, thinking about. By giving him some relief from the play-calling responsibilities you eliminate some of the pressure on him." It's the audibles that the quarterbacks are wont to call that cause the problems, Isbell laughs. "The hardest I ever got hit," he recalls, "was the result of a quarterback changing the play I had brought in.

"We were playing in a doubleheader in Cleveland in 1962. We opened against the Detroit Lions and later Cleveland played Pittsburgh. I came in to Don Meredith with a play and he got to the line and audibled off to a trap play. I thought I was supposed to pull and trap and Andy Cvercko, who was playing the other guard, thought he was supposed to pull and trap. What resulted was our running into each other head-on just behind the center right there in front of 80,000 people. It nearly knocked both of us out. What was even worse was having to watch it on film the following Monday. The whole team was howling and thought it was about the funniest thing they'd ever seen. Except for Andy and I. And coach Landry. Things like that never really amused him."

The one-time standout at the University of Houston can still vividly recall his one moment of glory as a Cowboys lineman. And even at that it was a moment shortlived and eventually rubbed from the record books.

"We were playing the Giants in the Cotton Bowl my rookie season," he remembers, "and Meredith threw this little screen pass that was really nothing more than a lateral. The pass was incomplete and the ball was just laying there. There was no whistle so I was certain that the official had determined that it was a lateral and therefore still a live ball. As luck would have it, I was nearest to it so I scooped it up and, still not hearing any whistle, ran 80 yards for a touchdown. That was my moment of glory. Man, I could already see the headlines.

"It turned out that the referee's whistle had jammed on him or something and he just hadn't been able to blow it. He finally ruled that it was just an incompleted pass and called my dramatic touchdown run back."

Following the 1965 season Isbell was traded to the Cleveland Browns and a year later was back in his hometown as a member of the Houston Oilers. He wound up his career in 1968 with the then-expansion Cincinnati Bengals.

"Having the opportunity to play under Tom Landry was a great experience for me," he says today. "He's one of the brightest men I've ever known. And, just as he does today, he's always thinking two or three plays ahead of the game when standing there on the sidelines. I never remember a situation where he was the least bit hesitant in making a play selection. He always had what he wanted in mind and was ready to give it to you just as soon as he knew the down and distance. Running back and forth from the sidelines to the huddle enabled me to learn a lot of football in a pretty short period of time."

AMOS BULLOCKS

✭

Records Made for Breaking

Young Craig Bullocks sat in the den of his Chicago home, watching as his favorite team, the Dallas Cowboys, do battle with St. Louis. Beside him was his father, Amos Bullocks, director of the social service operations of the Illinois Department of Corrections. They were keeping to their regular Sunday afternoon routine; namely, watching pro football, particularly should the Cowboys, a team for which the elder Bullocks played for three years (1962-63-64), be on the field.

On this particular afternoon a highly publicized rookie running back named Tony Dorsett slipped through daylight in the front wall, made a quick cut to the outside and was off on a 77-yard touchdown jaunt. The run completed and shown on instant replay, Craig Bullocks looked at his dad, smiled and said, "Well, there goes your name from the record book, Dad."

Amos Bullocks, once a 20th round draft selection out of Southern Illinois, back-up running back to Amos Marsh during the early days of Cowboys' history, shrugged, "Hey," he said in mock defiance, "they had to go out and pay a million dollars for a Heisman Trophy winner to get that record broken, though. It took them 15 years to find somebody who could do the trick."

Father and son both laughed.

It had been November 18, 1962 when Bullocks entered the game in the second quarter against the Chicago Bears after Marsh had hobbled to the sideline with an ankle injury, took advantage of an overshifted Bears defense and scored on a 73-yard dash in the Cotton Bowl. Until Dorsett's long distance jaunt against the Cardinals it had stood, rarely challenged, as the longest run in Cowboys history.

Bullocks does not hesitate to point to that record-setting day as his fondest competitive memory. "You know," he said, "I remember a great deal about that game, going in for Marsh and playing the rest of the day, the touchdown, the fact that it was being televised back in my hometown (Chicago), and all that, but I can't for the life of me remember whether we won or lost."

In a time when there were easily as many losses as wins — Dallas went 5-8-1 for the '62 season — the records show that the Bears, despite Bullocks' heroics, scored a 34-33 victory as only 12,692 fans looked on.

"It was a special play coach Landry had put in for Chicago since they had a tendency to overshift in certain situations. It worked just like it had been drawn up on the board. That was about it for me that day, though, because except for that one run they kept me pretty well bottled up. I don't remember how many times I carried the ball but I know I didn't end the day with 100 yards, so that should tell you something."

An All-America halfback at Southern Illinois, Bullocks contracted hepatitis in his third season with Dallas and was released and played a year with the British Columbia Lions in the Canadian League. "Actually," he says, "it was some kind of a trade deal as I remember, because the Cowboys got a lineman from B.C. when I went up there. After a year in Canada I came back to the NFL and finished out my career with the Pittsburgh Steelers in 1966 and '67.

"You know, we never had a winning season while I was there, but we all knew it was just a matter of time. With players like Bob Lilly and Perkins and Don Meredith and Cornell Green and a coach like Landry it was obvious that things were going to fall into place one day."

MONTE CLARK

Fast Learner

Speaking from his Pontiac, Michigan office, Monte Clark, head coach of the Detroit Lions, was answering questions about his team's just-won 27-24 victory over Dallas in one of the 1981 season's most controversial games. With just 27 seconds remaining, a Lions field goal had secured the win, but films would later reveal that Detroit had twelve men on the field at the time.

In the days following there were angry cries from the Cowboys and Clarke himself would admit they were not without good reason. Still, he pointed out repeatedly, it had been an innocent mistake. And, after all, a win is a win.

It was a philosophy he held throughout his playing career, including those days he himself labored in a Cowboys' uniform.

"I still enjoy talking about the year I spent with the Cowboys," he says. "I value the time I spent there. And, frankly, when I'm in a situation like I'm in now, trying to build a championship-caliber team, it helps to be able to look back and recall the composure Tom Landry kept in those days before he had developed Dallas into the winner it has become."

In his successful 11-year career as a professional, Clark spent one season working at tackle for the Cowboys; coming to Dallas in 1962 after a trade with the San Francisco 49ers.

"I came in on a Monday," he recalls, "and had a long talk with Landry. He told me that I would be one of the starting tackles just as soon as I was able to learn the offense. I studied like crazy, hoping I could get enough of a grasp on it to work my way into the starting lineup in three or four weeks."

In a move which may make Clark the fastest learner in Cowboys history,

50

he was in the starting offensive lineup the following Sunday, six days after signing on.

"And, you know," he says, "we had one of our best days ever rushing. Don Perkins and Amos Marsh ran the ball really well. Perkins, in fact, was always a back I greatly admired. When I was coaching in San Francisco I tried to hire him as a backfield coach."

During that '62 campaign the Cowboys would gain some degree of respectability, winning 5, losing 8 and tying one. "It was a matter of having a good day, then a bad one. We didn't have it all together then, but there was already an attitude building. The Dallas Cowboys, despite being just a couple of years old, were already thinking about being winners."

And that attitude indeed became prevalent the time he misplaced his playbook in the lobby of a Washington hotel prior to a mid-season game with the Redskins; upsetting himself and most other members of the Dallas organization. In addition to the sizeable fine awaiting Clark, there was concern that the Redskins might somehow have laid claim to the Dallas battle plan. "It was," Monte recalls, "a very unpleasant situation to be in." When, however, the Cowboys enjoyed their finest Sunday of the season, defeating the Redskins, 38-10, a good laugh was had by all. Landry, Clark remembers, even reduced the fine by 50 per cent.

"During the short time I was there," Clark says, "I developed some lasting friendships. I still stay in touch with the other offensive linemen who were there at the time. Just the other day I talked with (guard) Andy Cvercko on the phone and I see (guard) Dale Memmelaar and (center) Mike Connelly now and then. And it was (tackle) Bob Fry (now coaching for the Jets) who recommended me for my first pro coaching job."

The 42-year-old Clark spent six years as the offensive coach for Don Shula in Miami, sharing in two Super Bowl titles before being named head coach of the San Francisco 49ers in 1976.

His coaching successes would come, however, after he played in NFL championship games as a member of the Cleveland Browns in 1964, '65 and '68. "After that one year in Dallas," he says, "I was traded to the Browns for Jim Ray Smith. He had announced that he was going to retire if the Browns wouldn't work out a trade that put him closer to home. I guess you might say I'm the guy who cleared the way for Jim Ray to get his wish."

As it turned out, of course, Clark, once a standout player for Southern Cal, went on to championship games much sooner than did the Cowboys teammates he left behind. Among his teammates with the Browns was current Cowboys scout John Wooten.

"The Cowboys were still struggling when I was there," he says, "but you didn't see anyone pushing the panic button. They had a plan they believed in and they were dedicated to staying with it until it worked. That, perhaps more than anything, is the reason they made it to the top as quickly as they did. Landry would become frustrated, you know he had to. But I can't ever remember him showing it. The confidence that man showed — and continues to show — has been a big factor in his success."

51

It is, he admits, the same kind of success he would one day like to bring to Detroit.

DALE MEMMELAAR

★

Finding A Chance in Dallas

He had, by his own definition, been declared excess baggage by the St. Louis Cardinals, traded first to the expansion Minnesota Vikings, returned after just two weeks, and finally placed on waivers. Dale Memmelaar, a 28th round draft choice out of the University of Wyoming, was, at a very early stage of his professional football career, wondering if it was over before it had really been given a chance to begin.

Then came a call from Tex Schramm, general manager of a new team in the league, the two-year-old Dallas Cowboys. The Cowboys and the young offensive guard who was out of a job were, in a sense, both looking for a chance.

"Tex invited me to come down and try it in Dallas," Memmelaar, now athletic director at Washingtonville (New York) High School, recalls, "and I got in the car and started driving. It was a long trip and a lot of thoughts ran through my mind. I wondered to myself if maybe this was my last chance. One minute I doubted I would make it, the next I was confident that I would. By the time I finally got there, I had made up my mind that nothing in the world was going to prevent my making the team."

Let the record show that he did, starting in the offensive line for Dallas in 1962 and '63.

"Tom Landry gave me the biggest break of my career," he says. "Moving into a system like his really got me going. Getting traded can work several ways with a person; some have their spirits broken, others find a new enthusiasm. The latter was my case. Landry was looking for something different. He had his own ideas of how things should be done and I was much the same way. It was a great opportunity for me. After he saw what I could do, he told me he was going to give me the opportunity to play first team. And, in turn, I had the opportunity to prove to him that his decision was a good one.

"He treated everyone like a man; that's something that has stayed with me. It was always amazing to me what he could do to get people to play to the best of their ability, sometimes beyond. And he was such a student of the game. His whole system impressed me. In fact, when I finished with pro ball and got into high school coaching, I used basically the same things he had been using. Oh, I had to water them down considerably, but in principle they were the same, really."

Memmelaar's tenure with the Cowboys was a time of noteworthy offensive fireworks and a defense having more troubles than you could shake a stick at.

52

"One season," he recalls, "we led the league in scoring, but every time we would score and come off the field to rest it was right back to work because the other team was scoring more easily than we were."

It was a time in Cowboys history, he admits, when the enthusiasm he felt for the system was not shared by all. Dallas was a stopping place on the way to retirement for many players who had performed well on successful teams and were not eager for the changes Landry suggested. "It was a tough time," the guard who played at 250 pounds, remembers. "It took a great deal of mental toughness to stick with it because there might be as many as 40 or 50 new players coming through camp in a week's time. One day you might be first team and then they would bring in some veteran with better credentials and he would move ahead of you before he put a uniform on."

While he went on to play as a member of the world champion Cleveland Browns after being traded following the '63 season, Dale still looks to his first game as a member of the Cowboys as one of his career highlights. "It was a big deal for me because I was the starting guard. It was a game that was a big test for me. We were playing Washington in the Cotton Bowl and it was 105 degrees. The game ended in a 35-35 tie but that day I felt I showed what I was capable of doing; that I could play football in the NFL. It was a big moment for me."

GUY REESE
★
Cowboys' First Native Son

He was the first home grown Dallas Cowboy. A native son who played his high school ball at South Oak Cliff, was a college standout at SMU and in 1962, a 15th-round draft pick of the Cowboys.

Guy Reese then became a member of what is generally believed to be the most inexperienced defensive front four ever fielded by an NFL team. There was second year man Bob Lilly and rookies George Andrie, John Meyers and Reese.

"I don't remember," says head coach Tom Landry, "any time in NFL history that three rookies started in a defensive line. But, those guys did a good job. They put a lot of pressure on the quarterbacks simply because of their enthusiasm and ability. They didn't always get to the quarterback but they made him aware that they were coming after him."

It was their youthful enthusiasm, perhaps, which prompted the media to call them the Maverick Line. Maybe it didn't have the ring of Doomsday but as the former 6-5, 240-pound tackle Reese recalls, "It was one of the nicer things we were called back in those days.

"People have no idea what the transition is for a player coming out of college to play pro ball," he says. "One day you're playing against people your own age; then suddenly you're lining up against grown men. It's a traumatic experience."

Ironically, the most traumatic experiences Reese encountered in his two-year career with the Cowboys came not on defense but offense. And both involved the Pittsburgh Steelers.

It was the second game of the 1962 season and the Cowboys, playing one of their better games, trailed the Bobby Layne-led Steelers, 21-24 in the third quarter when Eddie LeBaron took over at quarterback for Dallas after Don Meredith injured an ankle. Jerry Norton had just intercepted a Layne pass at the Dallas one and LeBaron came on to put the offensive in gear.

Backpedaling into his own end zone, LeBaron lofted a bomb to Frank Clarke who gathered it in at midfield and sped toward what the 19,478 in the Cotton Bowl viewed as an apparent record-setting 99-yard touchdown pass. Few noticed the flag which had been thrown at the Cowboys goal line.

An official had ruled that offensive guard Andy Cvercko had been guilty of holding Pittsburgh defensive standout Big Daddy Lipscomb. The infraction had occurred two yards deep in the end zone, thus the Dallas touchdown was wiped out and the Steelers awarded a two-point safety (and eventually would win the game by that margin, 30-28). Even Pittsburgh coach Buddy Parker admitted he had never heard of the rule which stated "It is a safety when the offense commits a foul and the spot of enforcement is behind the goal line."

Obviously, Reese notes, it was a rule of which Landry was unaware.

"I've never seen Landry get as upset — before or since — as he did over that call. He really lost his poise. He yelled so loud and so long that when the game was over he had completely lost his voice.

"In fact, in the team meeting the next Tuesday he apologized to the team for his actions which, as far as I was concerned, weren't out of line. The Cotton Bowl had been a long way from being full, but you've never heard more booing than there was after that call.

"Still, Landry was obviously embarrassed about his reaction to the situation. I remember him saying, 'I felt I was right; I don't know why I was right, but I was certain that I was.' "

A year later he would have been. In the following off-season the obscure rule was wiped from the NFL books.

"Layne really played it for all it was worth that day," Reese remembers. "He would bring the team out of the huddle with all that booing and would throw up his hands and go to the sidelines. He would wait until the booing had just about died down and then run back out on the field and get it all started up again. He loved it."

Reese, who was later traded to Baltimore, where he spent two years before going to Atlanta in the expansion draft, says the highlight of his career came when he delivered a blow to the immortal Layne, causing the quarterback to leave the field for a few plays. "And, as you'll recall, Layne never missed much playing time."

His second traumatic occasion came in his rookie year while playing offensive tackle on the Cowboys extra point unit. Reese found himself lined up across from the 6-6, 280-pound Lipscomb.

"It was not the kind of situation you like to find yourself in," Guy remembers. "Big Daddy was kind of famous for the talking he did and when we lined up he looked me in the eye and said, 'Little man, Big Daddy's gonna block this kick.' "

Did you manage to block him out, Guy? "Well, let's just say he didn't block the kick."

LARRY STEPHENS
⭐
Fearsome Foursome to Doomsday

The 1963 season was just days away when Tom Landry, having already faced a lifetime of crises during the first couple of seasons with his expansion franchise Dallas Cowboys, was greeted with another helping of bad news. George Andrie, a respected member of his defensive front line was injured and the prospect of a young backup player moving in to replace him wasn't the kind of option Landry could parlay.

He sought a trade and placed a call to former New York Giants friend and cohort Harland Svare, then head coach of the Los Angeles Rams. Their defensive philosophies were similar, Landry knew, and if Svare could be persuaded to trade former University of Texas standout Larry Stephens to the Cowboys the vacancy could be filled with little loss of time. Svare agreed.

Thus in 1963 Stephens, an original member of LA's Fearsome Foursome along with Merlin Olsen, Lamar Lundy and Deacon Jones, changed addresses and gained the unique distinction of being a member of yet another defensive front four that eventually accrued national attention because of the tag — Doomsday — later placed upon it.

"Actually," Stephens recalls, "Dallas and LA were using about the same system then, so Tom got me because he felt I could step right in and play for him." He arrived in Dallas on a Wednesday and was in the starting lineup the following Saturday for a game against the St. Louis Cardinals.

The first couple of years would be difficult as the young and still struggling Cowboys searched for the first break-even season. In '63 they would go 4-10; the next year 5-8-1. "We could always see some improvement," Larry recalls, "but we always seemed to be a player or two away from having that solid unit that could help us put it all together." The 1965 season was, many felt, the year the Cowboys would swing upward at last.

"The defense was playing pretty good football that year," he says. "We

were holding people pretty good, but crazy things kept happening early in the year and we got off on a bad foot. We won a couple and then lost five in a row.

"I'll never forget, for instance, a game in Milwaukee against Green Bay. Our defense was outstanding that day. You'll remember that the Packers were awesome in those days but we really went after them. They didn't get but something like 50 yards rushing against us that day but beat us 13-3 after getting the ball down deep in our territory a couple of times. Even though we lost, there was a feeling among some of us that we had reached a level where we could play with the big boys. But, then, the following week we lost another crazy kind of game to Pittsburgh (22-13) for our fifth defeat in a row. Tom was really upset after that one; more than I'd ever seen him before or after. When I say upset I don't mean he was throwing things or chewing people out. The fact of the matter was that he didn't say anything. Not a word.

"Everyone was really searching, trying to find the answer to what it would take to get things turned around."

Quarterback Don Meredith had, by then, emerged as the team leader, Stephens remembers, and a meeting of the players was called. "No coaches, just the players," Larry says. "Back then Don and Tom were pretty close. Or it seemed they were most of the time. Close enough, at least, for Don to have some idea of what Landry's feelings about the state of the team were. We just got together and had a long talk among ourselves, reviewing what we were doing and what we weren't doing. One of the things that we all agreed on was the fact that if we were to make things work every man had to do his own job to the best of his ability. That, basically, was Landry's philosophy. If everyone does his work, then the whole thing comes together.

"Even today I don't think I could tell you exactly what turned things around, but the fact remains that we did turn it around. Not just that season, but maybe the whole direction of the Cowboys." That '65 season saw Dallas win five of its last seven games and end the year at 7-7 before advancing to the now defunct Playoff Bowl against Baltimore.

There have been no losing seasons in the Cowboys history since.

"Up until that season," says Stephens, who now makes his home in Lockhart but commutes to Dallas where he runs a trucking operation and service station, "we had the feeling, I think, that we were snakebit at times. There were days when we could play really good football and still lose. If that goes on long enough you get to a point where you start expecting bad things to happen to you. I think we were fortunate that we got past that stage when we did."

Before he ended his career following the 1967 season Stephens proved himself to be one of the most versatile linemen on the roster. In his early tenure, he worked at right end while Bob Lilly handled the left end. Later Lilly moved to tackle and Stephens switched over to the left end.

"In those days," he remembers, "Landry worked a great deal with the defense. We really didn't even have a defensive line coach as such. Or a linebacker coach. I know when I first got here a lot of my help came from Lee

Roy Jordan who was playing outside linebacker and Jerry Tubbs who was working at middle linebacker.

"I played two seasons in Cleveland, one in Los Angeles and then five in Dallas. They were all fine organizations, but even in the early days, Dallas had it over the others. I was at the exes reunion recently and it really made me start to think. An affair like that — first class all the way — is an example of the little extra things that the Cowboys provide. It makes you appreciate having been a part of the organization."

The organization, no doubt, appreciates what Larry Stephens and his teammates did in that 1965 season; in effect, setting the course that the team still sails.

JERRY NORTON

★

The Run That Angered St. Louis

Those who have done it, collectively agree that it is no easy task; that it causes a feeling unlike any other they experienced as a ball player. Returning to play against a team you once played for, says former safety Jerry Norton, is one part fun, one part sad, and, on occasions, several parts confusing.

After being a standout running back for Southern Methodist, the Texarkana native spent five years playing with the Philadelphia Eagles before being traded to St. Louis in 1958. "The first time I went back to Philadelphia as a member of the Cardinals," the Dallas-based wholesale electrical supplier recalls, "I was looking forward to seeing some friends. What I got was a cold shoulder and a knocking around you wouldn't believe. I couldn't understand it until after the game I went up to a couple of Eagles players and asked what in the world was going on. As it turned out there had been a story in the paper, quoting me as having said some pretty strong things about the caliber of the Eagles. I had never said any of those things, really, but they got me in a lot of trouble."

Then, there was his first trip back to St. Louis after becoming a member of the Dallas Cowboys in 1962.

"I had retired after the '61 season," Norton says, "and was living in Dallas. The Cowboys were about half-way through the exhibition season when I got a call one morning from Tex Schramm. He told me he had been in touch with the Cardinals and had permission to talk with me about coming out of retirement. We had lunch and I went to my first team meeting that night. That was on a Wednesday and I played quite a bit in a game the following Saturday."

Norton admits that it was a season in which he never fully managed to get in shape, inasmuch as he had done no off-season work prior to his sudden sign-up with the Cowboys. Later in that season he journeyed north to play against his former teammates in St. Louis. And, despite his lack of conditioning, he accomplished a feat that day which even now stands as something of an NFL rarity.

On December 9, 1962, Jerry Norton earned a spot for himself in the Cowboys record book; returning a St. Louis field goal attempt 94 yards for a touchdown. That historic run, he recalls today, accomplished two things: "It nearly killed me," he says, "and it really made the Cardinals mad. After that, they went on to beat us 52-20."

Such were the pinball highs and lows of the early day Cowboys.

It was a time, Norton recalls, of a revolving door passage of players, some over the hill, some misfits, a few troublemakers and many not quite up to NFL standards. "They were just doing whatever they could to put something together back then," he said. "It was a little confusing at times."

He remembers early in the season, sharing the deep secondary responsibilities with former player-coach Dick Nolan. Norton made a couple of interceptions but suffered a long dry spell before picking off another. Landry quizzed him about the problem. "Well," Norton told him, "I was doing pretty good until I began to learn the defense, then I got really confused.

"Actually, it wasn't so much the system as it was the fact I was never in really topnotch shape. I hadn't anticipated playing again and hadn't done a thing in the off-season. And those were days when you didn't get a lot of rest during a game. I came off the field cross-eyed every week."

A two-way performer at SMU, Norton had been drafted by the Eagles as an offensive back but his defensive performance in the annual College All-Star game against the Detroit Lions labeled him a safety. It was the job the Cowboys hired him to do.

Also an excellent punter, he would later be traded to Green Bay where he became the Packers' regular punter. That job was manned in Dallas by Sam Baker during Norton's tenure. "If nothing else," Jerry says, "being around Sam Baker for a year was fun. That guy's escapades are still legendary." Indeed, Baker was something of a Don Meredith-Pete Gent-Thomas Henderson rolled into one.

"The Cowboys," says Norton, "have come a long way from where they were when I was with them for that one season. But it was fun. I only wish I had been able to get in shape."

Maybe then he could have enjoyed his 94-yard touchdown run a bit more.

OLA LEE MURCHISON

★

A $50 Punch

One newspaper's account of the 31-10 defeat in the Cotton Bowl made mention of the fact that the only real punch the home team had displayed all day was the one thrown by Ola Lee Murchison, a kick return specialist. And although it was, unfortunately, a reaction that caused him to be ejected from the game, it was certainly not the deciding factor in the 1961 loss to the New York Giants.

Ola, who played at 6-3 and 225 and had managed to maintain the 9.4 sprinter's speed which enabled him to star on the University of Pacific track team as well as set numerous school marks as a wide receiver, had come to the Cowboys from the San Francisco 49ers. He had been a sixth round draft choice but when his name was called on draft day he was in the hospital recovering from his second knee operation.

Looking back, Murchison says about all the surgeon left him was his speed. Many of the elusive moves he had had at U. of P. were gone, never to return. After a year the 49ers let him go and the Cowboys, looking for help wherever they could find it, picked him up.

Though listed on the roster as a wide receiver, Ola's primary function was that of a punt and kickoff return man. He performed his task well but with few really magic moments. In that season there were no long, darting, dodging runs for touchdowns and no game-breaking plays. There were a lot of Ola Lee Murchisons on the team in those days.

"Still," he laughs, "I hate to think that the thing I'm best remembered for is punching a guy in the nose."

It isn't much of a legacy, really, but, as the man says, it makes a pretty good story. "Not to mention that it cost me a $50 fine," the Stockton, California, junior high principal recalls.

"This one guy," Ola recalls, "was after me all day. He kept hitting late, piling on, the whole bit. After a few times, I had had about all of it I wanted. I ran a kickoff back and one guy tackled me and then after I'm already down, here comes this fellow I'm talking about. He plows into me like the play was still under way. So, rather than get up, I just rolled over on him, pinned him to the ground, and let him have it. The next thing I knew the referee was telling me I was out of the game — and the other guy was running off to the bench with a big smile on his face.

"Then, when we went up to New York to play the Giants a second time it was made very clear to me that the incident hadn't been forgotten. We were

61

out for pre-game warmups and Sam Huff (the famed Giants linebacker) came over to me and made it clear that he and his defensive teammates had small tolerance for a kick returner taking swings at any of them. You can rest assured I was a model citizen that day."

Following that 4-9-1 campaign Murchison returned home to Stockton to finish work on his degree in music. "I was planning on returning to Dallas," he says, "but just for the heck of it I applied for a music teaching job and one as choir director of a local church. To my surprise, I was offered both jobs so I decided it was as good a time as any to call it a career. After all who ever heard of a music teacher getting a knee busted up or threatened by Sam Huff? It sounded like a good life to me."

And, indications are, it has indeed been good for Ola Lee Murchison. Today he is a junior high school principal, dabbles in real estate, gives private piano and organ lessons, is a flying instructor and will 'soon open a cafe-grocery in the nearby community of Forrest Hills.

"Having been a part of the Cowboys organization was fun," he says, "and something I'll never forget. The kids at my school all know that I played in Dallas and they're big Cowboy fans. In fact, the *Cowboys Weekly* is about the best read thing we have in our library. The kids really keep up with the team."

So does Ola Lee Murchison, a man who was never a household word but a representative figure from the early days when there were precious few highlights and even fewer wins; a time when a punch in the nose was big news.

JIM DORAN
★
Dallas' First Pro-Bowler

For nine years Jim Doran had been a key figure in many of the greatest moments in Detroit Lions history; a tight end on a team filled with gifted players like Bobby Layne, Doak Walker and Yale Larry just to name a few.

But as the 1959 season ended the former Iowa State standout did something he had never before done in his pro career. "When the season ended," he recalls, "I cleaned out my locker, took my shoes, and headed home. I just had a feeling I might be playing somewhere other than Detroit the following season."

He had no reason to expect, however, that he would move to a brand new franchise located in Dallas calling itself the Cowboys. When the other members of the NFL chipped in to help fill the expansion roster, though, Doran was among those players bound for Texas.

"We didn't win many the two years I was there," the Paton, Iowa farmer recalls, "but I enjoyed my stay in Dallas. I got to play, got some experience as a player-coach and learned a lot of football from Tom Landry."

He also realized a goal his first season in Dallas which had eluded him during his tenure with the Lions. In 1960, Doran was the lone member of the Cowboys selected to play in the Pro Bowl. "That was a big thrill for me," he says. "I had pulled a muscle late in the season, after being named to the team, but I didn't mention it to anyone for fear that I might be replaced. I knew that was probably my last chance at the selection. I was 33 at the time and knew my playing days were getting short."

Ironically, he would share playing time in the '60 Pro Bowl with a Detroit tight end named Jim Gibbons.

"Coach Landry had been totally honest with me when I joined the club. He told me that I wouldn't be around when he eventually put together the kind of team he hoped to have. He was looking for young players but needed a few veterans to help things along in the early going."

Doran responded by leading the team in receiving during that initial year, catching 31 for 554 yards and a 17.9 average per catch.

"The game I guess I'll always remember," he says, "is our very first league game. We played Pittsburgh in the Cotton Bowl and I was really anxious to perform well since Buddy Parker, my old coach at Detroit, was coaching the Steelers. And a teammate and friend, Bobby Layne, was their quarterback. You always want to make a good showing against people you've known for a long time, so there was every reason for me to be ready to play."

What resulted was a performance Doran today ranks as possibly the best he ever had as a professional.

While the Steelers would win the game 35-28 as a crowd of 30,000 looked on, Cowboys quarterbacks would hit the former Lion with touchdown passes of 75 and 54 yards. For the day, Doran caught seven passes for a total of 134 yards. In the aftermath of the defeat one dejected Cowboys player commented, "What we need on this team is eleven Jim Dorans." Unfortunately that was impossible and the NFL's newest entry limped home with a 0-11-1 season record in its premier year.

"In 1961 I played in every game," Doran recalls, "despite the fact I was having some knee problems. And, I was being used more as a player-coach by then. There were, you recall, only four full-time coaches on the Cowboys staff back then. It was a great opportunity for me to learn."

Following his retirement after the '61 season, Doran joined his old boss Parker in Pittsburgh where he served as receiver coach in 1964 and 1965.

"Of course, it wasn't all fun at the time — losing so often — but, looking back, there were some pretty crazy times. I used to get tickled at (Don) Meredith. He had a lot of trouble with Landry's system of check-offs and things like that. Pro football was good to me," he continues, "and I'm glad I had the opportunity to spend a number of years in it."

BILL HERCHMAN

A Two-Year Mystery

Looking back on it all, says Bill Herchman, the starting defensive right tackle for the Dallas Cowboys in the first two seasons of their existence, it was a time of great confusion. The lessons as taught by a young, energetic, demanding head coach named Tom Landry made sense in theory. On the field, there was — well — cause for many of the players to wonder.

"Quite frankly," says the man now in his third term as a member of the Duncanville (Texas) school board, "I was totally lost when I came to the Cowboys. I started for two years but what Landry wanted me to do was so different from anything I had ever done before that it was a big mystery to me."

Traded to the Cowboys by the San Francisco 49ers after four years of starting for a contender which weekly played to sizeable crowds, the former third round draft choice was excited about his move to the expansion Cowboys. A native of Vernon and a graduate of Texas Tech, it was like a homecoming. In addition to former 49ers teammates like Jerry Tubbs and John Gonzaga who had come to Dallas in the expansion draft, Herchman would be playing ball with several former Southwest Conference performers — Dickie Maegle of Rice, Mike Dowdle and Don Talbert of Texas.

"I was really looking forward to it," he says. "And, you know, when I saw the players we had, I honestly felt we would be capable of winning some football games."

In that regard, Herchman's two-year tenure with the Cowboys (1960-61) was a galloping disappointment. Only four times in the 24 games he labored with Dallas did it win. "Every week," he remembers, "we would go out and play a couple of good quarters, sometimes as many as three, but then we would break down and everything would go down the drain. Sure, it was a disappointing thing.

"It was the losing, I suppose, which made Landry's system hard for so many of the older players to accept. Frankly, there were a lot of the older players who didn't believe in it. They had been doing things their own way for so long — and generally with some degree of success — that they were frustrated because they weren't allowed to play the game the way they felt they could. When you're losing it's hard to accept something new and foreign. Maybe if we had been more successful, had won a few now and then, it would have made it all easier.

"In a sense, I was just as guilty as the next fellow. The truth of the matter is, I probably have more respect for Landry now than I did when I was playing for him. But, don't take that wrong: I had respect for the man the first time I met him and I knew that he knew what he was talking about, that he believed in what he was doing. He would stand up there at the backboard and go over and over things, saying, 'If you do such-and-such, this will happen 80 per cent of the time. I'll take the responsibility for the other 20 per cent.' And, more often than not, he would prove correct on his percentages. What it boiled down to was the fact that he was looking at things with more long range plans in mind, than most of us, who were just concerned about winning the following Sunday.

"It was a matter of patience on his part and a lack of it in some of the players. He was willing to make the sacrifice for the system he was installing. In truth, we might have been able to win a few more games if he had been willing to just let everyone do what they were able to do best; play their own style of games. But that wouldn't have allowed him the chance to build the foundation he was trying to build.

"It's really very easy to see the pattern in retrospect. Dallas today is doing a lot of the same things he was trying to convince us would work. And quite obviously, they're working and the players believe in them. That's what Tom was after, even 20 years ago. "Like I said, I didn't really appreciate Tom as much then as I do now."

After two seasons with the Cowboys, Herchman went to the Houston Oilers in the American Football League, where he could start as tackle along with Ed Husmann, another former Cowboy who had moved to the Oilers after the 1960 campaign. They would participate in one of pro football's most memorable title games, the AFL championship battle with the Dallas Texans in which Texans' running back Abner Haynes won a pre-overtime coin toss and not only gave Houston the ball but the wind as well.

"You know," laughs Herchman, "I've always said if Abner hadn't made that call we would have won the game. We were all so stunned that we never could get our heads together again."

After the '62 season in Houston, Herchman quit football and returned to Dallas and a job with a concrete company Cowboys owner Clint Murchison had helped him get during the off-seasons while still with the Cowboys. "In effect," he says, "Clint got me into the career that I would stay with for the rest of my life."

GLENN GREGORY

✫

Cowboys Handyman

He was, as a schoolboy, something of a Texas football legend, leading the Abilene High School Eagles to state championships and national winning streak records. He was All-America, All-State and written up in *Sports Illustrated* as a high school running back without peer.

His abilities as a catcher in baseball caught the eye of several major league scouts, but the promise of baseball bonus money did not sway Glenn Gregory from his ambition to become a college football player. Then, perhaps, a professional.

Selecting from more offers than he can now remember, he accepted one extended by SMU. As a Mustang he added to his list of All-This and All-That honors and was picked to play in the Hula Bowl, the All-America Game, the East-West Shrine Game and the College All-Star game.

And, to his delight, he was selected in the first ever draft conducted by the new team in town, the Dallas Cowboys. Officially, he was a ninth round draft pick but was actually the seventh player named since the Cowboys had neither a fifth or sixth-round pick. The 6-2, 195-pound halfback would never gain star status as a professional but says today he looks back on his two seasons with the Cowboys as one of his most pleasurable experiences.

"I thoroughly enjoyed it," says the highly successful Dallas insurance executive. "And it was quite a learning experience. You have no idea what a big transition it was from college to the professionals for me. For one thing, I had never even seen a real playbook. Oh, at SMU we got a few mimeographed pages of plays, but I'll never forget the first time I opened a Dallas Cowboys playbook. I felt like I was right back in a college classroom trying to get ready for another test. It was all strange; the terminology, the number of different variations which could be run off the same basic play. I thought I knew a little about football, but it occurred to me in a hurry that I had an awful lot to learn."

Not only from the playbook. "You know, back in those days we weren't doing much damage to anyone's won-lost records, so to be truthful there weren't many games that stick out in my mind. Certainly so far as my own accomplishments are concerned. But, there is one game that I'll never forget, or at least one play in that game.

"We were playing Minnesota up there and I was on our kickoff team. The Vikings had acquired (running back) Hugh McElhenny from San Francisco and had him running back kicks. So, we kick-off and the ball goes to him.

The only man who was to have blocked me must have completely missed his assignment because I had nothing but an open path to the ball carrier. I had visions of great things to come. I was really going to puncture the guy, maybe even cause him to fumble. All kinds of good things. So, I made a straight ahead dash for him.

"Now, the most fundamental thing they teach you in football is to stay under control, keep your head up, and that sort of thing. So, what do I do? Just as I got to him I ducked my head and plowed into him; only he wasn't there anymore. There I am with my head stuck in the ground, grabbing nothing but air, while he's off on a big gain. I would have given anything in the world at that particular moment if the ground had just completely swallowed me up."

Gregory's career was not, however, spent strictly on the kicking teams. In his two year tenure with Dallas (shortly before he was to have begun his third session he was called to summer military camp and then placed on the taxi squad for the 1963 season before retiring the following year), Gregory worked as a Jack-of-all-trades, playing wide receiver, defensive halfback, flanker and safety.

"It never really bothered me that I was working at several positions all the time," he insists. "In those days we didn't really have too many athletes, so I could understand why it was necessary. Mainly, I just wanted to play, wherever, whenever, just like most athletes."

His preference was wide receiver, where he normally served as a backup to Billy Howton and Frank Clarke. Defensively he started several games during his career, but spent most of his time subbing for Don Bishop and Warren Livingston. "For a couple of weeks," Gregory remembers, "I would work at wide receiver and then someone would get hurt in the secondary and I'd move over there. Then in a couple more weeks the secondary would be pretty healthy but one of the receivers would be limping so back to offense I'd go. It got a little confusing at times, but it was fun."

Any particular individual performance that he remembers with fondness?

"Well, yes and no," Gregory says. "In 1962 we went up to St. Louis and I had a pretty good game at defensive halfback, knocking down a couple and intercepting one. But, it was pretty easy to forget, really. We lost the ball game, 52-20."

MIKE DOWDLE
★
Yabba, Dabba, Do, Wilma!

In the younger, more carefree days, Mike Dowdle was explaining, the Dallas Cowboys still looked like a poor man's three-ring circus. The only real pressure being felt by those who managed to remain with the team during those formulative years was finding where practices were to be held and when the next team meeting was scheduled.

"I'll never forget the first day I came to the Cowboys," the former University of Texas fullback says. "The San Francisco 49ers had released me after the final exhibition game of the 1960 season and I arrived in Dallas the Sunday before the regular season was to begin. The day I got here they had a scrimmage and cut 16 people. They were keeping everyone at the Ramada Inn and it looked like Grand Central Station . . . there were so many Cowboys and would-be Cowboys in and out of there."

"Quite honestly," the Dallas resident says, "in those first few weeks I really went through culture shock. I had been with the 49ers (who had drafted him as a fullback) just long enough to see that they were a pretty organized outfit. Then I came to the Cowboys and it was madness. Everyone was running around trying to figure out what to do next.

"For instance, we never knew for sure where we were going to be practicing. Normally, we would be at old Burnet Field where the facilities were worse than any high school facility I ever saw. But at times we wound up at some city park. It seemed we practiced just about wherever they could find room."

A standout fullback for UT, Dowdle did not play a single down of offense with the Cowboys in his rookie season. "It was a circus that first year. But it was a circus I badly wanted to be a part of. I worked my tail off and made the team as a specialty teams player and a backup fullback who never saw a down of action."

Tom Landry, who was then doing a great deal of the defensive coaching, had plans for the 235-pounder from Graham, Texas. "After the '60 season he came to me," says Dowdle, "and told me to start thinking about playing linebacker. Shoot, I hadn't played any defense since high school days but if that was the way I was going to make it in pro ball, that was what I was going to do."

The following season saw Dowdle listed as the backup left linebacker behind Chuck Howley. Jerry Tubbs was in the middle and Gene Babb, another converted offensive back, was the right linebacker. Not too many games passed before Howley moved to the right side and Dowdle earned the vacated linebacker job. For good measure he also filled in for Tubbs in the middle when the current Dallas linebacker coach was injured and unable to play.

"Up until I got that starting job," he said, "my pro career was kind of a hope-and-pray sort of deal. But after that it became fun. And, too, the organization of the team was beginning to show some in that second year. We didn't win but we had some good times . . . and learned a lot.

"I can honestly say that everything that I ever learned about defensive football, I learned from Tom Landry. He was an amazing man, even then. He tried his best to do it all, to coach the entire team. There was never any question that he was the man who was running the team."

By the end of the 1962 season the college draft was beginning to pay off for the Cowboys. They drafted a youngster out of Alabama named Lee Roy Jordan about the same time the San Francisco 49ers were putting out feelers for a man with experience who could play middle linebacker for them. Landry made a deal and Dowdle was back with the team he started out with. He would be the 49ers' middle linebacker until the end of the 1966 season. "I got in a little squabble with the front office," he recalls, "and told them to trade me. I also told them that if they traded me to Pittsburgh, I would retire. They did and I did."

But not before he had a number of run-ins with his old teammates on the Cowboys.

"There were several of us on the team who, for whatever reason, got hooked on a TV cartoon show called 'The Flintstones.' We even got to calling each other by the names of the characters on the show. For instance, Meredith was Fred Flintstone and I was Wilma Flintstone.

"We (the 49ers) were playing Dallas in an exhibition game in Portland, Oregon one night and I was at middle linebacker right across the line from Don. He came up to the line of scrimmage and looked at me and burst out laughing. He said, 'Well, yabba dabba do, Wilma!' and I yelled back, 'Aw, shut up and just call the play, Fred.' Every player on my team wondered what in the world was going on."

After his four years with the 49ers, Dowdle returned to Dallas to open his highly successful Federal Oil & Gas Leases, Inc.

"I've kept up with the Cowboys pretty closely," he says, "and sometimes I'm amazed that it is the same organization that started out back in 1960. But, you know, it was fun. And gratifying to know that I was once a part of it all."

FRED CONE

Want-Ad Kicker

For seven years Fred Cone had worked as a fulltime kicker and part-time running back for the Green Bay Packers, then he retired to become a high school football coach in Mobile, Alabama. Cone had been out of the game for two full seasons when he noticed a story in the local paper that told of a new NFL franchise in Dallas scheduled to compete in the 1960 season.

Coach Cone read the story and got the itch to make a comeback.

"I contacted them, actually," he admits. "I had known Don McIlhenny at Green Bay and understood he was going to be playing with Dallas, so I called him and asked him to put in a word for me with Tex Schramm and Tom Landry. I told him to tell them that I had been kicking regularly since I had left Green Bay. Which, of course, was a flat-out lie.

"I got a call later from Tex, asking if I was serious, and I told him that not only I was serious, but that I was kicking better than ever. Which was another lie. As soon as Tex told me they were going to send me a contract, I hung up the phone and went out and started kicking like crazy."

And, despite the fact his performance in the early stages of that first training camp was proof of his fib, Cone earned the job and that season became the first Cowboys scoring leader; connecting on six of 13 field goals and 21 extra points for a grand total of 39 points.

"You have to understand," the current assistant director of intramurals at Clemson says, "that we weren't exactly the highest scoring team in the league back then."

During his one-year stay, Cone hoped to persuade Landry to allow him some playing time in the offensive backfield but had no real success. "In training camp, they agreed to let me have a go at it and when a couple of backs got hurt I got some playing time in one of the intra-squad scrimmages. One afternoon, I broke, literally running over this one defensive player, and went about 45 yards for a touchdown. I thought I had it made after that, but instead of making me a running back they cut the guy I ran over, the next day. I never did get a chance to play running back."

Still, as the season wound down, the urge to carry the ball one final time remained. "We were playing in Detroit and it was really cold," Cone says. "Before the game, I went up to Landry and told him that if the game got out of control — meaning if Detroit really got a big lead as so many teams had done that season — I would like to run one kickoff back. I told him that was going to be it for me, and that it would mean a lot for me to carry the ball one last time. He said it would be okay with him if the situation arose."

Which, alas, it did. "They had us down 23-14 with just a few seconds to play and were getting ready to kick off to us again. I was sitting on the bench, wrapped up in a parka, trying my best to stay warm. I said to myself, 'This is it,' and got up to get ready to go in the game. I was so cold and stiff that I couldn't even walk. Suddenly, the idea of running the ball once more for old time's sake didn't sound so great. I sat back down and wrapped the parka over my head, hoping Landry would either have forgotten about our agreement or wouldn't be able to find me."

Whatever the case, Cone was not called upon to run back the kickoff. It, perhaps, saved him some embarrassment inasmuch as he feels he might well have been injured for life had he been allowed to carry out his wishes.

"Of course, it wouldn't have been the first time I looked a little foolish on a football field," he says. "There was a time when I was with Green Bay that I would have loved to have found a hole to crawl into. We were lined up for a field goal and Tobin Rote was holding for me. The snap was bobbled and I decided I was going to save the day by running out into the flat and having Tobin throw to me. I did, waving my arms furiously, and, sure enough, he threw it to me. I could smell touchdown from the moment he threw, but this defensive back stepped in front of me, picked it off, and went the length of the field. Oddly enough, that game was against Detroit, too."

Following the 1960 season, Fred Cone was never again forced to face any more Detroits. He retired and returned to his alma mater, Clemson, to recruit and work with the kickers for the next 12 years before moving into the school's intramural department.

Every now and then, he admits, he wonders if maybe, just maybe, he shouldn't have carried the ball that one last time. "It's probably best that I didn't," he says, "still . . ."

GENE BABB
⭐
From Honeymoon to the Landry Mile

After a short and eye-opening year of coaching football at Ranger Junior College in 1959, Gene Babb was ready to do two things: get married and, if things worked out right, return to professional football.

Drafted by the San Francisco 49ers in the 19th round after finishing up his career at Sherman's Austin College, he had played two seasons, had gone back for a third but, when released, had taken the coaching job in Ranger.

"The minute I drove onto the campus," he recalls, "I knew I had made a mistake. I decided immediately I was going to do something else, but I stayed a year there just because I felt obligated."

During that time he received several calls from AFL teams, including the Houston Oilers, asking him to return to work as a professional fullback. The idea of playing with the Oilers interested him. After all, as a native Texan, raised in Odessa where he played high school ball under Hayden Fry, the idea of playing in front of home folks appealed to him. First, though, there was the matter of marrying his fiancée Gerry in a ceremony in Waco. There would be ample time after that to decide between coaching football and playing it, or so he thought.

"The day before we were to be married," Gene says, "this guy from Dallas named Vance Jobe caught up with me and said he had been looking all over. Anyway, he takes my bride-to-be and me out to dinner that night and, in the middle of the meal, says he wants to know if I would be interested in playing for the Dallas Cowboys, the NFL's new franchise. We talked about it a little and I explained to him that I was pretty close to an agreement with the Oilers and he points out to me that San Francisco had traded the rights to sign me to the Cowboys.

"Later that evening he got Tex Schramm on the phone — the Cowboys were already in Oregon at training camp — and we talked for a while and made a deal. The next day we got married and drove straight to Dallas to look at an apartment that Jobe's wife had found for us. A checking account had already been opened for us and everything.

"That same evening we got on a plane to Denver where Bedford Wynne, one of the owners, had reserved the honeymoon suite at one of the nicest hotels in town for us. Jobe, who I finally found out, was one of the Cowboys photographers, went right along with us. It was a little strange, but the treatment we were getting wasn't bad. "The next day we flew to Portland where Gil Brandt met us at the airport, gave us the keys to a car and told us he had rented a cabin for two or three days so we could have a honeymoon, after which, I was to report to training camp."

The honeymoon was over, Babb found out, when he reported to camp and was immediately ordered to run the infamous Landry Mile. "Honeymoon and all," he says, "I made it."

In that first season with the Cowboys he worked at fullback, and in his second year moved to linebacker at Landry's request. "There were times," he recalls, "when I actually went both ways, which was unusual even back then."

Following the '61 season, Babb made his way to the Houston Oilers where, for two more years, he labored as a two-way professional.

His playing days over, he returned to his alma mater, coaching at Austin College before moving to SMU to join the staff of his former high school coach, Fry. He would later move to Oklahoma State and would end his association with football by serving as a scout for the Atlanta Falcons for four years until 1976.

DAVE SHERER

★

The Student Punter

He, as well as anyone, can find sympathy with the occasional problems head coach Tom Landry and the Cowboys have had in the past finding a punter. Dave Sherer, now a commercial realtor in Dallas, has long been a student of the art of punting. Such was the case long before he gained the distinction of being the Cowboys' original punter.

Today, 20 years removed from the life of a professional athlete, the one-time SMU end and punter, who was the second round draft selection of the Baltimore Colts in 1959, still ranks second on Dallas' all-time punting list. First is the colorful Sam Baker who maintained a 45.1 average in his two seasons (1962-63) with the Cowboys. Sherer, in that first season, booted the ball 57 times for a healthy 42.5 average.

"Punting was always easy for me," he says. "In fact, I never felt there was any great science to it. It was just a matter of getting into a groove, of doing it the same way every time and not pressing for the boomer every time. I think today there are too many kickers, particularly the young guys trying to make a team, who press too hard, trying to impress the coach with the long punt.

"When I was in Baltimore Weeb Ewbank told me that the way I was going to make the team was to kick the ball 40 yards every time and not allow any runbacks. During camp I averaged 41 yards and a half yard runback per punt. That's how I got the job, not by booming it 50 yards every so often."

Though he did that, too, his longest as a Cowboy being an impressive 67-yarder.

After spending two years at New Mexico Military Institute, (the same junior college which produced quarterback Roger Staubach), he transferred to SMU where he doubled as a tight end and punter. Drafted by the Colts, he saw little action at end, but was impressive in his kicking efforts. So much so, in fact, that it may have hurt his chances to play more regularly. "I played end some in a backup capacity in Baltimore," he says, "but when I came to Dallas in the expansion draft it was made pretty clear to me that it was the Cowboys philosophy that kickers didn't do anything but kick. Oh, if I had come in and proved to be a standout kind of end they probably would have used me, but I didn't impress them in that area so I did the punting."

It was a different era in pro football, he recalls. Hang time was not a part of the general fan's vocabulary. "The only time I ever heard the word," he says, "was when we would practice the kicking game. Now you hear the TV announcers talking about it every time someone kicks the ball. Today it's a stat everyone wants to know. Back when I was playing pro ball the only people who watched punters were their wives or girl friends."

Today, however, a punter is considered a major weapon on any championship caliber team.

"The only reason I was very visible that first season," Dave says, "was because our offense was having so much trouble moving the ball. I got a lot of work, but it was a fun time.

"In fact, I was tickled to death to get the opportunity to get back to Dallas even though I had been on a championship team in Baltimore my rookie year. I loved Dallas and knew I wanted to make it my home, so I was anything but upset when the chance came for me to work for the Cowboys."

It would be a short career, however. The numbers caught up with Dave Sherer, much as they do with players today.

"When I went to camp the next summer," he says, "I was told that my chances of making it weren't too good unless I could develop as a placekicker as well. I'd never been a placekicker, so that made it a tough battle for me. They had to have someone who could do both punting and placekicking, so Allen Green got the job. Coach Landry told me when he let me go that if it had been a situation where the Cowboys were shooting for a championship he would have kept me. But they were desperately trying to build something then, doing everything they could to get the best possible people on the field.

"It was kind of hard back then, but now it makes sense. The older you get, the easier it is to understand some things. For instance, from a fan's point of view, I can't see why Landry doesn't go ahead and let Danny White continue to do the punting. He's outstanding and he's consistent. But, by the same token, I can understand Landry's philosophy. If he loses his quarterback, he loses his punter. And obviously he considers the punter a valuable weapon."

Dave Sherer should know. If only he could have kicked field goals as well.

JERRY TUBBS
⭐
Coca-Cola's Loss, Cowboy's Gain

In the spring of 1959 Jerry Tubbs was back in his hometown of Breckenridge, Tex., teaching in the local junior high school. He had made up his mind that he'd had enough of professional football. Drafted in the first round by the Chicago Cardinals in 1957, he had played for them for a season and a half before moving on to San Francisco for a two-year stay with the 49ers.

Having planned to play at the pro level for no more than a couple of years, he decided to call it quits. Coca-Cola had been negotiating with him concerning a regional public relations position complete with title, a handsome salary and an expense account, and Tubbs, weary of both linebacking and teaching, was just waiting for word that details of his new career had been ironed out.

In the meantime, 49ers head coach Red Hickey, aware that he would lose some of his players in a special expansion draft benefitting the newly formed Dallas Cowboys, telephoned Tubbs to interest him in playing again in 1960. Tubbs declined Hickey's offer, citing his soon-to-blossom position with Coca-Cola.

And so it followed that Tubbs' name was on the list of players the 49ers made available to the Cowboys that year. And Dallas, desperate for any manner of experienced talent, quickly chose the former All-America University of Oklahoma player (along with 49er teammates Fred Dugan and John Gonzaga). Which, frankly, was no big deal to Jerry — until the Coca-Cola deal fell through.

"I wasn't particularly thrilled about the idea of playing for a brand new team," Tubbs says, "but when the other thing fell through it was either Dallas or teaching junior high school in Breckenridge. I made up my mind that there was no point in looking back; that I'd just do whatever I could to make the best of my new situation."

Tubbs' first difficulty came in trying to convince head coach Tom Landry that he was better suited to play middle linebacker than one of the outside positions. It was the same argument he had waged unsuccessfully at Chicago. "Tom was concerned that I wasn't big enough (at 210 pounds) to play in the middle. So, for the first couple of games that first season I played outside linebacker and Jack Patera was in the middle."

Only after Patera was injured did Tubbs, the man who eventually became the backbone of the early Dallas defenses, get his chance at the highly revered (then and today) position.

Playing where he felt himself most effective, however, was not the solution to all the problems he found in Dallas because for Jerry Tubbs, losing was a unique experience. As a schoolboy in Breckenridge he played on one of Texas' most storied high school teams; winning two state championships. At Oklahoma he never experienced defeat as Bud Wilkinson's teams established a collegiate winning streak record and claimed a couple of national championships. In his senior year Tubbs received the Walter Camp Award as the nation's outstanding college player, was everyone's All-America and finished fourth in the 1956 Heisman Trophy balloting.

There are those, in fact, who will tell you that the Sooner linebacker would have won the Heisman over eventual winner Paul Hornung of Notre Dame that year had it not been for a mid-stream change of heart on the part of the OU public relations department. For the first half of the season Tubbs was the man being promoted. But by mid-season, Tommy McDonald, the OU halfback who was running wild, was also a legitimate contender. The PR wheels changed directions and began beating the drum for McDonald. What resulted was a dramatic split of the vote with McDonald getting third in the balloting and Tubbs fourth.

Such rare air made life on a winless team difficult for Tubbs. "I'll never forget," he says, "when we tied with New York, 31-31, in the next-to-last game of the season. On the plane coming back to Dallas everyone was really celebrating. It was as if we had won the Super Bowl. I didn't say much, but I couldn't understand it; couldn't believe that tying one stinking game was enough to get excited about."

In time the frustration grew out of control. "Through my high school, college and early pro career I never thought of myself as a dirty ball player," Tubbs says. "But I got so frustrated in those early days with the Cowboys that I did some things I'm not too proud of."

It was during a 1964 disaster against the Cleveland Browns that the frustration reached a new high. "The Browns were beating us pretty good," Tubbs remembers, "and they were back in scoring position late in the game. On the particular play I'm talking about I was supposed to blitz. I did, but as I got past their center he turned and slugged me in the stomach and knocked the breath out of me. I was furious — that he'd cheap-shotted me, that no penalty had been called, and that the quarterback had gone on to score on the play. I was still boiling when they lined up for the extra point so I just told our defensive linemen to get out of my way and positioned myself right in front of the center. As soon as he snapped the ball, I brought both hands down in a karate chop to the back of his head. It knocked him cold.

"As soon as I'd done it I was scared to death. John Wooten, who was playing tackle for the Browns, was yelling that I'd killed the guy. I was never so glad to see a guy get up in my life. It was a foolish thing for me to do and I made a vow there and then that it would never happen again. It didn't."

Following that '64 season Tubbs announced his retirement but was eventually persuaded by Landry to return for another year. To boost Tubbs' salary, the new contract was written for the dual role of player-coach.

By the end of the '65 season, with Dallas seemingly on its way after a 7-7 season and a spot in the Playoff Bowl, Tubbs again publicly announced he was through as a player, confident that newcomer Lee Roy Jordan was ready to assume the role of middle linebacker.

For some time, in fact, Tubbs had been applauding the abilities of the No. 1 draft pick from Alabama. Introducing Jordan at a team meeting shortly after his arrival, Tubbs said, "I feel a little like Eddie Fisher introducing Richard Burton."

Before the '66 season would begin, however, Landry again spoke with him, pointing out that there was dire need for a backup for Jordan. Again Tubbs scratched his retirement plans. He played a great deal in the early part of the season but then suffered a back injury and watched as Jordan carried the entire load for the remainder of the year.

"The next year ('67) I was to become a full-time coach," Tubbs says. "It was the year that Landry really felt we had a legitimate shot at the championship, however, so once again we talked about my remaining on the active list. I told him my back was a mess and that I didn't think I could help much. He said if I could play one or two games it might make the difference. So, I agreed. I was active that entire year but never had to play a single down.

"I bet if you'll check, I'm the only linebacker in the history of the NFL to be active for a full season and not get off the bench for even one play."

The following season Tubbs did put his uniform away for good and became a full-time member of Landry's staff. As the linebacker coach today, he and Landry remain the only original members of the Cowboys team to have stayed with the organization throughout every minute of its history.

"If anyone had told me I was going to be around pro football this long," he says, "I'd have told them they were crazy. Shoot, I wouldn't have even stayed with Coca-Cola this long."

BOB LILLY

★

From Broken Bones to Canton

As his spectacular 14-year career with the Dallas Cowboys was winding to an end, drawing him closer to the day he would be summoned to Canton for induction to the National Football League Hall of Fame, Bob Lilly never wished for a return to times past. Rarely, in fact, did he ever speak nostalgically of the infant days of the Dallas franchise when he, the first No. 1 draft pick in the team's history, was the cornerstone upon which the Cowboys defense would eventually be built.

"When it was getting about time for me to retire," he remembers, "people would ask me if I ever wished I could start my career all over again. The question always amused me.

"In the latter stages of my career I was rarely hurt, for the simple reason I finally knew what I was doing. My first year in the league was a little different story. That (1961) season I broke five ribs, a wrist, a thumb, hurt my knee and sprained both ankles."

The fact that he earned a spot on the All-Rookie team that season as a defensive end, a position at which he never felt comfortable, hardly overshadowed the pain and the frustration of those hardscrabble times.

Through those early, struggling years the big TCU All-America from Throckmorton, Texas, was the proof that there was hope for the future. Seven times an All-Pro defensive tackle, the first Dallas player inducted into Texas Stadium's Ring of Honor, and the first from the franchise to be named to the Hall of Fame, he is still "Mr. Cowboy" to many who have witnessed the team's championship climb.

As Dallas gained in power and prestige, he was there, leading the way. And when finally the Cowboys managed to win the big one many doubted they could, it was Bob Lilly who celebrated most enthusiastically; understanding, perhaps better than any other member of the team, the significance of a world championship.

It is no surprise, then, that the game which remains most vivid in his mind is the one in which Dallas accomplished a goal it had been working toward for over a decade.

"I can think back to some pretty doggy days during those early expansion years," he says, "as well as some pretty high times, like winning our first Eastern Conference championship in 1966. There were some gripping disappointments even in that time frame, though: losing to a couple of great Green

Bay teams in '66 and '67 and the sick feeling of losing to Baltimore in our first trip to the Super Bowl in 1970."

It was a time of a unique brand of frustration; a time when the Cowboys were winners but not champions. It was a time when a great deal of attention was dealt to the negative performances that were coming with far less regularity than they had years earlier. The Cowboys, the critics howled, were a team of great talent but simply weren't able to win the big one.

"And for that reason, if nothing else, the game I'll still be able to call to memory years and years from now will be our Super Bowl victory over the Miami Dolphins. On that day — January 16, 1972 — the Dallas Cowboys set to rest a lot of the conversation about our previous failures. That 24-3 victory was far more than a big payday and a diamond ring to me.

"I can't really describe the feeling that comes from winning the Super Bowl. It's something you can only share with the players and coaches on your own team. I can only say that it was the greatest thrill of my playing career. The Hall of Fame thing was nice, something I'll always cherish, but finally winning the championship after all we'd gone through for so many years. It made a lot of hard work worthwhile."

Lilly recalls that afternoon in New Orleans as one on which the Cowboys came as close to perfection as is possible in a game where the human element plays such a demanding role. "We were as prepared and ready to play as any team I've ever been on ever was. We arrived in New Orleans with a ten-game winning streak and were playing outstanding football. We felt that all we had to do was continue doing the things we'd been doing for weeks. There was such an atmosphere of confidence.

"Looking back, I'd say that on that given day we were almost flawless. I remember reporters coming up to me afterwards and asking me to single out players who had done exceptional jobs. Generally, I don't mind doing that sort of thing because in a lot of games there are certain individual performances that make the big difference. That wasn't the case in Super Bowl VI. It might sound a little trite, but that was a tremendous team effort, the kind of thing you feel proud to have been a part of."

For Lilly, it was a day that wiped away years of disappointment and it was a day when a man he regards highly received a just reward.

"After the game our dressing room was a mad house. Tom Landry's face was one big smile — and I don't have to tell you how unusual that is — and everyone was slapping each other on the back and yelling. Someone gave me a cigar and I lit up. I was happy for me, and I was happy for the guys on the team, but what I felt for Landry finally winning the Super Bowl — well, I can't tell you how I felt. But I'd been with him for a long time and thought I knew him pretty well. And I think I had a pretty good idea what winning the Super Bowl, finally winning the big game, meant to him.

"Somehow, he had known way back in the early '60's that our day would come. Along the way there were a lot of us who wondered. That day he made believers of us all."

THE
✭ WINNING ✭
YEARS

By the mid-60s they had come further, faster than any expansion team in sports history, growing in stature and popularity. The dog days behind them, they had become a feared force in the NFL. And although the Dallas Cowboys had the ammunition to win big, they still possessed a frustrating lack of experience that led to big losses as well.

The long-awaited turnabout prompted the first sellout in the club's history in 1965 as 76,251 turned out to watch them play Cleveland in the Cotton Bowl. The Cowboys failed to seize upon the opportunity, however, losing 24-17.

On paper they had, in fact, become winners, but their fandom wanted more. Twice they came close to cracking the mid-60s dynasty of Vince Lombardi's mighty Green Bay Packers, but twice they came up short, losing the title game in '66, 34-27, and again the following year in what has come to be known as the Ice Bowl. Playing in minus-13 degree weather, Dallas' 1967 dream of championship glory was exploded by a late game quarterback sneak that lifted the Pack to a 21-17 victory.

The Cowboys then labored under another form of stigma. They became the team that couldn't win the big one, always next year's champions. Wrote Steve Perkins: "No other pro football team had ever been quite like them, at one and the same time so rich, so dazzling, so young — and so tragic. They were the first expansion team to challenge for a championship, and when they lost two years in a row they lost dramatically and heroically . . . But how glorious to lose, and how poignant to keep the conviction in the hearts of Cowboys fans that their team was best, as only time would tell."

In that sense, they were champions even before they had the trophy to prove it.

CORNELL GREEN

★

Basketball to the Corner

Despite the fact the thermometer still registered a brain blistering 94 degrees as the 8 p.m. kickoff neared, a crowd of 54,000 had gathered in the Cotton Bowl to witness an exhibition game involving the up-and-coming Dallas Cowboys and the reigning world champion Green Bay Packers.

Rookie cornerback Cornell Green was oblivious to the heat and the number in attendance. A series of training camp injuries had reduced the cornerback roster to a point that he, a man who would later admit he had never tackled anyone in a football game before, was opening at the strong side position.

That night in 1963, however, would hardly be any indication of what was to come in the ensuing years in which he would be a four time All Pro selection (1966-67-68-69) and named to the Pro Bowl on five occasions (1966-67-68-72-73).

"It wasn't the fact that I was all that nervous," Green, who later became a member of the highly successful Cowboys scouting corp, remembers. "It was just that I didn't know a heck of a lot about what was going on."

And with good reason. Green had done what an Ohio State basketball player named John Havlicek had almost accomplished with the Cleveland Browns. Havlicek, with only high school football experience, had survived the Browns training camp until the final cut before going off to the NBA Boston Celtics. Green, a standout basketball player at Utah State, had approached Dallas player personnel director Gil Brandt about a tryout. After all, he said, he had played a little running back in high school. Already known as a man willing to take on an athlete with size, speed and ability, Brandt signed the player whose basketball jersey would later be retired by his alma mater.

And there he was, starting against the awesome Packers and facing highly regarded Green Bay receiver Boyd Dowler. "One of the good things about it all," Green says, "was that I didn't know enough about pro football at the time to be all that shaken by the fact it was the Packers we were playing."

In fact, it looked for a brief minute or two as if his new career was going to be a piece of cake. "Early in the first quarter," Green remembers, "Dowler came out in a short pattern, caught the ball, and I tackled him. He fumbled and I recovered. I remember coming off the field with a big grin on my face, thinking, 'Hey, this isn't going to be so tough.' "

He changed his mind before the game ended with the Packers on the long side of a 31-7 score. "I thought the night would never end," Green says.

"I don't even want to think about how many times Paul Hornung ran over

me or slipped out of tackles. Twice Dowler got behind me for bombs and caught more than his share of shorter passes. The entire night was unbelievable. I was a physical wreck before the night was over. After that game I was nervous before every other one I ever played."

Green insists the initiation of his first game will be hard ever to forget.

"Oh, there were some exciting times that come to mind too; like the first championship game against Green Bay when the big excitement was simply the fact that we had made it to that level. Then the Ice Bowl game against the Packers. That was one of those that was hard to lose because we honestly felt we should have won the game. That kind stays with you, regardless of how hard you might try to forget it. And, of course, the whole Super Bowl experience is something special. Actually one of the most satisfying accomplishments we ever made when I was playing came in the 1965 season when we finished 7-7. That was the year we got over the hump, became a solid football team. We had to win our last four to end the year at .500 and everyone set their minds to doing it."

For the 6-3, 210-pounder who had once set scoring records in basketball, there was a long series of satisfactions before he announced his retirement following the 1975 training camp. After having established himself as the premier cornerback in the NFL in the mid-to-late '60s he moved to strong safety and earned his fifth trip to the Pro Bowl.

Which is a long way from the day in the dressing room when, as a rookie, he complained to a teammate that he was having a tremendous amount of trouble adjusting to wearing hip pads. After a quick check, the helpful teammate pointed out the problem. "Maybe," he suggested, "if you wouldn't wear them backwards it would help."

Green, a quick learner, never had equipment difficulties thereafter.

And long before his career ended he had put that dismal performance against Dowler and the Packers behind him. During one of his trips to the Pro Bowl, Green was asked by a reporter if he could recall how many times a receiver had beaten him on a pass route.

"None," Green snapped.

"Come on now," the reporter argued, "not even last year or the year before?"

"No, never," Green said. "Aw, well, maybe one of those guys did beat me once in awhile, but as I was walking off the field I managed to talk myself out of it."

SAM BAKER

★

Kicker From Camelot

In the brief two-season tenure he spent in a Dallas Cowboys uniform (1962-1963), Sam Baker accomplished a great deal. He is still No. 1 on the all-time punting list with a 45.1 average on his 128 punts. His longest traveled 75 yards from the line of scrimmage — almost 90 yards from the point of the kick — and never was one of his attempts blocked. He led the Cowboys in scoring in his two seasons with 92 and 75 points respectively and he hit on 23 of 47 field goals, twice booming three-pointers from 53 yards away.

Such were the on-field heroics of the former Oregon State running back ("I was All-Coast, almost," Sam used to say, laughing) who had come to the then still fuzz-cheeked Cowboys. On Sunday afternoons he was a solid, respected performer: as reliable a player as ever checked out a uniform.

The rest of the time he resembled a three-ring circus.

"For some reason," says Baker, now a junior high physical education teacher in Tacoma, Washington, "I could never take it (pro football) as seriously as I was supposed to. I never was able to convince myself that I was a part of a million dollar enterprise. Football is a nice thing to do while you're young."

It was Sam Baker who, in his first season with Dallas, established a rather lofty record when he was fined $1,000 for missing the team plane back to training camp after an exhibition game in Cleveland. To his everlasting credit, however, he did manage to catch a later flight which got him back in the wee hours of the morning. Gil Brandt picked him up at the airport. "Coach Landry wants to see you," he said. "Figured he would," said Baker.

So, wearing a suit very much in need of attention from the cleaners and holding a folded copy of the *New York Times* under one arm, Baker knocked on Landry's door at 4 a.m. When the awakened coach answered, his kicker snapped to attention, clicked his heels and reeled off a happy salute. "Baker reporting, sir," he said. Landry reportedly almost smiled, then informed the tardy Baker of his penalty.

Looking back, Baker says, "I don't think Tom really disliked me, but it is probably safe to say he didn't have the respect for me that I did for him. I seemed to always say or do the wrong thing at the wrong time when I was around him."

To wit:

"We were in a team meeting one time and Tom was talking about his philosophy of team dedication. He said, 'If I thought it would help this team in some way, I'd climb on top of this building and sing Glory to God.' Bill Howton was sitting in front of me and said, 'Hallelujah!', and I started laughing. Landry turned just in time to see me crack up and, obviously, thought I was laughing at him.

"Then, there was another meeting I didn't fare too well in. Tom was telling us how he had to have more harmony if we were going to accomplish anything." Baker, heeding his coach's words, then tried setting the harmony in motion with a loud, resonant, "Hmmmmm . . ."

It was Sam Baker who found a loop-hole in the demand that everyone reporting to camp run the infamous Landry Mile. Showing the coach the letter he, along with all other players, had received, Baker pointed out that the letter specifically stated that "all backs and linemen" would be required to run the mile. "There was no mention whatsoever about kickers having to run the thing," Baker explains. (Note: In the interest of preserving the peace, however, Baker did, in fact, run the Landry Mile, almost. He ran the straightaways and walked the curves, completing the distance in the slowest time ever recorded by a member of the team.)

"You know, though," Baker says, "I did have a lot of respect for the Cowboys organization. They were the only team that ever fired me (traded, actually) and sent me a letter afterwards saying they hoped I did well in my future endeavors. That really impressed me. Tex Schramm wrote the letter. I've always held him in very high regard."

Football as it is played today, however, disturbs Baker somewhat. "Vince Lombardi," Baker says, "left us a legacy we may never be able to overcome. Anytime a boy between the ages of 12 and 15 has to win every game or perish, something's wrong. The emphasis is being placed on the wrong values. When team camaraderie and social values are overlooked, things aren't as they should be."

ED NUTTING
✮
The Impatient Lineman

Though it was a year which revealed the first faint signals of better days to come for the Dallas Cowboys, 1963 was, in some respects, a carbon copy of the three previous seasons in the new franchise's history.

Ed Nutting, the starting right offensive tackle for most of that '63 season, remembers it as a time when the linemen were always angry at the backs, and vice versa; the receivers were speaking ill of the quarterbacks, the quarterbacks were bent out of shape at the receivers, and so on.

"Actually," the Atlanta, Georgia realtor says, "you could see that things were beginning to take on a positive form that year but, still, there were the frustrations of not getting down the road quicker. The objectives were great, the people were great and Tom Landry's leadership was outstanding. He was more patient than anyone on the team. He was able to see things coming together before we as players were."

Still, says the former All-Southeastern Conference lineman, things could have been better than the 4-10 mark accomplished by the Cowboys in '63. "I think we were a better football team than we looked on most Sundays. Part of the problem was the frustration of the players. And a lot of that was brought on by the constant experimenting that was still going on in those days.

"Landry wasn't settled on a quarterback so he had Don Meredith and Eddie LeBaron alternating plays, for instance. No one was really crazy about that, particularly Don and Eddie. But it was Landry's way."

Nutting himself was part of the swinging door operation in the offensive line. After a year with the Cleveland Browns, who had made him a second-round selection in the 1961 draft, Ed had come to the Cowboys and was injured in the exhibition season of '62. After rehabilitating as an injured reserve that season he opened the '63 campaign as the starting right tackle while Bob Fry started at left.

"At the first of the season Billy Ray Smith was playing behind Fry at left tackle. The coaches became disenchanted with my play and moved Smith over to the starting right tackle job. Then, later, they got down on Fry and moved Smith back to the left side and elevated me back to the starting spot on the right side. That's just the way things were handled back then. They were looking for the right combination.

"A lot of it was simply the fact that everything was so new. The players, the team, the organization. The '63 season was the first for (offensive line coach) Jim Myers and he was in a position of feeling his way along too. It made it hard for anyone to feel really comfortable about what we were trying to accomplish. Anytime you have that much newness, you've not got much chance for things to run really smoothly."

The following year Nutting made it clear he was not happy in Dallas and refused to report, asking instead to be traded. Dallas made no such effort. "What we wound up with was a stand-off," he says, "so I retired."

Looking back, he says, he has a better understanding of what it was Landry and the organization were trying to accomplish. "When I speak of the frustrations," he points out, "I'm not telling the whole story of that season. In a way it was exciting to see something developing. And you definitely could see that things were going to right themselves and the Cowboys program was going to be a good, solid one. It's just hard to take things like that into consideration when you're young and eager to win, to show that you're better than people think you are.

"I don't think my feelings were much different from most of the guys on the team. It's just that we lacked the kind of patience Landry had. Somehow, he knew all along that it was going to finally come together. I'm glad that it did. And glad that I was there to see it begin to happen."

FRANK CLARKE
⭐
Much Better Than He Thought

In his seven years as a member of the Dallas Cowboys, wide receiver-tight end Frank Clarke firmly established himself as one of the bonafide standouts of a team still in search of its true identity. Before he closed out his career following the 1967 season he caught 281 passes for 5,214 yards and scored 50 touchdowns. In 1963 he led the team in receptions with 43 and again in '64 with a career-high 65. That '64 season, in fact, saw him named to the Associated Press All-Pro team.

Even today he ranks third among the team's all-time receivers. Yet only in recent years, with the advantage of considerable retrospect, has Clarke come to feel he was perhaps something more than an average football player.

"When I was playing," he says, "I never really was able to recognize my own talents. For reasons I'll probably never be able to completely explain, I always placed unreasonable expectations on myself, and felt I should be better than I was at the time. With that kind of personality and attitude, it makes it difficult to really appreciate some of the good things that come your way.

"For instance, when I was named All-Pro in '64 it should have been a very exciting thing to me. But I was more excited over the fact that Bob Lilly had also made it. He deserved it more than I did, I thought, so I didn't really enjoy the status of being All-Pro the way one should. In fact, I was always running scared, afraid of losing my job. Looking back, it's foolish, I guess. But I had it in my mind that because people like Tommy McDonald and Buddy Dial were around I was likely to be traded.

"As time has passed and I've had a better chance to review things that have taken place in my life, I'd have to say I'm a little disappointed that I didn't make a little bigger deal out of being named All-Pro. Today I look back on it as one of the highlights of my career and I'm far prouder of it now than I was at the time. That season I was a very consistent ball player; I came up with a lot of third down catches, I blocked well. I had a nice flow going all season, and a nice harmony with the quarterbacks. I was lucky, and you know, that always plays a part in an individual's having a really good season. It was one of those situations of my being in the right place at the right time."

Throughout his professional career, which began in 1957 with the Cleveland Browns and ended after seven seasons with the Cowboys, Clarke, by his own admission, was an athlete constantly in search of approval. "What

I would do," he reflects, "is look to other people to tell me that I was good."

It was something head coach Tom Landry had begun trying to tell him as early as 1961.

"The most discouraging time in my athletic career was early in the 1960 season," Clarke recalls. "Because Dallas was an expansion team the league allowed it to keep more players than the other teams. Still, only the regulation number could suit up for games and each week a list of those who would play was posted. I can still remember one week looking at the sheet and not finding my name. We were to play Baltimore in the Cotton Bowl and I wasn't to be a part of it. I recall going to the game, sitting in the stands, and not really paying much attention. It was all a blur to me. I was afraid my pro career was over."

Today, however, all that is behind him. Confident and successful, Frank Clarke enjoys what he calls a full, active life. "I'm comfortable with myself now. I like myself." It is part of the message he spreads as a member of the Cornucopia Institute in St. Mary, Kentucky.

"Looking back now," he says, "I'd have to say that I'm thankful for the opportunity I had to play professional football. It was always a serious thing to me and, in retrospect, I'm glad I approached it that way. I was coachable, I had a good body, good speed and good hands. And in 1964 I made All-Pro."

Today that means a great deal to him. As it should.

JERRY OVERTON

He Learned the Hard Way

It was a career too soon ended, one which hinted at promise just before an off-season accident prematurely brought it to an end. Still, Jerry Overton looks back on his brief tenure with the Dallas Cowboys fondly. He had, after all, earned himself a place in the starting lineup.

A fifteenth round draft choice in 1963, the 6-2, 192-pounder with 9.8 100-yard dash speed was one of only four rookies to make the roster that year. There was first round pick Lee Roy Jordan, Harold Hays, Tony Liscio and Overton.

"My speed, I think, was the thing that got me a spot on the team," says the man who is currently vice-president of the Denver-based Brinkerhoff Signal Petroleum Company. "In an early pre-season game I managed to return a punt something like 70 yards and that seemed to catch (Tom) Landry's eye. I was just hoping to make the team any way I could and if it was as a kick return specialist, that was fine with me."

A standout defensive back at Utah, he would get little chance to earn game experience at safety until veteran Cornell Green was ejected from an exhibition game against San Francisco. "He was involved in a fight and when he got tossed out, I got to play the last three quarters of the game. I didn't do anything really outstanding, but I didn't goof up too badly either, so I have to think my case was helped along by Cornell's misfortune."

By the seventh game of the regular season, however, Overton's performance was such that he was elevated to the starting free safety position over roommate Jim Ridlon. "It was a big moment for me," he remembers, "and even today I can remember at least one play in the game quite vividly. I got beat on a deep play action pass by Red Mack for a touchdown — a touchdown that enabled the Steelers to win the game, 27-21. After the game, Landry came up to me and said, 'Well, you learned the hard way.' I was convinced that it would be back to the kicking teams after that, but I went on to start for the rest of the season. And with each game I gained a little more confidence. By the end of the season I was already thinking ahead to the next year. I felt like I had made a place for myself and had a pretty promising future."

Indeed he did, until a skiing accident in the off-season dashed his hopes. "I had gone back to school to do some graduate work and went skiing and hit a fence which was buried in a drift. I shattered a bone in my leg and they had to put pins in it. I laid out the entire 1964 season and then tried to come back in '65. I made it until the final cut before Landry called me in for a talk. He said he was going to have to let me go, but if I wanted to continue trying to play he thought I might have a good chance of helping out the new AFL franchise in Denver. I thought about it for a while, but I finally told him that if I wasn't good enough to play for Dallas, it was time for me to call it quits. The leg felt okay, but the injury took away some of my speed. And without it I was a very ordinary football player."

Ending his career as a player, Overton launched a nine-year career as a high school coach. He worked for two years at a school in California as an assistant and then moved to Casper, Wyoming where he served as a head coach for seven years before going into the oil business.

"When I was coaching," he says, "I tried in a lot of ways to follow in Landry's footsteps, to handle things the way he had handled them when I was playing for him. I've always been very impressed with him, from the first day I met him to this day. I admire him a great deal.

"Back when I was with the Cowboys we were still in the building process and we had our problem areas. But you could see it coming together, particularly the defense. In those days, Tom worked very closely with individual defensive players and it was a big help to me.

"When you get down to it, there was a willingness to help on just about everyone's part. Cornell and Ridlon helped me a good deal as did (receivers) Frank Clarke and Billy Howton. And Pettis Norman. And there were fun times. Like the first trip to New York's Yankee Stadium where Mickey Mantle waited for the arrival of the team. Or coming off a two-game losing streak on the road to play in the Cotton Bowl. "When the introductions were made people began booing like crazy. Don Meredith looked over at me and said, 'It's sure great to be home, isn't it Jerry?'

"Sure, I would have liked to stayed around longer, but things just didn't work out. I thought I had a pretty good future ahead of me and then, all of a sudden, it was over."

Overton is among those who get back from time to time for the annual player reunions. "I was there a few years ago and talking with (wide receiver) Golden Richards. I had just moved to Denver and he was telling me how much he liked that part of the country. I suggested he come up and we would go skiing sometime.

"Tex Schramm overheard the invitation and came rushing over. 'No deal, Golden,' he said, 'one ski idiot on this team is enough.' "

JIM RAY SMITH

Final Days of an Old Warrior

Like so many others in that particular period of Dallas Cowboys history, he had come to finish out a career which had already been outstanding. His heart and his most shining hours were elsewhere. The prospect of joining a team still struggling for a sense of direction was rarely the kind of thing to which an old warrior accustomed to triumph eagerly looked forward.

In the case of offensive guard Jim Ray Smith, in fact, there was a point in time when he decided against it. After his four years as an All-Pro and five appearances in the Pro Bowl, the powerful Cleveland Browns had traded him to Dallas. Having cleared holes for the immortal Jim Brown before sellout crowds, he found it difficult to consider becoming a part of a team which, the year before, had won only four games.

Even the fact that the big Baylor-ex had called Dallas home during his days with the Browns failed to brighten the prospect. Traded in 1963, he decided to retire. "I had played seven years for the Browns," Smith remembers, "and had a great experience. I had owned a home in Dallas since 1957 and was getting into the real estate business pretty well. It just seemed a good time to call it a career."

Jim Ray Smith, however, did not count on the persuasive abilities of men like Tex Schramm and Tom Landry. They invited him to dinner, told him of the plans they had for their new franchise, and made it clear that he could help move them along toward their goal by filling a spot in the offensive line. The competitive juices began to flow, and soon the old warrior was ready to have another go at it.

The memories the current president of Jim Ray Smith Realtors, Inc. has of the two seasons he spent in a Cowboys uniform are framed with frustration. Two years, two knee operations.

"The only real fun in being a part of a football team, any football team, is participating. When you can't, for whatever reason, it becomes a very frustrating experience. The first year I got hurt in the fourth or fifth game and did some cartilage damage to my knee. I tried to continue playing but the cartilage buckled over into the joint of my knee so I had to have surgery. The next season, '64, I had surgery again in October and the doctor told me I was through with football."

It wasn't the way he would have liked for it to end. Still, with the advantage of retrospect, Smith does not begrudge those last two professional seasons. "It's just that I would have liked to have been able to do more. I've never been a very good spectator, particularly when they were paying me to be a player."

Not that he didn't have his moments on the field prior to his untimely physical problems. "I guess the games I remember most were the ones we played against the Browns. It's hard to explain the feeling you have when you play against a team you were a part of for so long, one you felt so strongly about. Things were good for me in Cleveland, you understand. Even today, I can't help but pull for them. Oh, I want Tom to win and I've got some good friends on the Cowboys that I enjoy seeing do well; I'm a Cowboys fan so far as that goes. It's just that there's still a little bit of the Cleveland Browns in my blood."

In his appearances against his old team, he and the Cowboys lost both times in '63 (41-24 and 27-17) and in '64 were defeated 27-6 and 20-16. "When you play against your old teammates," he says, "you want to be sure you aren't embarrassed. You want them to still have respect that you can still play the game. I like to think the Browns felt that way about me after each of our games."

Playing with the youthful, still-developing Cowboys — after having spent so much time with the established winning tradition that was so much a part of the Browns of the time — Smith was in a position to compare the old guard with the new kid on the block.

"Cleveland had more team spirit than any team I was ever on, high school, college or professional. There was a strong, almost family-like feeling. Dallas, on the other hand, was still a team of strangers in those days, with a lot of guys like myself who had come from other teams and other ways of doing things. They were in a period of adjustment and, frankly, there were a number of people on the team who had their doubts about some of the things we were trying to do. It's hard, after playing several years, to suddenly begin changing techniques and philosophies.

"I think it says a lot for Landry's convictions that he stayed with his master plan even in the struggling times. He knew all along that it would eventually pay off for him. And, goodness knows, it has."

Smith remembers 1964, a 5-8-1 campaign, as the one in which the Cowboys, who had just moved an impressive young defensive end named Bob

Lilly to tackle, were given the "kiss of death" by *Sports Illustrated*. The national magazine not only predicted they would be winners but pictured members of the defensive line on the cover. It was a prediction ahead of its time.

"They (S.I.) were going mostly by what they felt the defense would be able to do," he says. "You just can't separate units like that, though. It's always been my belief that you aren't going to have a good defense until you have a strong offense. I've always felt if the offense doesn't move the ball or it fumbles or is intercepted too often, the defense is going to suffer. After a while they're going to look over at the guys on offense and say, 'Hey, why should I work my tail off when you guys keep turning the ball over or aren't putting any points on the board?' Things like that happen quickly and they spread like a cancer.

"We (Dallas) just hadn't reached the point then where we could say we had two strong units. And, while some people were trying to be leaders, they were having a rough time of it because they really didn't know how to carry out the job. The proper team spirit hadn't quite developed in those days — but you could see it coming. By the time I left I felt very strongly that Dallas was going to be a team to reckon with very soon."

The very next season, in fact, they made their first playoff appearance, traveling to Miami to play Baltimore in the now defunct Playoff Bowl. He doesn't say it, but Jim Ray Smith talks like a man who would like to have been there for that one last season. Still, as he points out, he had his moments.

JOHN ROACH
★
He Came Out of the Stands

Having spent six years as a well-paid backup quarterback, first for the Chicago Cardinals and later for three seasons behind Bart Starr at Green Bay, John Roach retired after the 1963 season and came home to Dallas. For the former Highland Park High School and SMU student, it was time to put football aside and get down to the business of making his place in the "real world."

"Our youngest child," he recalls, "was getting ready to begin school and I was placed in a position of deciding whether I wanted to continue for several more years as a backup quarterback or get into a career. It was time, I decided, to come back to Dallas to stay."

He is quick to point out that he didn't find himself aching to return to the game when time came in '64 for players to report to their respective training camps. He did, however, look forward to attending the annual Salesmanship

Club game that year which would match the Dallas Cowboys and his old teammates on the Green Bay Packers.

Sitting in the stands in the Cotton Bowl that evening, he watched the Pack romp to a 35-3 victory. He admits he was glad to see Green Bay looking so sharp so early but could not help but feel sympathy for the Cowboys, particularly when starting quarterback Don Meredith suffered a knee injury. He knew that Eddie LeBaron had retired after the '63 season, leaving the signal calling duties to Meredith. With the former SMU All-America limping, Roach knew, Dallas was facing some long Sunday afternoons. As he paid a visit to the Packers' locker after the game, Roach ran into Dallas receiver Buddy Dial.

"John," Dial said after greetings had been exchanged, "we could sure use you." Roach laughed. The laughter died the following Tuesday when he received a call from Tex Schramm, informing him that the Cowboys had spoken with Green Bay and were prepared to make a deal for him. "We need another quarterback in a hurry," he said, "and we think you can do the job for us."

The former third round draft choice of the Cardinals pointed out that he had made no concerted effort to stay in playing shape but was willing to give it a try if the Cowboys wanted him. The following day he signed.

"You have no idea how far out of shape you can get in such a short period of time," he says, now occupying the president's chair at Murray Investments Company. "One of the first things I did was go to the trainer (Clint Houy) and ask him to put me on some kind of a program that would get me back into condition. He very candidly explained to me that he couldn't put me on the kind of program I needed for the simple reason that if he did, I would be too sore to play.

"It didn't take me long to realize that there is no way you can really get into shape in a season. As much as I disliked it, training camp is the only way. So, while I didn't exactly set the world on fire that year, I did the best I could while never really feeling I was properly conditioned for the job."

With Meredith suffering a variety of ailments off and on during the season, Roach saw considerable action, starting a couple of games. He spelled Meredith often, and on a couple of occasions the two alternated.

"You know," Roach says, "it was thrilling to be on a team where a win really was a big thing. Dallas hadn't won much up to that time but in '64 we did win some (the Cowboys went 5-8-1 that season). In Green Bay it had been just the opposite. We had been expected to win them all and if we didn't do it big there was the feeling that we had failed. I really got caught up in the enthusiasm in Dallas."

It should be noted, however, that Roach did not threaten any club records nor was he selected to any All-Pro teams. "On the other hand," he notes, "we did some positive things that year. We beat Washington early in the season (24-18) and came back later in the year and won three in a row, which was a club record at the time."

Then, however, came Roach's encounter with his former teammates, the Packers, in the Cotton Bowl. "I still have nightmares about that one," he admits.

"You know how it is, wanting to really perform well against the people you had played with for several years. Well, suffice it to say I didn't. The play that comes to mind was one that Coach Landry sent in from the sidelines. We were pretty deep in our end of the field and he sent Tommy McDonald in with a pass play that was to go to him over the middle. McDonald told me that Landry had said I would need to release the ball quickly.

"I did. And as soon as I let the ball go I knew that Ray Nitschke (Packers linebacker) was going to get to it before McDonald did. He picked it off and ran it in for a touchdown."

The Pack went on to defeat the Cowboys, 45-21 in a game John Roach would love to forget.

BUDDY DIAL

✦

He Brought Devotion to Dallas

As a member of the Pittsburgh Steelers he had earned recognition as one of the National Football League's premier receivers. Over a four-year stretch, the former Rice standout averaged over 1,000 yards in receptions per season. His career average with the Steelers was 26.8 yards per catch. There was one game in which he caught 11 for 297 yards. He once had a string of 12 straight games in which he scored at least one touchdown.

Thus it was no surprise that great enthusiasm surrounded wide receiver Buddy Dial's arrival in Dallas prior to the Cowboys' 1964 season. No one, however, was more enthusiastic than Dial himself. Delighted to be back in Texas, he had long viewed the city of Dallas as a place he would like to live.

His first training camp as a member of the Cowboys, however, marked the initial step toward what he now looks back on as the most disappointing time of his athletic career. "In Pittsburgh," he says, "there was never much pressure to report to camp in anything near top shape. The philosophy there was to gradually work yourself into condition. Dallas, on the other hand, wanted its people ready to go full tilt on the first day of camp. I felt the way I had done it those five years in Pittsburgh worked pretty well for me, so I didn't really bother to get in shape. I was just going to do things my way regardless of what the Cowboys wanted."

On the fourth day of camp Dial tore a leg muscle and would miss all but the final game of that 1964 season. Things would never be the same thereafter.

The next summer, again in camp and this time in good shape, Dial began to miss passes. He had never had such a problem before, not at Rice where he made All-America in 1958 or with the Steelers where he was a Pro Bowl selection and even today ranks fourth on the club's all-time receiving. Former Steelers quarterback Bobby Layne, in fact, often insisted that the game had no better receiver than Dial.

"I couldn't really understand what had happened," Dial recalls. "All my life I had heard other receivers talk about how the ball came to them in a bouncing manner. As they ran their routes, their own movement made the ball appear to bounce in flight. To me it had always come in steady and smooth. Suddenly, I was seeing it bounce toward me, too. And I wasn't making the catches.

"It was Jerry Tubbs who finally suggested to me that the problem might be the fact I was running differently because of my leg. Looking back, I think that might have had something to do with it. Don Meredith and I were roommates and we both talked about it a great deal. We were both frustrated. I think we got to a point where we were each trying too hard.

"While I was with the Cowboys I had a couple of good days, but I never really felt I made any real contributions to the team. I had come to Dallas with really high expectations and flopped. There's no other way to put it. I never experienced as much disappointment in my athletic career. To be honest, it's something I've never gotten over. The good years at Pittsburgh seem to take a back seat to the bad years with Dallas. I feel I let the fans down, my teammates down and I let (Tom) Landry down."

Now living in Tomball, Texas, Dial does admit pleasure in the fact that he left something of a legacy, however. Not just with the Cowboys but the entire NFL. A devout Christian, he had been active in church work while in Pittsburgh and one day approached Steeler coach Buddy Parker with the idea of having a minister come to the hotel for a Sunday morning devotional. "We always stayed in a hotel on Saturday nights, even when we were at home," Dial recalls. "I went to Buddy with the idea, not sure at all what his reaction would be. But he said fine and told me to make an announcement about it at the Saturday practice."

The following Sunday morning, 25 of his teammates showed up for the devotional, and a tradition, which would eventually spread throughout the NFL and eventually all professional sports, was born. "When I came to Dallas," Buddy recalls, "one of the first things Coach Landry asked me to do was organize the same thing for the Cowboys. Even today I have guys coming up to me, saying how much they appreciate the fact I had a part in getting the devotionals started."

Buddy Dial, then, did make his mark. It just doesn't show up in the record books.

PERRY LEE DUNN

He Still Wonders

It has been 16 years now and still Perry Lee Dunn wonders. He wonders if maybe he hadn't gone duck hunting on that day in 1964 when the NFL draft was under way things might have been different in his professional career.

He had been an outstanding quarterback since schoolboy days and had wound up a noteworthy career at the University of Mississippi. He wanted a shot at playing quarterback professionally but the more he talked with pro scouts the more he was made aware that they felt his future was as a defensive back. Gil Brandt of the Dallas Cowboys was one of them.

"I never fully understood why people didn't think I would be able to make it as a quarterback," the Brandon, Mississippi, resident says today, "but I wanted to play professionally so I was ready to agree to whatever." He told the Cowboys he would sign with them if they drafted him. And went duck hunting.

The first player Dallas picked in that 1964 draft was an Oregon running back named Mel Renfro, another player they planned to convert to defense. Next they selected Dunn. "I found out later in the day from one of the Ole Miss coaches that San Francisco had been trying to get in touch with me all day. They wanted to draft me as a quarterback if I was interested. When they couldn't get in touch with me they picked George Mira instead. It's just the way things work out sometimes, I guess. But looking back I feel I had what it took to play quarterback in the pros. I'll never know, though."

Instead he came to the Cowboys after playing in the College All-Star game and found that plans for him had suddenly changed again. In the All-Star game it had been his fate to defend against Chicago Bears tight end Mike Ditka. It wasn't, Dunn says, a pretty story. "When I got to camp, Coach (Tom) Landry told me maybe I'd better work at making the team as a running back."

Which he did. And toward the end of his rookie season he moved into the starting lineup when regulars Don Perkins and Amos Marsh were injured. "I played fullback and Jim Stiger (Washington) played halfback."

There is, however, one performance with the Cowboys specialty teams that stands out in his mind. "There are few things that I experienced in my life as an athlete," he says, "that affected me as much as the first trip I made to Yankee Stadium. I had always been a great admirer of the New York Giants and it was something to walk out onto the field in that stadium. I had a pretty good day, making quite a few tackles and recovering a fumble. And the fact that we won the game (31-21) added to the excitement of it all."

In his second season in Dallas the Cowboys drafted an Oklahoma State running back named Walt Garrison. Dunn could see the handwriting on the wall. "I wasn't blessed with a great deal of speed," he admits, "so it was pretty apparent that I was going to have a hard time." Still, he played regularly in the '65 season, the breakthrough year in which the Cowboys finished the regular season at 7-7 and went to the Playoff Bowl.

"That's where it all really started for the Cowboys," he says. "That's when it was obvious that things were beginning to come together. There was never any doubt in my mind that Dallas was going to be a strong team. It was just a matter of the players getting to a point where they could do the things Landry wanted them to do."

Dunn, Don Talbert and Billy Lothridge went to Atlanta in the expansion draft in 1966 and he played three seasons with the Falcons before going to Baltimore in 1969.

"I went to the Colts after the exhibition season had already begun," he remembers, "and played immediately. (Johnny) Unitas would call the play in the huddle and then tell me what I was supposed to do. There again, the fact that I had been a quarterback for so much of my athletic career made the transition relatively simple for me. We came into Dallas for the final game of the pre-season and had a really good game against the Cowboys (winning 23-7). In the second half I went 25 yards for a touchdown, right over Lee Roy Jordan. He had been a good friend of mine while I was in Dallas and I really got a kick out of that touchdown. He was cussing and stomping around after the play. I got a big kick out of that too."

TOMMY McDONALD

The Artistic Receiver

The 1963 NFL season was history. And for reasons many Philadelphia fans still wonder about, Eagles coach Joe Kuharich began to methodically dismantle his championship team. Noting to the puzzled press that he felt it necessary to trade away quality players to get a better balanced team, he said goodbye to a quarterback named Sonny Jurgensen and a Pro Bowl wide receiver named Tommy McDonald.

McDonald, the magic-making 5-9 receiver from Oklahoma, had spent all eight of his professional years in an Eagles uniform. He learned he had been traded when he heard the news on his car radio enroute home one afternoon. He had, the announcer was informing the world, been traded to the Dallas Cowboys.

He accepted the news with mixed emotions. His pride had been dealt considerable damage yet the prospects of moving south, playing in the Cotton Bowl where he had performed on several occasions while an All-America member of the all-winning OU dynasty, lightened his spirit.

He played as a Cowboy only one year — the season of 1964 — and by his own admission it was light years removed from some of the campaigns he had known before, yet it was not a time without fond memories.

"You know, it's funny," he said, speaking from his home in King of Prussia, Pa., "I played with Dallas just that one year, but I find myself thinking about that time often. One of the things I suppose I'll always regret about my athletic career is the fact that I didn't perform as well for Dallas as I felt I should." And while he logged duty as a starter along with receiver Frank Clarke, there are few statistics one can argue with the Albuquerque native. During his dozen years as a pro he caught 84 touchdown passes, one every sixth time the ball found its way into his hands. Yet few of those marks were during his stay in Dallas. There were times, however, in that 5-8-1 season that quarterback Don Meredith found him and McDonald was able to show the form which had earned him six trips to the Pro Bowl.

"Frank Clarke had a fantastic year that season," recalls McDonald. "He led the receivers — Buddy Dial and I were the others — with 65 receptions that year for over 900 yards. I still believe that he was and still is one of the most underrated ends ever to play pro ball."

Even today McDonald, now in the oil portrait business with 21 artists under contract to him, vividly recalls his encounters with Philadelphia during that season. Despite Kuharich's trades, the Eagles were not yet a team to be taken lightly. And for McDonald they represented the kind of challenge only a pro athlete traded away can fully explain.

"The first time you go back to a town where you previously played, where you established your reputation as a pro, you hope to do something special. It isn't a matter of wanting to show your former teammates up, but you want them to know that you're still performing well. And you want to give your old fans something to think about."

What Tommy McDonald wanted to do on that next-to-last game of the '64 season when Dallas travelled to Philly, was to impress on Kuharich that he had made a mistake in trading him away. "We had played them in Dallas earlier and they beat us by three (17-14) and I hadn't done much in that game. I knew that there would be a lot of people paying close attention to my performance when we went up there to play them.

"The night before the game they almost had to tie me down, I was so anxious to play. I don't think I've ever wanted to play well in a game so badly. It didn't turn out like I had hoped it would," he continues, "since we lost the game (24-14), but I was able to leave the field that day feeling that I had performed well. I caught a pass from (Don) Meredith for one of our touchdowns and remember one of our players — I'm not sure who it was — telling me I should run over to the Eagles bench and present the ball I had caught for the score to Kuharich. I thought that was funny, but it wasn't in my nature to do anything like that. In fact, I never even said 'boo' to him all afternoon.

"I suppose it may be silly to react to a situation like that, but I had enjoyed playing in Philly. I liked the town, I had a lot of friends there. It's only natural, I guess, for a man to want to prove to people that he still has a few good days left in him. And, despite the fact we lost the game, I felt I showed them that afternoon."

He would never, however, feel he was a vital part of the Cowboys team, and after the season asked Tom Landry to trade him. "I can't pinpoint it," he says, "but I just didn't feel I had helped the club that much. I hadn't caught that many balls and, frankly, Don didn't seem inclined to throw it to me very often. It was just one of those things.

"And, too, I was disappointed in myself. Dallas had traded three players for me, flew me down for a big press conference after the announcement and all, and then I went out and had a very mediocre year. I get to thinking about it today and think I should apologize to the fans of Dallas for not producing the way they had expected me to."

Following that year with Dallas, McDonald was traded to Los Angeles for kicker Danny Villanueva.

JIM RIDLON
★
The Embarrassed Punter

Professor Jim Ridlon well remembers his first training camp as a member of the Dallas Cowboys. It was, in a word, a shock.

"I had been with the San Francisco 49ers for six years before I was traded to Dallas," says the former defensive back who later became the youngest full professor in Syracuse University history, "and in one of our first team meetings Coach Landry looked around the room and asked who had the most NFL experience. He decided I was the man, so he asked me to come to the front of the room and draw up the six basic ways offensive teams run the sweep in pro ball. I had no idea there were that many. It was embarrassing.

"Later that evening Tom came up to me and told me he was sorry he had put me on the spot like that. Then he said, 'Jim, you're going to enjoy playing ball here because you're going to start playing it with your mind as well as your body.' "

The two seasons (1963-64) Ridlon played in the Dallas secondary were to prove Landry's promise.

"Looking back," says the professor of visual and performing arts and highly successful abstract artist, "I've only known two geniuses in my life. One is a professor here at Syracuse, the other is Tom Landry. Frankly, I think it is a waste of time for Landry to be in football. A man with his mind and abilities could be incredibly successful in so many areas — as head of a major corporation, as a political figure — you name it.

"On the other hand, football is fortunate to have a man of his caliber. He's revolutionized the game and amazingly enough seems to get better each year at what he does. One of the things that stands out in my mind as a good example of his innovative coaching style is his invention of contemporary confusion: having people shifting all over the place before a play finally gets under way. It's fun to watch."

Landry's intellectual approach was challenging and enjoyable to Ridlon. "By the end of my fifth season with the Cowboys," he says, "I was comfortable with his style of coaching. It was a great experience to learn from him. To be honest, I don't think there were a lot of people in our group who fully understood what he meant by playing the game with the mind. What it boiled down to for me was first the fact that we (the Cowboys) were going into the game with far more information than players on other teams. We were prepared; knew what we were expected to do and had a pretty good idea of what to expect the other team to do. When you've got that kind of information, you've naturally got to be more confident. You play the game without the element of fear getting in the way."

Ridlon, who called defensive signals on occasion, has written a 400-page text titled "Keying Defenses," and plans to publish it at some future date when Landry is no longer coaching. "Right now, it wouldn't be right simply because it details a lot of the things the Cowboys are still doing," he says. "But, some day I'm going to release it. In Landry's scheme of defense, everything you see the offense do is familiar. You're never surprised. You see exactly what the other guy is doing and you know how to deal with it. What he wanted you to do was use logic, conception and reaction. He didn't want a team going on the field all excited. In his style of play emotions get in the way. Stability is the big factor."

Which is not to say Ridlon always played the game without emotion. An afternoon in Yankee Stadium in a game against the New York Giants is a good example.

"Playing well against the Giants, Landry's old team, was always a big deal," Ridlon remembers. "Well, I got an interception in Yankee Stadium and ran it in for a touchdown. I was so excited about it that I punted the ball into the stands. Now, bear in mind Landry never re-ran good plays, just the bad ones he wanted to have corrected. But he gets to my interception and he runs it back. Then he runs it back again. He didn't say anything, but I could feel it coming. I nudged Cornell Green who was sitting next to me and said, 'Hey, I'm fixin' to get a compliment.' Sure enough Landry runs the play back a third time and after I had done my little hot dog number of punting the ball into the stands, he says, 'Nice punt, Ridlon.' "

Following his football career, Ridlon returned to his alma mater to serve as coach of the freshman and defensive backs at Syracuse for six years before moving into the classroom on a fulltime basis. And while he is still a close

follower of the game (he does the color commentary on radio broadcasts of Syracuse games), most of his efforts and time are now dealt to teaching and painting.

In addition to his work at Syracuse, Ridlon has, for the past four years, been director of the New York State Summer School of Art, a program for gifted high school students. He has also written three art-related textbooks. And for kicks, his home in Syracuse is a renovated firehouse.

"Growing up," he says, "I had two ambitions. To be an athlete and an artist. Fortunately, I've been able to realize both with some degree of success."

He made no further mention of his punting abilities.

JIM COLVIN

A High Grade for Courage

In the office of his West Texas Cadillac dealership, former Cowboys defensive tackle Jim Colvin proudly displays a game ball presented him by his teammates following a 27-13 victory over the St. Louis Cardinals in the waning stages of 1965's break-even (7-7) season.

It is not the only game ball he was awarded during a pro career which began in Baltimore and wound through Dallas, New York and finally New Orleans, but he is quick to point out it is the one which he treasures most. At the same time he questions his teammates' decision.

"Don (Meredith) threw three touchdown passes that day. He couldn't miss," Colvin says. "The only thing I did that was all that outstanding, really, was to tackle St. Louis' Bill Triplett in the end zone for a safety." What he fails to mention is the fact that on that Saturday afternoon in the Cotton Bowl he played a key role as an improving Doomsday Defense held the explosive Cardinals running attack to only 88 rushing yards for the day.

Nor does he mention the fact that if the doctors had had their way he would not have been on the field at all. Three weeks earlier he had re-injured a knee in practice before the Cleveland game. Doctors suggested surgery should be performed. Colvin, who prides himself in the fact that he never failed to start a game during his three-year Dallas tenure, said he would wait until the season ended.

"They had been after me for quite some time to get the knee fixed," he says. "I tore it up pretty good in the first half of a game in Milwaukee earlier in the year. I remember coming back home, hearing the doctors planning to operate the next Thursday. I listened for a while, then told them I wasn't going to be able to make their surgery because I planned to play the next Sunday.

"Looking back, I'm not all that sure it was such a smart thing to do, but I really had this thing about playing hurt. I felt strongly that that was what a professional was supposed to do. So, there I was out there most of the year, hobbling around on a torn up leg, trying to prove I was the toughest guy in town. Probably the reason they gave me that game ball after our win over the Cardinals was more because they felt sorry for me than because they thought I'd played such a great game."

If, in fact, Colvin didn't succeed in proving his toughness he did get a high grade for courage. In the same season he suffered a fractured elbow on a first down situation against the Washington Redskins. Rather than summon a trainer, he remained in for the series, the Cowboys held, and he trotted off the field. "I told the trainer I thought maybe I had broken something and he examined it, padded it a little, and I went back in and finished the game. The following Monday they X-rayed and found out that there was a break."

Colvin finished the season with the injury dealing him almost constant pain.

He launched his professional career as a rookie with Baltimore in 1960 and became a regular for the Colts in his second season. He came to the Cowboys in 1964 and suffered through the only losing season (5-8-1) he experienced during his pro career. "But," he says, "even then there were some high points. We went into Yankee Stadium and beat the Giants there. That was the first time I had ever played in Yankee Stadium and it was something I'll never forget. There's just something about that place, its history, I guess, that really gets your motor running."

In 1966 he was traded to New York where, despite his bad legs, he had a few good games before deciding to retire. In '69 he reported to the New Orleans Saints briefly but realized his playing days were behind him and gave it up for good.

An unsung hero, perhaps, but Jim Colvin can take stock in knowing that in his office sits a symbol of determination and character; a game ball richly deserved.

J. D. SMITH
★
Doing What Comes Naturally

For eight seasons he had been a standout performer for the San Francisco 49ers, All-Pro in 1959, a 1,000-yard rusher in that same year, and twice had been selected to participate in the Pro Bowl (1960 and '63). J. D. Smith, the fleet North Carolina A&T running back, had assumed he would end his playing days in the uniform of the 49ers.

Even today he finds it hard to describe the sensations he felt when informed that he and teammate Leon Donohue, a guard, had been traded to the still-growing but seldom-winning Dallas Cowboys for third and fourth round draft selections respectively just before the opening of the 1965 season.

"I knew Dallas had Don Perkins and liked what he did, so I was making a move to be a backup running back. That's never any fun for a guy who is used to seeing a lot of action. So, to be quite honest, it was tough to sit around and wait Sunday after Sunday when I knew I was capable of playing. Particularly that first year. I had missed training camp so I had a lot to learn about Coach Landry's system."

It wasn't the end of the world, however. "Oh, no, not at all. In fact, after I got to Dallas I liked what I saw. They were a team that was just about ready to make people take notice of them and there were some great guys on the team — Don Meredith, Jerry Rhome, guys like that. We became close friends. Shoot, I never miss Monday night football for the simple reason I get such a kick out of listening to Meredith's comments. And I'm delighted to see Rhome doing so well for Seattle as a coach."

Now living in Oakland and working as a security supervisor for Sears, Smith is quick to point out that his accomplishments as a member of the Cowboys were modest. "What it amounted to," he says with a booming laugh, "was that I stayed around for a couple of years, standing there on the sidelines just in case something happened that they would need me. As I said, the only thing I didn't like about my two seasons with the Cowboys was that I didn't get to play enough."

Ah, but there was a moment of glory lived by J. D. Smith in his tenure as a Cowboy. A game ball which is displayed in the living room of his home stands as testimony.

"We were playing Philadelphia up there my first season," he remembers. "We were still in contention for the Playoff Bowl, which was a pretty big thing at the time for a team which had never gone into any kind of post season play. Perkins got hurt that day and Landry put me in. I'll never forget what he told me after Don was injured. He said, 'J. D., forget all the stuff I've been trying to tell you and just go out there and play your kind of ball game. Just do what comes naturally. You're a pro, you can handle it.' "

Indeed, with a minute and 45 seconds remaining on the clock Dallas' 21-19 lead was far from being an assured victory. Eagles quarterback Norm Snead had shown a hot hand, particularly in the second half. The Eagles, in fact, were on an impressive march when Snead was intercepted by Obert Logan at the Cowboys two yard line. If the Eagles could force the Cowboys into a 1-2-3-punt situation there was still the likelihood of getting into range for a field goal which could win the game.

Landry instructed Meredith to keep the ball on the ground and do whatever he could to run out the clock. On five consecutive plays the Cowboys quarterback handed off to J. D. Smith. When the fifth play was completed the clock had run out — and the ball had been advanced out to the 40 yard line.

"That," Smith recalls, "was a great feeling. That day I felt I made my contribution. And, as you'll remember, we went on to the Playoff Bowl that season (which Dallas ended with a best ever regular season mark of 7-7).

"Then the next year we went 10-3-1 and lost the championship to Green Bay. But in those couple of years Dallas was on its way. It was great for me to be there to do whatever I could to help them get started in the direction they've been going ever since."

Still, however, he wishes he had been able to play more.

OBERT LOGAN

⋆

Two-Time Cowboy

Obert Logan frankly admits that he was in awe of the surroundings. It was his first trip to New York, to Yankee Stadium, where he and his Dallas Cowboys teammates faced the opportunity to do something in the final game of that 1965 season that had yet to be accomplished in the franchise's infant history.

With a win over the New York Giants, Dallas could finish the year at 7-7, .500, and earn a trip to the Playoff Bowl.

"I had heard about Yankee Stadium all my life," he recalls, "and when we stepped out on that field it was like walking through a dream. I went over and saw the bronzes of Babe Ruth and Lou Gehrig, the whole bit. It was really something."

That Dallas would triumph over the Giants, 38-20, was thrill enough for the young safety from little Trinity University. His personal heroics were icing on the cake. In the third quarter the Giants had driven into field goal range and Logan and Cornell Green lined up on opposite ends of the defensive line to rush the kick. Green got there first, blocking it. The ball bounced into the air and Logan fielded it and returned it 60 yards for the first and only touchdown he would score as a professional.

"That," says Logan, who now lives in San Marcos, Texas, where he operates a floor covering supply firm, "was one of those days you don't forget. By winning that one we got over a hump, got to .500 and into the playoffs. I was so excited after scoring that touchdown that I threw the ball into the stands. There wasn't a fine for things like that then, but even if there had been it would have been worth it. Like I said, it was my only touchdown in the NFL."

His rookie season, he recalls, was the first year in which the still-new Cowboys began to gain national attention. "We were just on the verge of becoming what the team would eventually evolve into. People in Dallas were really beginning to take notice. It was the first year we ever had a sellout, for

instance. And there was a positive feeling among the players. The older guys, those who had been around through some of the real struggling years, were beginning to see that Tom Landry's philosophy was working. It was a fun year."

Even if it included spending one long afternoon having to try to bring down Cleveland's famed Jim Brown. "Today," Obert says, "I can look back and tell people that I played against the guy, that on one particular safety blitz I went blasting in and tackled him all by myself. But back when it was happening I was wondering if I was going to get out of it alive.

"And the defense was beginning to build a reputation for itself. With guys like Cornell and Bob Lilly and people like that it was hard not to. One thing that we seemed to do better than any team in the league was block kicks. I was talking with (Cowboys special assistant) Ermal Allen not long ago and he reminded me that we still held the NFL record (15) for blocking the most extra points, punts and field goal attempts." (In the same year that Logan ran his blocked field goal 60 for a score, teammate Mike Gaechter did the same for the same distance against Washington.)

In his two seasons with the Cowboys, however, Logan admits that there were times when he questioned the Landry method. Only after he went to the New Orleans Saints in the 1967 expansion draft did he gain a real appreciation for what he had learned in Dallas. "When I got there and saw how they were operating it gave me a whole new appreciation for what Landry was doing, for what the entire Cowboys organization was doing."

Logan's tenure in New Orleans would be short-lived since the Saints drafted University of Houston standout Bo Burris as a safety in that same season. They would soon tell him of their intentions to trade him and he just as quickly told them he was not interested in playing for any team in the east. "What I really wanted to do," he says, "was get back to the Cowboys if there was any way. I told them, and they explained that for that to happen they would have to place me on waivers. 'Fine,' " Logan said.

It was at a time in the season of 1968 when Dallas was crippled by injuries to defensive backs Mel Renfro and Dickie Daniels. They needed help in the secondary and when Logan appeared on the waiver wire, they picked him up. Thus was added another milestone to his career. Not before or since has a player ever left the Cowboys, played with another team, and returned to a Dallas uniform.

"When I left in '67," he says, "I knew I was leaving a winner. It was good to get back and I felt very good about the fact they wanted me back. What I found when I returned was even more maturity on the team. When I left there was a feeling that we could win, but there was still some lingering doubt. When I got back I was aware of a feeling that the Cowboys believed they could win, period. There were no longer any doubts."

For the duration of that year Logan labored as a backup safety and wide receiver. "I didn't play a great deal, but I learned a lot of football. That had been one of the reasons I was so glad to get the chance to come back; to learn from Landry."

He would eventually put those lessons to use. Prior to the 1969 season it had come down to keeping either Logan or Bobby Jo Conrad as a backup wide receiver. Conrad's experience edge won out. Landry called Logan in for a second time to advise him of the decision. "He asked if I wanted to play some more. He said that Cleveland, New England and the New York Jets had expressed interest," Obert says, "but I told him I thought it was time for me to retire."

While it would end his NFL career, the urge to play again struck in '69 when the semi-pro San Antonio Toros of the Continental League offered him a spot as a wide receiver, and eventually as the team's head coach. "I had gone down there to play and they asked me if I would coach. I thought about it and decided, 'Why not?' I put in a very simplified version of the Flex defense and we allowed only 153 yards per game all year. We wound up going to Indianapolis to play them for the league championship and lost the game in overtime. It was a lot of fun."

Not, however, quite like returning a blocked field goal for a touchdown in Yankee Stadium. "No," Obert says, "that would be hard to top."

COLIN RIDGWAY

The Infamous Kicker

He gives no indication that the distinction, however negative, bothers him. Colin Ridgway lives with the story, tells it himself, laughs about it. It is, in a strange sense, his professional football legacy. "Let's face it," he says, "it's what people remember me for."

It is safe to say there are few sports trivia fans in Dallas who realize that in 1956, in Melbourne, Australia, his homeland, Ridgway was the youngest track and field athlete to participate in a modern Olympic Games, finishing sixth in the high jump with a leap of 6-7¾ at the ripe old age of 16. You have to look hard to find those who remember that as a student at Beaumont's Lamar Tech he became the first Texas-based jumper ever to clear seven feet, going 7-1 at the Border Olympics.

"As a professional football player," the Dallas resident says, "I had my highs and lows." The high came in an exhibition game against the Green Bay Packers when he made his very first appearance in a Cowboys uniform, punting six times for an almost 50-yards-per-punt average.

Ah, but that day in San Francisco's Kezar Stadium; that's different. The story, which Ridgway claims has all the necessary elements of truth, goes something like this:

He and Danny Villanueva were battling for the punting job and the competition had become fierce by that windy afternoon on the bay. Danny, it seems, was manning the headphones on the sideline when the call came from the pressbox that it was his time to punt. Inasmuch as the Cowboys offense had bogged down deep in its own territory and was going into the wind, Villanueva thought better of the situation and calmly strode over to Ridgway and informed him that it was *his* time to punt. Colin took the field.

"Everything felt right," he recalls, "I thought I got into the ball well and the trajectory was high." Too high. All of the distance was straight up. Never downfield. There was, in fact, a moment when it appeared the kick would go for minus yardage. Instead, it was caught by an opposing linebacker just three yards from the line of scrimmage. For a moment it appeared that Ridgway might even get the opportunity to field his own punt. "I was talking to one of the writers after the game," he says, "and I told him that I was wishing I was a bit more familiar with the rules of the game. For a moment I considered calling for a fair catch."

That moment, taken from the pre-season of 1965, has become part of the Cowboys lore. "Boomer," as he was called, left his mark.

He had come to the United States at the request of a Lamar Tech recruiter who saw him performing in England, and he brought national attention to the small Gulf Coast school much as an imported tennis player named Cliff Drysdale had. He had played some soccer, had demonstrated a strong leg and had caught the eye of then Houston Oilers coach Bones Taylor. When he went up to Houston and drop-kicked several 50-yard field goals, the Oilers offered him a contract. Dallas' Gil Brandt, in the meantime, heard about Ridgway and suggested he pay a visit to the Cowboys before signing anything.

"At that time," Colin says, "I knew very little about football, but I did know the Cowboys were winners so I came up and gave it a try. It was all new and exciting to me. I think the thing which impressed me most was the high caliber of young men on the team. There was a great deal of polish and class; people like Craig Morton and Obert Logan, Don Meredith and Bob Hayes. Super people. And Bob Lilly; he helped me a great deal as did Meredith. Both of them were very interested in Australia, in fact, and spent a lot of time with me talking about it. Meredith even made a trip down there and visited several of my friends.

"Playing with the Cowboys was a wonderful experience for me. I loved it. I loved the game, the spectacle of it. I always thought that part of it set it apart from any other kind of sports event — the stadium, the crowds, the uniforms, the sideline activities — and to have been part of it was a great thing."

Now working for a travel wholesale company which packages tours, Colin Ridgway is an admitted fan of professional football, and indoor stadiums; where wind is no longer a factor kickers have to face.

A. D. WHITFIELD

✪

An Educational Experience

To those who report to the Dallas Cowboys training camp as free agents, former Dallas Cowboys running back A. D. Whitfield can offer his empathy.

"There's nothing in the world that can give you the kind of feeling you get when you get to camp and look around at all the guys who are bigger and from bigger schools and come equipped with ready-made reputations and fat signing bonuses.

"The year I went out there (1965) there were 80 rookies and 20 of them were running backs. The first few days I wondered what in the world I was doing there. I was certain that I had made a big mistake. But I decided that I'd better just make the best of the situation and see what I could do."

What he did was make the squad, going head-to-head with Danny Reeves in practices until a pulled hamstring gave the current Denver Broncos coach an edge. "For a while I thought I was going to make it," the North Texas State ex says, "because I was having some good practices and the coaches were really encouraging me. But I pulled that hamstring and was less than 100 percent for three or four weeks and I thought I was gone."

Head Coach Tom Landry, however, chose to keep the 5-10, 215-pounder placing him on the taxi squad along with the likes of a big kid from Elizabeth City College named Jethro Pugh. In the fifth week of the regular season Whitfield was activated and played out the year as a backup running back and return man. "Needless to say I didn't get much playing time as a kick returner with Mel Renfro and Bob Hayes in front of me, but I learned a great deal.

"In fact, I learned from the day I walked into camp. My year with Dallas proved to be very important to me. And it was enjoyable. I was a part of the first Cowboys team to make it into post-season play, going to the Playoff Bowl. 1965 was a real turnaround year for Dallas and it was fun being a part of that.

"And I got the best coaching I'd ever had. I learned a great deal of football." It was that education, he says, which enabled him to spend four more years in the league.

"The next season Coach Landry called me in and told me he was going to have to let me go. He was very honest. But he also told me that he felt there was a place for me in the NFL," A.D. says.

Indeed there was. From Dallas he went to the Washington Redskins where he advanced to a starting role and played four seasons. "It's ironic," he says, "but in that year I was with the Cowboys I spent most of my time working on the specialty teams. In the regular season I carried the ball just one time against Washington for no gain. Why they were interested in me, I'll never know, but I went up there and started running circles around everyone."

"I feel very fortunate to have been able to play in the league for five years," the Dallas-based New York Life Insurance agent points out, "and I would never have had the chance had it not been for the Cowboys. When I was a senior at North Texas I was really certain that I was going to be drafted. I remember sitting by the phone both days, just waiting for it to ring. I had talked to any number of pro scouts and was just so sure. This is going to sound really naive, but when I wasn't picked, I was convinced there had been some kind of mixup and called (NFL commissioner) Pete Rozelle's office to ask what happened. He told me to sit tight and someone would probably be in touch with me. Sure enough, the next day the Cowboys signed me."

Today Whitfield's loyalties are mixed. As a Dallas resident he follows the Cowboys and is a strong backer. But, the fact remains that he spent four years eating at the Redskins' table. "I'd be happy if they split every year," he says, laughing. "I know I have a lot of fun with people in the office when Dallas and Washington are getting ready to play.

"I tell them that if they've never been in RFK stadium for a game they have no idea what Dallas is up against. But, frankly, I have to say that with Tom Landry on the sidelines Dallas is never going to be much of an underdog, no matter where the game is played. His composure is a big plus. I think that was the deciding thing in that great (35-34) game at the end of the 1979 season."

For several years he's worked with the Cowboys, helping to sign free agents. "I was the one who went up to Howard University and signed Steve Wilson," he says.

Free agents, one must assume, have a special bond.

MAURY YOUMANS
★
Birth of the Flex

If, in fact, former Dallas Cowboys defensive end Maury Youmans' theory is correct, he was among those who, in the season of 1965, witnessed the birth of The Flex. It was the year in which the expansion franchise began to make quick, giant strides, he recalls, and one of the big reasons was a new defensive concept which Landry had installed to take advantage of the remarkable talents of defensive tackle Bob Lilly.

"I really think Tom put it in for Lilly," the Treasure Island, Florida, realtor says. "Bob was so quick in those days that he would move up on the (offensive) guard's nose and if the guard pulled he would just go with him and run the back down from behind. By doing that, though, he left a pretty big gap so the defensive end, who normally would play on the tackle's outside shoulder, had to move in to a head up position to fill the hole." Thus, he notes, began the coordination of what is now regarded as the most highly publicized defense in pro football.

Youmans, who spent four years with the Chicago Bears before coming to Dallas in a trade prior to the 1964 season, says he had his doubts about it in the early going. "I really didn't think it would work. In my case, for instance, it took me off the direct course to the ball I had always been used to. I had always felt I was being paid to put the quarterback on his tail. Frankly, there were a lot of the defensive players wondering what was going on. At that point, the defense had been carrying the load. The people in the stands would boo the offense when it came off the field and cheer us. We felt we were doing a pretty respectable job and, suddenly, we were changing things. There was some uneasiness.

"But, as the year progressed and we began to see the effect it was having, people began to believe in it.

"Before all was said and done, I was one of its biggest boosters. What I liked about it was that you knew full well what your responsibility was on every play. It was, in a sense, a comfortable feeling to know what to do rather than have to make the decision on whether to cover inside, outside, or middle on every play. The hardest part of it all was learning to react at the snap of the ball, to not hesitate like you do in some defensive alignments.

"The trade to Dallas really worked well for me," he says. "I was coming off knee surgery after our championship season ('63) in Chicago and thought I might be traded and had made it known I wanted to go to the Giants. When you've been in the league a while and know you're going to make a move, you naturally want to make it to a team that's a contender. It goes without saying, then, that I had my doubts when they made the trade with the Cowboys.

"But it turned out great. I learned more in two years with Dallas than I did in four at Chicago. In Tom's system you are allowed to prove yourself. Even my first impression of things was good when I arrived. It was a better situation than I had been in in Chicago. It was a young team and had already developed a good feeling of togetherness. There were no cliques running through the organization like there had been in Chicago. And it was Landry who held it all together. He was one of those unique individuals who could get up in front of a Monday team meeting, after you had gotten whipped pretty good the previous day, and have you believing there was no way you were going to lose again the next week."

Youman's first season with Dallas was a "learning year," he says, one in which he backed up the likes of Larry Stephens and George Andrie. Then, in his second year he became a starter, moving from the right side to the left.

"I came to the Cowboys in a real time of transition," he says. "In '64 we showed signs of progress, having some good games, but still were losing more than we were winning (5-8-1). Then, the next year we really began to come

in. People began to believe Tom's theory that it was possible to play a perfect game. They began to believe in the system and the people working in it. That was the year we finished at 7-7 and went down to Miami to play in the Playoff Bowl against Baltimore. It was a big step for the franchise."

JIM BOEKE
★
Type-Casted Actor

It was a part he felt uniquely qualified to play. Jim Boeke, an offensive tackle for the Dallas Cowboys from 1964 to 1967, had been there.

The scene, early in the movie *North Dallas Forty,* is the team meeting room of the North Dallas Bulls, a fictional football team created by former Dallas wide receiver Pete Gent. Films of an early pre-season game are being shown and a lineman named Stallings, played by Boeke, is badly manhandled on a particular play. The coach, livid, turns up the lights and says, "Stallings, what in the hell were you thinking about on that play?" Stallings, obviously embarrassed, says he isn't sure. The coach explodes again.

And, finally, when the meeting ends and the players are dismissed, Stallings is asked to remain for a moment. It's over. He is released. Fade out . . . and cut.

In a sense, the real life of Jim Boeke was being recreated briefly on the screen. There was, he remembers, a day in Dallas much like the one on the screen. Oh, there was no yelling, no cursing, but the axe fell just the same.

The Cowboys were in the second or third week of training camp when Boeke, who had come to the Cowboys after spending three seasons with the Los Angeles Rams, began to get bad vibes, something more than an inkling that bad days were coming. "You just know things like that," he said recently from his Fountain Valley, California home. "It's a feeling you get. I knew it was coming, but there was no one who would enlighten me about what was in the works. I even asked (offensive line coach) Jim Myers if there was some kind of trade in the works and he told me he didn't know anything about it.

"But, when they take you off the wedge (the front line of the kick return team), there's no place else to go. I had no idea what day or what hour it would be, but I knew it was coming."

Finally it did one afternoon after practice. "Coach Landry called me in and told me I had been traded to New Orleans. He explained to me why and wished me luck. That was it."

119

It was, he admits, an unnerving blow. But it was not as difficult to deal with as had been his release from the Rams three years earlier. "I really didn't know what to do when they told me I had been traded to Dallas," he recalls. "For a couple of days after the trade I just hung around the Rams camp for a couple of days, like a lost puppy. Finally, it occurred to me that I had better get on with it, so I reported to the Cowboys."

The move, it turned out, was not a bad one at all for the former Heidelberg standout. By the time Dallas advanced to the NFL championship showdown against the Green Bay Packers in 1966 he was the starting left tackle. And a good one. Fate, however, dealt him a legacy he still carries. It was, history shows, Jim Boeke who moved ahead of the snap, drawing a penalty when the Cowboys had the ball on the Packers one-yard line. It is not one of his fondest memories.

After Dallas and New Orleans, Boeke was traded to Detroit where he stayed only through four exhibition games and played very little while trying to make the adjustment to right tackle. Then it was to Washington briefly and finally the Rams' taxi squad for a while. There his career ended. "My pass protection became a problem," Boeke flatly admits, "and while I still had the quickness, I lacked the strength some of the younger players coming up had. It was time to get out."

And into teaching on a fulltime basis. Today he is a teacher at Westminster High School and pursuing an acting career when time permits. Enrolled in the South Coast Actors Studio in nearby Newport Beach, he aspires to serious acting. "I'm really into it; I enjoy it," he says.

North Dallas Forty, was the second football movie he appeared in, having also worked as one of the players in the highly successful *Heaven Can Wait.*

"I knew they were planning to do *North Dallas,"* he says, "and Tom Fears (the former Rams Hall of Famer) was coordinating some of the football scenes. He called and asked if I would be interested and pointed out that they were planning to shoot it in Houston. When he said I'd have to be in Houston for two months, I told him no thanks. I said that would be just like going to training camp again. I just didn't want to be away from home for that long.

"Then, however, they ran into some problems in Houston and decided to film in California. When they called again and told me about the part and said they would just need a guy for a couple of days, I was excited about it. Like I said, I knew the feeling the guy was supposed to have."

DANNY VILLANUEVA

★

A Victory Won, A Tragedy Averted

There is, in the Danny Villanueva home in Los Angeles, but one souvenir from his days as a professional football player. Now busy with the myriad activities of vice president and general manager of Spanish International Communications Corporation, owners of television stations in five states and director of Magna Verde Corporation which promotes TV soccer and boxing, the former Dallas Cowboys kicker has put his playing days behind him. No scrapbooks, no trophies, no faded pictures. Seldom even a wistful look back at the way it was.

Except for the one game ball he has kept. It is a memento too special to hide away. The memories it calls up are too pleasant to want to forget. It is a game ball which represents a beginning of something still ongoing among the Cowboys, Danny says. It is the ball he kicked 30 yards for a last minute field goal which defeated the Washington Redskins, 31-30, and vaulted Dallas into the franchise's first playoff game. It was the beginning in a sense of all that was to come.

It was a game which also had all the earmarks of defeat for the Cowboys, then still shouldering the stigma of not being able to win the big one. The fading minutes of the clock were fast escaping when Washington punter Pat Richter, protecting a 30-28 Redskins lead, punted the ball inside the Cowboys' five-yard-line.

On the sidelines Danny Villanueva had no reason to be nervous. This one, he knew, would not come down to him. There was simply not enough time.

Obviously, it was an opinion with which Cowboys quarterback Don Meredith begged to differ. He first hit Pete Gent on a long pass, then came back to connect for yet another first down to Pettis Norman. Next he threw to Dan Reeves coming out of the backfield. The miracle was beginning to take form.

It became a very real possibility when Meredith, rolling out to his right, was knocked out of bounds and tackled by an over-zealous Redskins defender after he was clearly off the field of play. As the official stepped off the 15-yard penalty, 11 seconds showed on the clock. It had, in fact, come down to Villanueva.

"It was," he remembers, "just over 30 yards. But it looked like 80. Then Reeves bobbled the snap and I had to wait. There was absolutely no timing on the kick. I just tried to nurse it over the goal posts. I've never in my life been so relieved to see an official raise his arms."

In the aftermath of the stunning victory, a visitor arrived at the door to the Cowboys dressing room, asking to see Villanueva. He was Pete Richert, the former Dodgers and Washington Senators pitcher, who had been seated in the end zone with his son. He had caught the ball and thought Villanueva might like to have it as a souvenir. "It was a great gesture on his part," the former kicker says. "I could tell that his boy — just a young kid — had hopes of keeping it, so I got another ball from our equipment manager and traded him. The exchange made both of us happy."

Villanueva remembers the thundering welcome home the Cowboys received. Fans waited behind crowd-control barriers to offer personal congratulations to the players as they stepped from the plane. "Meredith," Danny remembers, "finally got away by climbing into an ambulance and getting the driver to take him away from the airport. It was unbelievable."

Members of his family, including then two-year-old son Jimmy, had gathered at an apartment to watch the game on television. While the celebrating following the game winning boot was in full bloom, Jimmy made his way outside and fell into the swimming pool. A resident of the apartment, who had been waxing his car nearby and had put aside his task long enough to go inside and watch the final dramatic moments of the game, returned to his job and noticed the young Villanueva, unable to swim, bobbing in the water. He jumped in and saved his life.

"When I got home and heard about it," Danny says, "the first thing I did was find the guy. I gave him a blank check and told him to make it out for whatever amount he wanted. He handed it back to me and said he would gladly settle for a couple of tickets to the playoff game."

Thus it was a day which would forever be chiseled in Villanueva's memory. Few people were ever aware of the near personal tragedy, yet everyone who followed the Cowboys with even casual interest knew the details of the final minute of the game in Washington.

"It was one of those situations you find yourself in," Danny recalls, "where you really don't have much time to think about what you've got to do. It was just suddenly time to do it. You know, that was a really big win for Dallas. That was the first time the Cowboys made it into the playoffs, the first of what has developed into an impressive string. You might say that was the day the dynasty began."

And what if he had missed? "I already had it figured out," he says. "We were already in Washington, so I would have just taken a taxi to the Mexican Embassy and asked for immediate asylum."

HAROLD HAYS

☆

First Specialty Teams Captain

Earlier in the season of 1966 the Dallas Cowboys, riding the five touchdown performance of Don Meredith, had buried the Philadelphia Eagles, 56-7, so there was little reason to expect what transpired the second time the two teams met that year. Again the Dallas offense did a respectable job, putting 23 points on the board, and the defense showed no drastic letdown. Yet the Eagles won the game, 24-23.

They did so primarily on the kick return efforts of Eagles running back Timmy Brown who went around, over and through the Cowboys specialty teams to account for the upset victory. Needless to say Tom Landry was less than pleased. He also needed little review of the disaster to come to the decision that there was a need for more leadership on the specialty teams. Thus he went in search of a player who might serve as the bell cow of the vitally important unit; a man who would assume the responsibility of seeing to it that future "Philadelphias" were avoided.

The man for the job — the player who became the first captain of the specialty units in the club's history — was a third year player who had been a 14th round draft choice out of Southern Mississippi in 1962. Today Harold Hays looks back on his 1963-67 term as a Cowboy (he finished his career with a two-year stint on the San Francisco 49ers) and points to his time spent on the specialty teams as the most memorable.

Oh, there were some big games: the Green Bay Ice Bowl; his first game as a rookie, (when he started a pre-season affair against the Los Angeles Rams in the LA Coliseum which seated more people than lived in his Mississippi hometown) but going down on kickoffs and guarding against punt returns was Hays' thing.

"I was one of those guys who really get hooked on playing professional football," he points out. "That game against the Rams in the Coliseum in my rookie year was the first pro game I'd ever even seen. And since Lee Roy Jordan was playing in the College All-Star game and late getting to camp I got to start. I even intercepted one of Roman Gabriel's passes. But as time went on I really wasn't getting to play all that much with linebackers like Jordan and Chuck Howley and Jerry Tubbs and later Dave Edwards around.

"I wanted to make a contribution and saw that I could do it on the specialty teams. A lot of guys take that duty simply because they think that's the only way they can make the team. That wasn't the case with me. In fact, for

125

quite a long time I was the only reserve linebacker on the roster so I was pretty well assured of a place on the team. But it didn't assure me of that much playing time so I made a special effort to do as much as I could as a member of the kicking teams.

"It was a big thrill to be named a captain," he admits, "though after it came about, I would always tell people who mentioned it to me, that the only reason Landry did it was so he would have one person he could get steamed at rather than having to spend his time getting mad at all 11 guys."

During his tenure with Dallas, Hays had a front row seat from which to view the Cowboys' methodical advancement toward becoming a championship caliber team. "In the time I was with Dallas we won a lot of games but in some of the early years I would have to say we did it without the benefit of a lot of real quality football players. We had a lot of players with limited ability who were made to look maybe a little better than they were, simply because of Landry's system.

"He got a lot out of what we had; and in the process continued to add more quality each year. The draft system of the Cowboys was beginning to pay off by the mid-60s, and each year there would be a few more quality players. It was a gradual thing; hardly noticeable to a lot of people, I suspect. But, those who watched the Cowboys closely could see it happening.

"It was disappointing to come so close and not win it all," Hays notes, "but there was a foundation built in those years which has carried the Cowboys ever since, I think. In that respect, those were very important years to the club."

Though he would spend his final two seasons of pro ball as a member of the 49ers, Hays continued to call Dallas home. He still does today, operating a highly successful sporting goods concern. Traveling a four-state area (Texas-Oklahoma-Arkansas-Louisiana) as a manufacturer's representative, he deals primarily in fishing equipment. "We handle some sporting goods, a line of athletic shoes and basketball goals, things like that," he says, "but my main thing is fishing equipment."

In a manner of speaking, Harold Hays is still specializing. And thoroughly enjoying it.

DICK DANIELS

Product of the Cowboys Classroom

He learned lessons, he says, which have stayed with him. And, as the director of college scouting for the Washington Redskins, they are the creeds he still follows; the tools of his trade, so to speak. And although it has been ten years since Dick Daniels last played football professionally, he has never left it. Today, in fact, he is more involved than he was during those years he labored as a player.

Once a defensive back for the Cowboys, he got his basic NFL education in Dallas. He learned what coaches require from young athletes attempting to make the team, and he realized what an athlete must prove to convince coaches that they are, in fact, in need of his services. He also learned how important a player's abilities — in all phases of the game — are if one expects to break into pro ball.

He looks for the same characteristics in candidates today — as he travels in search of new talent for the Redskins — that he sought when he began his scouting career in 1971 with the Miami Dolphins. Scouting for the Tampa Bay Buccaneers (1976-77) and the San Francisco 49ers in '78, he attracted talented players through his knowledgeable observations. Observations, he claims, he would not likely have made without the thorough tutelage of Coach Landry.

"The thing that stands out in my mind as I look back on my playing days with the Cowboys," he says, "is the kind of preparation Tom Landry and his staff demanded of everyone. Every week, regardless of the opposition, every little detail was dealt with. Landry, more so than any coach I ever played for, realized the importance of preparation. In that particular phase of putting together a game plan, he was years ahead of his time."

Daniels, one of the many Cowboys' finds from the small college ranks, was called to the attention of the scouting department by cornerback Mel Renfro. Like him, Daniels had come from Portland and Renfro was keenly aware of his abilities as a running back as well as a secondary performer.

"I was very fortunate to have spent a couple of seasons (1968-69) with the Cowboys, seeing how things were done right. And, frankly, it made it a little tough for me at times when I went to other teams."

Before he would end his career, the former free agent out of Pacific University, (located in Forest Grove, Oregon where the Cowboys trained prior to locating their summer activities in Thousand Oaks) would spend the 69-70 season with the Chicago Bears and close out his playing days in the '71 season with the Miami Dolphins.

"The Dolphins did things quite a bit like the Cowboys, so far as setting up an outstanding game plan and making everyone familiar with what to expect from the next week's opposition," Daniels says. "And I would have to say, that reflects directly on the coaching records established by Landry and Don Shula. It has never been any mystery to me why those men have enjoyed such success."

"What we learned in Dallas," Daniel recalls, "as we prepared for games, was a basic understanding of what the opposition was going to try to do to us. We learned their strengths and their weaknesses, both as a team and individually. Then things were further broken down. After we had a grasp of the overall concept, various aspects of the game plan were broken into components that each individual would put to use. That was where Dallas was different.

"Most people have about the same approach to a game plan, offensively and defensively, but with the Cowboys it was a more isolated kind of thing. You dealt primarily with what your specific role in the overall plan was and you concentrated your efforts on being as well prepared to do your particular job as possible. What you did was learn what parts of the plan you could use. The coaches already knew and they saw to it your attention was focused in the right area rather than trying to see that you knew everything about everyone's job.

"Looking back, I'd have to say one of the greatest jobs of preparation we ever did was to get ready for the (NFL) championship game against Green Bay that first time in '66. Personnel-wise, we were no match for them at that time. We were still a young, inexperienced team and they were a team of veteran superstars. Yet we played an outstanding game against them (despite eventually losing, 34-27).

"The coaches did an incredible job. We were very well prepared and when there were situations when adjustments were necessary, they were made quickly and without any confusion."

Twice Daniels would see the Packer dynasty deny him the thrill of being a part of a championship team. Then, in his final year with the Cowboys, it would be Cleveland which turned Dallas back in the Eastern championship game. Following that year he would be traded to the Chicago Bears for whom he would play for a season and a half.

Eventually, he would, however, make it to the Super Bowl. Not as a member of the Cowboys but rather as an opponent of the team he had once played for. He was a member of the Miami Dolphins which would lose 24-3 to Dallas in Super Bowl VI.

LEON DONOHUE

Ired by A Lady Columnist

The article remains vivid in the mind of Leon Donohue. Authored by Joan Ryan, wife of then-Cleveland Browns quarterback Frank Ryan, it had been a strong condemnation of the Dallas Cowboys in general and quarterback Don Meredith in particular. As a columnist for the *Cleveland Plain Dealer,* she had written her observations after having watched Dallas and St. Louis battle to a 10-10 tie the week before.

"I don't recall too many specifics about the column she wrote," the former Cowboys offensive guard (1965-67) says, "but there was one line that I can still see: It said, 'Don Meredith is a loser.' That made us all mad. Well, everyone except maybe Don himself who never really got too upset about it. We all knew he was the leader of our team and when someone said he was a loser, it was as if they were saying we were all losers."

Vindication, then, would be far too long in coming in that season of 1966. In the first meeting of the two clubs, just a few days after Mrs. Ryan's "Backseat Brown" column appeared, the Browns won 30-21 and, almost ironically, Meredith had one of his worst days of the season. He was intercepted four times and the Eastern race tightened as St. Louis, Dallas and Cleveland were separated by just a game and a half at the season's midway point. "Right now," head coach Tom Landry had said, "the Browns are the best team in the East."

It would be Thanksgiving Day before the Cowboys would have another opportunity to prove their coach — and Joan Ryan — wrong.

The holiday game was to be a twilight affair, beginning at 5 p.m. in the packed Cotton Bowl, for the benefit of a national television audience. "I don't remember ever being in a quieter locker room before a game," Donohue recalls. "Everyone realized that if we had any chance of winning the championship it would have to come by defeating the Browns. And, there was that thing Ryan's wife had written still staring us in the face."

Indeed, few Cowboys fans had forgotten. One of the largest banners visible was one stretching across a section in the upper deck saying, "Ryan's a Loser."

And on that evening the losers would be Ryan and his Cleveland Browns. Kicker Danny Villanueva kicked field goals from distances of 11, 12, 13 and 31. Dan Reeves took a short pass from Meredith in the second quarter and scored from the six. Don Perkins, who would rush for 111 yards against the Browns defense as Donohue and Co. repeatedly opened holes, added the clincher in the final period with a 10-yard touchdown run.

The Cowboys won the game 26-14 and headed for their first-ever NFL championship appearance (which they would eventually lose to Green Bay, 34-27).

Looking back on the Cowboys' first winning season (10-3-1), Donohue says, "It was the win over Cleveland that got us to the championship game. That was the one we had to win. It was one of our first really big, really significant wins. Up until that time I don't think we had a very good idea of how good a team we really had. Once we got that far, though, we suddenly became aware that we were something more than a team of Don Merediths and Bob Hayes. We began to feel we were a solid unit, capable of playing with anyone in the league."

Donohue, now head football and wrestling coach at Shasta College in Redding, recalls his days with the Cowboys as a "fun time" in the club's history. "We had some really good athletes," he remembers, "and some real characters. Like Dandy, for instance. He was fun just to be around on a day-to-day basis. I would have to guess that things are a little more serious with the Cowboys these days. Still, I like to think maybe they're having a little fun with their winning."

As head football coach, Leon has seen his team capture Golden Valley Conference titles. "You know," he says, "there were times when I was playing that I really wondered about some of Landry's thinking on various things. Now, though, I can see why he did a lot of the things he did. They make a lot more sense when you're looking at them from a coach's viewpoint. Things are just naturally different on the other side of the fence."

The former San Jose State standout, whose career from high school through the pros was constantly detoured by knee surgeries, recalls that when he first applied for an assistant coaching post at the college where he has now been for eight years, one of the things which helped him get the job was a letter of recommendation from Tom Landry.

"It was really a nice letter," he says.

Nothing at all like the column written by a lady journalist named Joan Ryan. "But, you know," Donohue says, "that column might have been one of the best things that ever happened to us."

PETE GENT

★

He Didn't Show Up on the Film

Things, says former Dallas Cowboy receiver-turned-best selling novelist-screenwriter Pete Gent, aren't always as you remember them. He points to the well chronicled and still oft-discussed 1966 NFL Championship game matching the Cowboys and the Green Bay Packers as a textbook example.

It went as follows: There, in the jam-packed Cotton Bowl the Cowboys, having ended the regular season 10-3-1, got their first chance at winning all the marbles. Under the artful direction of the quarterback Don Meredith they had come from behind and moved near the Packers goal line in the fading seconds of play. But the hopes died with a pair of tragic misfires. First, left tackle Jim Boeke jumped offside on a second down at the two. Then, on fourth and two Meredith was pressured while trying to throw a roll-out pass and was intercepted by Green Bay's Tom Brown in the end zone.

There it ended with Green Bay declared World Champions by virtue of a 34-27 victory.

"Your memory," Gent says, "can really play strange tricks on you. All these years I've sworn I was in there on that last play, watching Meredith get that pass off, seeing it intercepted. But recently I saw films of the game and it was Buddy Dial in there instead of me. He and I were alternating then. Obviously, I was on the sidelines."

On the field or not, Gent is not among those who believe the Dallas defeat on that afternoon was the fault of teammate Boeke's drawing a five-yard penalty. Or, for that matter, Meredith's throwing the ball up for grabs on the final Cowboys offensive play.

"It is hard, in any game, to isolate a single thing and say it is the reason you lost," Gent points out, "but a couple of things come to mind more quickly than Boeke's jumping offsides.

"First, we seemed to break down in the third quarter, making mental mistakes. I dropped one I should have caught, and we fumbled. We seemed to lose some of the momentum we had gained in the first half after coming from 14 down to tie things. Then, it was a mistake to have Bob Hayes instead of Frank Clarke in there on that fourth-and-two play at the end of the game. Hayes had never been in on goal-line situations before. It was just some kind of a mix-up." Accounts of the game later noted that Green Bay linebacker Dave Robinson had breezed past Hayes and applied the fatal pressure to Meredith, forcing him to throw the ball up for grabs.

"I honestly think," Gent continues, "that the main reason so much attention was dealt to Boeke's mistake was the fact that NFL films got some really good shots of it. They played that thing over and over; using several different angles. And there was always that deep bass voice dramatically saying how the 'Cowboys' hopes had died with that play.'

"They didn't. Shoot, we moved the ball back down to the two. Like I said, if we had played better in the third quarter we would have never been in that position late in the game anyway."

While it would end in disappointing defeat, Gent, a member of the Cowboys from 1964 to 1968, remembers it as the season in which Dallas got over the expansion hump and became a winner. "We had come on strong at the end of the '65 season, winning five of our last seven games," he says. "There was a strong feeling in the club that the next year was going to be a good one. And it was. We went 10-3-1 and came very close to beating Green Bay for the whole thing. That was the year a lot of us — Don Perkins, Danny Villanueva, Boeke, Meredith — sort of reached the peaks of our careers. Don really blossomed that year. He was an outstanding quarterback and had gained full confidence of the team."

Another person who gained the players' confidence was head coach Landry. "The biggest difference in the Cowboys now and the Cowboys I knew in the first couple of years I was playing for them," Gent says, "is that now they think Tom is right. When I first joined the team there were a lot of guys on the team who questioned what he was trying to do. There were a lot of personality conflicts, between players, coaches, and coaches and players. But Landry stuck to his beliefs and finally won everyone over. You could see the confidence in him growing toward the end of the '65 season. By 1966 he was in charge of the situation.

"I can remember having a long talk with Meredith about it," he says, "and at the time I was a little surprised to hear Don defending Landry so strongly. He said, 'Hey, the guy has shown me a lot.' "

By the same token, Meredith showed Gent a lot in that '66 season. "For one week," he recalls, "I held the club record for the longest touchdown pass

132

— an 84-yarder from Meredith against Pittsburgh. But the next week he threw a 95-yarder to Hayes to set the record which still stands."

Now safely removed from football, Gent makes his home in Wimberely, Texas, near Austin, where he is working on two novels. One, he says, is a detective story; the other will tell the story of what might happen should a critical NFL game be "fixed" by gamblers.

The success of *North Dallas Forty,* a book which prompted fellow Texas author Larry L. King to write, ". . . Gent is not a football player who happened to become a writer; he's a writer who happens to have played football," made him an instant literary celebrity. The book sold 70,000 in hardback, went over the million mark in paperback, and the movie version which Gent did the script for was a box office success several times over. His second novel, *Texas Celebrity Turkey Trot,* also earned him warm praise.

Which is to say the former Michigan State basketball player-turned-pro football player-turned writer has come a long way.

"A lot of good things have happened to me since I got out of football," Gent admits, "but it was a really fun time in my life. And, you know, despite what the films show, I'm almost sure I was in there on that last play of the Green Bay game."

JOHN WILBUR
⭐
His Fan Club Loved Him

To many, the season of 1967 will be remembered as the one in which the Dallas Cowboys won a big one; capturing the Eastern Conference championship by bombarding the Cleveland Browns, 52-14. For one former member of that team, however, it is best recalled as the season of the Great Fan Club Blitz, a well organized movement led by a group of young fans who had decided for whatever reason to see to it that the sporting world became aware of a relatively obscure second year lineman named John Wilbur.

"It was really kinda crazy," Wilbur was saying from his home in Honolulu recently. "All I had done the year before was play on the specialty teams and then, in my second year, these kids got together and formed a John Wilbur Fan Club. They had this banner they brought out to the games and they made up bumper stickers and everything. Then they got busy stuffing the ballot boxes on the Oak Farms Favorite Cowboys contest.

"I wasn't even aware all this was going on but at the end of the year, I got this call telling me I was invited to attend the Favorite Cowboys awards program. Now, Bob Lilly had already been announced as the winner so I wasn't sure what in the world they wanted me there for.

"When I got there they told me that I was the second place winner and they gave me a check for $500. That, so far as I know, is the only time they ever named a second place finisher and gave him a prize. The more I think about it, I have to wonder if maybe all those kids didn't get enough ballots stuffed into the boxes for me to win and the people at Oak Farms wondered what in the world they would do with a winner named John Wilbur: a guy who was about as far from being a big name as you can get in the NFL. I figure what happened was that it was close enough that they decided to go with Lilly, but felt they had to acknowledge me, too. It was a crazy kind of thing and I had a lot of fun with it."

It was, in fact, heady stuff for a former Stanford free agent who literally had fought his way onto the Cowboys roster a year earlier — after head coach Tom Landry had persuaded him not to quit during his initial summer training camp. "I went to camp scared to death," he recalls, "and it didn't take me long to convince myself that I didn't have a chance in the world of making the team. I went to Tom and told him I was ready to check it in, and he talked me into trying a little longer; said that he thought I had a chance. I decided to give it all I had."

The following afternoon during drills he got into a fight with veteran middle linebacker Lee Roy Jordan. Wilbur says he won, Jordan disagrees. Regardless, it gained the young guard notice.

"A few days later I got the first indication that I might have a chance when Pete Gent and I were showering after practice. He told me not to worry, that I was in." Looking back on it all, John points to one critical mistake he made. "When I talked to them about quitting," he laughs, "they asked me if it was the money. I told them that wasn't it at all. That was a big rookie mistake."

All in all, however, it was a good time for the California native. As a rookie he distinguished himself on the specialty teams as the Cowboys went 10-3-1 in their 1966 regular season play. "The only thing bad about that year," he recalls, "was the fact we had a great opportunity to go to the first Super Bowl and missed out on it. But, then, we came back the next year and won the East. We were walking on a cloud. Anytime you do something for the first time, it's great. Those first couple of years were great, a lot of fun."

While he has fond memories of his four seasons with the Cowboys, Wilbur admits that one of his biggest moments came in '72 when, as a member of the Washington Redskins, he was on the winning side of a 26-3 Cowboys defeat, a game that earned George Allen and his 'Skins the NFC title and a berth in the Super Bowl VII.

After ending his career with the Redskins in 1974, Wilbur played for the Hawaii franchise in the now defunct World Football League and has remained in Honolulu where he serves as a part-time coach for the University of Hawaii, owns a restaurant and operates Wilbur Enterprises, a real estate and development firm.

"I enjoyed my time with the Cowboys," he says. "They gave me a chance, they trained me to play professional football, and they gave me a couple of the greatest years of my career."

CRAIG BAYNHAM

★

He Helped Make Christmas Merry

It was Christmas Eve in the season of 1967 when Craig Baynham, then a rookie running back from Georgia Tech, heard Dallas Cowboys quarterback Don Meredith make the call . . . I Left, Drive 28, G Take.

"Funny, isn't it?" Baynham says, "how you remember all the things that terrified you in your past."

The scene was the Eastern Division playoff game against the Cleveland Browns and Baynham, a 12th round draft choice, had little reason to believe he would see much action beyond his specialty team duties and running back kickoffs. After all, he was listed third on the depth chart behind fellow running backs Danny Reeves and Les Shy. Third team rookies seldom get much playing time in championship games.

Then, however, Reeves suffered a pinched nerve in his neck early in the game and coach Tom Landry summoned not Les Shy, but instead, Baynham.

"Usually," Craig remembers, "when a new back goes in they don't call his number right away. The thinking is to let him block on a couple of plays to get the feel of things. Man, I couldn't even speak, my mouth was so dry. Then he called 'I Left, Drive 28, G Take,' and my knees almost buckled."

For the record, the 6-1, 200 pound running back picked up a first down on the play, keeping a drive alive which led to the first Cowboys score; that, in fact, came on a short Meredith-to-Baynham pass. "I was the safety valve man," Baynham remembers, "and Don just flipped a little lob pass over to me. I was still nervous as I could be about being in there and the ball looked about the size of a house coming toward me."

It was the beginning of what was to be one of the Dallas Cowboys' most historic offensive showings. In the first 25 minutes Dallas had bolted out to a 24-0 lead. By the end of the third quarter Meredith had directed his team to a 45-7 advantage and was replaced by Craig Morton. Morton put the finishing touches on a 52-14 victory which caused an overhauling of the Cowboys record book.

"Don was incredible that game," Craig says. Before leaving the action he hit on 10 of 12 passes and two touchdowns: the short ones to Baynham and an 86-yard bomb to Bob Hayes. Hayes was also putting on a big show, hauling in five passes for 144 of Meredith's 212 yard total. Not satisfied with his pass catching performance, "Bullet Bob" also returned punts for 64 and 68 yards to set up two of Dallas' touchdowns.

And in the midst of all those superlatives was the rookie Baynham. "Hey," he says, "it was one of the best games I ever played. I ran for something like 60 yards and scored three touchdowns, the one on a pass and a couple of short runs to score, and to be quite honest what I did wasn't hardly noticeable.

137

Everyone else was doing such an incredible job that just an average performance by a running back wasn't going to get much notice."

The mood of the team prior to that game, Baynham says, was hard to explain, yet there was an almost electric tension built up by game time which gave hint of what was to come. "If ever a team was ready to play," he says, "we were that day.

"You know, it's great to get caught up in something like that; to be able to be a part of it. It was especially pleasing to me since I got to play a great deal and felt at the game's end that I had made a contribution. A lot of athletes will play out their whole career and never have an experience like that.

"It sure made for a nice Christmas the following day."

Baynham played two more years with the Cowboys before he was traded to Chicago where he spent two more seasons. He completed his professional career with a year's service with St. Louis.

Now living in Canada, he is an associate pastor in a church currently pastored by Bill McRae.

"It is a calling," he says, "even more demanding and rewarding than 'I Left, Drive 28, G Take.' "

LANCE RENTZEL
Remembering the Turn-Around

It began, Lance Rentzel remembers, with the infamous Ice Bowl, the 21-17 defeat suffered in sub-zero weather in Green Bay, Wisconsin. And it would linger for three long, frustrating seasons. The Dallas Cowboys, a team of no small abilities, could not, the critics would repeat all too often, win the big one.

Wide receiver Rentzel, who led the Cowboys in receptions three consecutive years (1967-68-69) and went over the 1,000-yard mark in '68 (1,009), notes that it was a period in Cowboys history when they were ever so close to gaining a grip on professional football's brass ring — but for a variety of reasons were unable to quite make it.

"That game in Green Bay started it," he says from his home in Beverly Hills, California, "and it seemed to go on and on. We were so close that day. In fact, when I caught that 50-yard pass from Dan Reeves and we went ahead, I thought we had it.

"What people never seemed to mention about that game — and I'm still asked about it a great deal — was the fact that the weather conditions hurt us a great deal more than they did the Packers. Speed was our game and we simply couldn't use it when everything was coated with ice.

"I'll never forget that plane trip home. Nobody said anything. Everyone was in a state of shock. Then, long after it was over we were still constantly being reminded of it, of the fact that we hadn't won the big one.

"That game had a tremendous effect on the Dallas Cowboys for years."

So much so, he contends, that it would hamper the Cowboys in their ongoing bid to win the big game. "The next year," he recalls, "we played Cleveland for the Eastern Conference championship and lost it, 31-20, and the tag was with us again. Then in '69, we met Cleveland for the Eastern championship again. There was a great deal of emotion leading up to that game. Everyone was ready; it was time, we felt, to prove the critics wrong. We stopped them early, forcing them to punt and you could literally feel the confidence grow. They punted and the ball hit Rayfield Wright's leg and they recovered.

"I looked over at our bench and could see heads hanging. I knew right then that we were whipped."

Indeed they were. A team which couldn't win the big one, fell with a thud, 38-14. And with the defeat came more pressure than the Dallas Cowboys have ever experienced, before or since. Throughout the NFL they were looked upon as a team with multiple weapons and multiple ways of self-destructing.

How, then, did Dallas manage to finally shake the albatross from its neck? Not, says Rentzel, by finally winning a big one, but, rather, losing big.

The former University of Oklahoma standout pinpoints the Cowboys turnaround in 1970 when, playing before 69,323 in the Cotton Bowl and their first Monday Night TV audience, they were humiliated by the St. Louis Cardinals, 38-0. The defeat dropped the Dallas season record to a limp 5-4, and signaled the end in the minds of many Cowboys followers. In retrospect, Rentzel points out, it was the beginning.

"After that," he says, "everyone relaxed. The pressure went off. We forgot about trying to prove things and just went out every Sunday and had a good time. What happened was we won seven in a row and made it to the Super Bowl. We lost to Baltimore, 16-13, but long before that we had passed some big tests in winning the division title (5-0 over Detroit) and the NFC championship (over San Francisco, 17-10). That season, I believe, was the culmination of a string of events set in motion that day in Green Bay in '67.

"What it boiled down to was the fact we had to sink to the depths we reached that night against the Cardinals before learning how to play the game. I think it's to Landry's credit that he didn't overact to the situation and make wholesale changes in his philosophy. By staying with what he believed in, he has become one of the game's most successful coaches. And the Cowboys have become one of the most successful teams in history."

SIMS STOKES

★

Almost A Hero

No other game in modern NFL history has merited as much re-creation. One need only to refer to the Ice Bowl and followers of professional football know immediately that the subject is the Dallas-Green Bay NFL championship game of 1967, a game played on the coldest December 31st on record in Green Bay, Wisconsin.

The names of the participants have become legendary: Landry and Lombardi, Starr and Kramer, Meredith and Lilly. The folklore that has accompanied the record is now a full-fledged part of the NFL legacy; minus 20 degrees (down from the 13 degree reading at kickoff) when the Packers scored late to go ahead and win, 21-17.

And there, for most, the story stops. In the minds of most, the game ended there, with Bart Starr sneaking and Jerry Kramer blocking Jethro Pugh.

There was, however, more. To Sims Stokes, a rookie sixth round draft pick out of Northern Arizona that season, there has, and probably forever will be, a might-have-been.

Generally relegated to specialty teams play — he had been the man who returned the historic game's opening kickoff 35 yards — Stokes went in as a wide receiver on the game's final play. After scoring, the Packers had to kick off to Dallas, giving the Cowboys one final opportunity.

"I lined up on the right side," the successful Dallas real estate executive remembers, "and ran a fly pattern. I was open deep, but the ball was underthrown. I never even got a hand on it. But, that's a part of the game.

"It was a great call by Landry. The plan was to go deep with a fresh receiver. It was a big gamble in one sense, but not in another. If I had gotten deep and we had connected, maybe we would have scored. Or, if we had been able to get an interference call downfield, we would have still had one more shot since a game can't end on a penalty.

"I got bumped pretty good coming off the line by (Green Bay and later Dallas cornerback) Herb Adderley — that may have messed up the timing of the play somewhat — but, still, I did get open. I guess it wasn't to be, though."

Stokes insists he went into the play confident that it would work, however. "One of the things I learned from Tom Landry, a man I greatly admire, was that you play every down of a football game. It often takes just that one play to win it all, and that's the kind of attitude we had that day. Really, though, we should never have been in that kind of position. The public seems to think that Starr's touchdown was the biggest play of the day, but I've never thought that was the case. The biggest play in my mind took place a couple of series before when we had them backed into a second-and-23 situation and we let (Green Bay running back) Donny Anderson get loose with a pass out of the backfield. I remember standing on the sidelines, watching him pick up that yardage, and thinking, 'There went my ring.' That, to me, was the big play of the game."

The tenure of the 6-1, 198-pound wide receiver with the Cowboys would last just that one season. From Dallas he would go to Baltimore and be the last man cut before the Colts got down to the 40-man limit in '68.

"I could have tried somewhere else," he says, "and may have been able to hang around somewhere in the league for a few years, but I've always been a man who calculated my odds pretty well. That was one of the things I liked about the Cowboys organization. It treated football like a business, so you generally had a pretty good understanding of where you stood. I've never felt that America affords equal opportunity to everyone. It simply affords an opportunity. From that point, it's up to the individual. That's pretty much the way the Cowboys worked it."

Stokes has not done badly since choosing to call his professional football career over. Today he owns in excess of $1 million in property, is highly successful in the commercial real estate field, and is enthusiastically involved in Republican politics. Twice he has served on Washington-based committees, serving once on the president's advisory council on minority businesses.

"You know," he says, "as a wide receiver I only caught one ball as a Dallas Cowboy."

Ironically, it was for a touchdown against the Green Bay Packers in a preseason game. And it was called back because of a penalty.

PETTIS NORMAN

Close to Perfection

It has been 11 years now, yet when former Dallas Cowboys tight end Pettis Norman stands to speak to gatherings of businessmen or educators as he quite often does, the game comes back to mind. It is Norman's example of what teamwork can accomplish.

"In the nine years I played professional football with the Cowboys," says Norman, owner of several fast food restaurants, public speaker and successful real estate investor, "the closest we ever came to perfection was the day in 1967 when we beat the Browns 52-14 for the Eastern Conference championship. That was the most total team effort of which I have ever been a part."

It was not a day when Norman caught a lot of passes. His name would be in no headlines following that Christmas Eve performance before 70,786 in the Cotton Bowl. The heroes would be quarterback Don Meredith (who,

despite playing with a broken nose, directed the Cowboys offense to 401 yards before he left with the score reading 45-7), receiver Bob Hayes and defenders like Bob Lilly and Lee Roy Jordan.

"When Tom replaced Don," Norman recalls, "Don stopped to shake hands with each of the offensive linemen before he left the field. It was one of those rare kind of days. The offense couldn't do anything wrong. Everyone was tuned in on the same thing, like there was some kind of mental telepathy going on. There's no doubt but it was one of Meredith's greatest games. He may have thrown one pass that was off all day and his overall execution was outstanding.

"Personally, I didn't do anything that was outstanding. Oh, my blocking was sharp and I helped the backs pick up some yardage, but that isn't the thing that makes the game stand out in my mind. The personal satisfaction of being a part of that kind of group effort was a tremendous thrill. Cleveland was a good football team and we totally dominated them. We were ahead 24-0 after the first 25 minutes of play. Meredith threw for 212 yards, completing 10 of 12 with a couple of touchdowns.

"And the defense — Lilly, George Andrie, Jethro Pugh, Willie Townes, Green — simply refused to let the Browns do anything. Cornell intercepted one and ran it back 60 yards for a touchdown. In fact, we were scoring just about every way you could think of. Hayes set up a couple of scores with punt returns of over 60 yards (64 and 68), caught five passes for about 150 more; one of them an 86-yard TD pass from Meredith. In all, Bobby accounted for something like 285 yards. Rookie Craig Baynham, who was in for Danny Reeves who had a pinched nerve in his neck, played like a veteran, scoring three times himself."

It was, Norman remembers, a pleasure to view the game film the following Tuesday. Even coach Tom Landry told the press, "It was our greatest game ever, considering the strength of the opposition. We've never had so many things going for us — defensive line, offensive line, quarterbacking, receiving, running, secondary, the kicking game — all phases."

Even the eventual 21-17 ice-station loss to Green Bay in the NFL Championship has not dulled the memory of the Cleveland victory. "Win or lose," he recalls, "it would have been impossible to play a technically good ball game in the conditions we had in Green Bay."

While the team effort against the Browns holds the No. 1 spot in Norman's recollections, he is also fond of an individual effort which came against the St. Louis Cardinals in 1965. It was a game Dallas eventually won 27-13, but only after coming from behind to do so. Norman, who still ranks high on the list of all-time receivers with 124 catches for 1,672 yards (a 13.5 yards per catch average) in his 1963 to 1970 career, made what he considers the best catch of his professional life. "Don called a Fake 92 Roll Left which is a pattern where I go across the back of the end zone. Don was throwing from about the 15 yard line and got hit pretty good just as he let the ball go. The pass was a little behind me and I turned, leaned out the end zone, keeping my feet in bounds, and made the catch for the touchdown. For a moment there, I

144

was convinced that I was about the best receiver around.

"Making catches like that are a great thrill, a lot of fun and, yes, satisfying. But nothing, no amount of circus catches or touchdowns, could ever compare to being a part of that game against Cleveland. That," says the man who came to the Cowboys from Johnson C. Smith College, "is the type of thing that comes once in a lifetime — if you're lucky."

GEORGE ANDRIE
★
You Never Forget Losing

In Green Bay Packers terminology it was called 31 Wedge. It would, on that bitterly cold afternoon in 1967, find its way into NFL playoff history. To most, though, it would be called simply a quarterback sneak with Bart Starr nudging his way two feet into the end zone.

To the Dallas Cowboys who had fought across a frozen field in 13 below zero weather into a late 17-14 lead in that memorable NFL Championship game, it was, after all was said and done, a day of ultimate frustration. Starr's score lifted the Pack to a third straight NFL championship, 21-17, and Dallas players went home with frostbite and bitter memories.

George Andrie, a longtime member of Dallas' famed Doomsday Defense now retired and living in Arkansas where he has a Coors distributorship, remembers the game a bit differently. But with no less disappointment.

"You never forget losing one like that," he says. "Time makes it easier to live with, but you never forget. It will always be there.

"Everyone who talks about the game remembers it being won by Starr's sneak in the last seconds (Starr scored with 16 seconds remaining). That wasn't how they won the game. No, they won it with a fantastic drive that led to that two-foot quarterback sneak. Starr did an incredible job hitting his backs on short swing passes and screens. He moved them down the field by isolating Chuck Mercein and Donny Anderson on linebackers, one on one. He did a brilliant job. That was what decided it."

That and the weather. "Every coach will tell you that bad weather and frozen fields affect both teams the same," Andrie points out, "but I don't buy that. The frozen field definitely worked to our disadvantage ... we weren't used to those kinds of conditions. There was no way people could go out in weather like that and not be a little distracted by the almost unbearable cold. And, too, everytime we needed to come up with the big play to keep a drive going or something, we'd have someone slip or fall down or miss an exchange."

Recalling the trying situation, Andrie remembers waking the morning of the game to be made aware of the temperature. "I couldn't believe it," he says. "It had been nice the day before."

Andrie insists he wasn't one of those who suffered frostbite but he does say that it was several weeks before normal feelings returned to his fingers. He also recollects that his seven yard run to the end zone with a Starr fumble for Dallas' first touchdown felt like it was an 85-yard full-out sprint. "I never thought I would get into the end zone," he says. "I would run a couple of steps, slip, slide, and finally fell in. It was unreal. But at that point it gave us a lift and I was pretty elated about it."

The play came late in the second period with Green Bay operating on its own 26. Starr had retreated to pass when Willie Townes hit him, knocking the ball loose. Andrie picked it up on the seven and went in for the score. A couple of minutes later Willie Wood fumbled at the Packer 17, and kicker Danny Villanueva moved Dallas closer with a field goal from the 14 with 36 seconds remaining before the half. Halfback Dan Reeves later shot the Cowboys into the lead with a bomb from midfield to Lance Rentzel. With just eight seconds gone in the final period, Dallas led finally, 17-14.

But then would come the errorless Packer drive that would spell victory.

"I can't say enough about that drive. Under those conditions it was an almost impossible accomplishment. They didn't drop a pass, no ·penalties. And we helped them along a little when an interference call against Dave Edwards allowed them to keep the drive moving. By all rights, however, they should never have gotten into position for Starr to sneak it in.

"We had kept good pressure on Starr all afternoon, had played a solid defensive game, in fact. And then that happened. In my career I went through some emotional peaks and valleys but there is no question but that I felt worse after that loss than any I was ever involved in.

"The weather was no real factor so far as I was concerned. Being from Michigan, I knew what it was like and had, in fact, played in similar conditions. But a lot of our players, particularly our offensive guys, weren't prepared to cope with the conditions.

"Back then, the NFL title was the big game. The Super Bowl was looked upon by everyone as something anti-climactic. So it wasn't so much the fact that we had missed a shot at the Super Bowl as it was missing out on the league title.

"But, Dallas was always a team which adversity made better. It always caused us to pull together. The only thing you can do after a loss like that is to reflect on it and try to see where you can improve and do better. That, I think, is what we did over the next years."

Still, Super Bowls that were to come would never totally erase the memory of that bleak day in Green Bay.

MIKE JOHNSON

★

Finding A Friend and A Father

The Dallas Cowboys were into the final stages of warmup for the 1967 season, playing the Houston Oilers in the Astrodome in a game they would eventually win, 33-19. In the stands, Robert Wiley, a long-time employee of the Houston Parks Department and avid football fan, watched and, unlike most of those seated near him, cheered for the Cowboys. For no particular reason, really. The Cowboys were winners. He liked that and figured it cause enough to be a fan.

That a talented young man named Mike Johnson was the starting right cornerback for Dallas made no real impression on him. That would come years later.

Try as he might to remember, there is nothing about that game against the Oilers which stands out in Johnson's mind. No big plays on his part, no fumble recoveries, nothing special like his interception the previous season against Philadelphia, or the steady days he would have over a three-year period as a Cowboys starter. It was just a game, an exhibition which didn't even go into the record book. Mike Johnson, in fact, doesn't even recall the score.

What he would learn just recently, however, was that his father — a man he had been told was dead while being raised by his grandparents back in Garden City, Kansas — had been in the stands to see him play. At the time, however, Robert Wiley, the Cowboys fan, had no idea the Dallas cornerback was his son. It would, in fact, be years later before he even began the search for the son he had never seen.

"I was living in New York, working for a food broker," Johnson says, "and through some relatives I got word that my father was trying to locate me. At first I couldn't figure out what it was all about, but after speaking to my mother about it she told me the whole story."

His father had been a serviceman, stationed near Garden City. By the time he was born, his father had been transferred to another base. Then another. Mike's mother built a story to protect her son.

"When it all came out," he says, "she was glad I knew. She said she felt much better that the truth was known."

Johnson who had been informed of his dad's search by relatives living in Denver, began a search of his own, found where Robert Wiley was living, and placed a long distance call. "I never had butterflies playing football like I did when I made that call," he says. "My stepmother answered the phone and I identified myself. In the background I could hear her telling him who it was. There was what seemed like a long silence before he answered the phone. Man, it was something. I couldn't wait to meet him. In fact, he flew me down to Houston that next weekend so we could get together."

On that weekend several other relatives stopped by to participate in the reunion. More than one took Mike aside and asked if he didn't feel the need to give his long lost father a swift kick in the seat of the pants. Nothing like that ever entered Mike's mind.

Instead, they sat for hours, talking football. Mike told his father of playing the same backfield with Gale Sayers at Kansas, of his tenure with the Cowboys (1966-69) and of his brief stay with the Chicago Bears before being released.

Johnson told him of how he spent but one practice as a running back before being moved to the secondary. "When the rookies reported for the first day of training camp practice," he says, "I worked with the offensive backs in the morning and then Ermal Allen told me I was a defensive back before the afternoon practice started." It was a move that obviously worked, since he would eventually work as a member of a starting secondary which included Cornell Green at the other corner and Mel Renfro and Mike Gaechter at the safeties.

"Mel was always a big help to me," Mike says. "From the time I was a rookie until the time I got knocked out in a game against Washington, and Mel was the only one on the field who realized I had been knocked out and was trying to signal the bench to get me out of there. Nobody understood, though, and suddenly it was time for the next play. I kept asking him what to do and where to go and he would tell me and then I'd just stare at him and ask again. Finally, he said, 'Mike, just stand back here and cover somebody, anybody.'

"Well, Bobby Mitchell ran a post pattern and somehow I managed to step in front of him and pick it off. It was the next day before I even knew it."

He told of being a starter for three years before developing concentration problems and feelings of self doubt. "For some reason I still can't explain," he says, "I suddenly found myself saying, 'Hey, what am I doing here? Am I really good enough to play for the Cowboys?' Coach Landry gave me plenty of time to correct my problems, but I just couldn't seem to. Finally, I forced him into a position of making a move himself. I was traded to Chicago and was there for the pre-season before they put me on waivers."

There is no sadness in his voice as he reflects. Robert Wiley is glad of that. He wanted to hear his son's athletic story from beginning to end. "I think he's proud of the fact I was a pretty good athlete, and that I played for the Cowboys. It's something, but even today when I tell someone that I played for the Cowboys, they hit the ceiling. It's a big deal to a lot of people."

Nothing, however, like finding a father you had spent all your life believing was dead, Mike says. He's now moved to Houston, taking a job with Frito-Lay, so that he can be close to Robert Wiley. "We're having a great time, getting to know each other," he says.

"As soon as I met him for the first time, I wanted to bring him to the (Cowboys) reunion with me to introduce him to Coach Landry. He came up to Dallas with me and the first person we ran into when we walked in was Tom. It was a big thrill for Dad, and for me.

"You know, when I was a kid back in Garden City, I had three dreams. I wanted to play football for the University of Kansas. I wanted to play professional football and, though I never mentioned it, I wanted to have a dad like most of my friends."

It's taken a while, but Mike Johnson has finally realized all three.

WILLIE TOWNES

★

Battle of the Bulge

In those years Willie Townes served as a member of the Dallas Cowboys front four, he and head coach Tom Landry spent a good deal of time debating over the proper weight a 6-5 defensive end should carry. They discussed it over post practice and wind sprints, at the Fat Man's Table in training camp and as specialized conditioning programs were drawn up to keep Townes' weight somewhere on the minus side of 280.

It was a battle rarely won by the congenial University of Tulsa ex who was a second round pick in the 1966 draft. Eventually, it got the best of him when a knee problem developed in the early stages of the 1968 season. The subsequent operation forced him to the injured reserve list and resulted in his reporting back for duty out of shape and overweight.

"The adhesions in my knee never broke after the operation," he recalls. "I just couldn't get around well enough to get in shape. A man on one leg can't be much of a football player."

It is not, however, the twilight of his three-season career that Townes, now a division manager for Miller Beer, thinks back on. As he was then, Townes is a fun-loving guy who looks to the good times.

Among those was a Christmas Eve in 1967 when he and the Cowboys stunned the pro football world by defeating the powerful Cleveland Browns, 52-14, for the Eastern Division Championship.

On that one, Townes and Landry agreed. The Cowboys coach, in fact, stated following the victory that "it was the greatest game we've ever played, considering the caliber of the competition." Townes seconds the motion. "That was the one," he recalls, "that proved to a lot of people that we could win the money game. Before that there were a lot of people who said we weren't ready to play well in the games that really counted. That day we did. We were almost unbelievable.

"I was a second year player, still learning what it was all about, but even I could tell there was something different about that game. It was a feeling I'd never had before. The enthusiasm was really high. And, one of the things that really stands out in my mind was the fact that the game plan Landry put together for that one was one of the most simple we ever had. He told us the game plan was no big deal, to just go out and play as well as we were capable because it was a game we had to have.

"It was," he continues, "the first time we really got everything together, offensively and defensively. We had always had a hard time with the Browns before. On that day, though, we did just about whatever we wanted. Shoot, that was the only game in my life that I ever got in enough rest on the sidelines. Dandy (Don Meredith) was out of this world. By midway through the second half I had time to turn around and wave to friends in the stands."

Indeed, it was a tremendous collective effort on both sides of the Cowboys' attack; for in-between offensive romps came periods when the defense throttled the highly respected Browns.

"We really shut them down," Townes remembers. "I got to (Browns quarterback) Frank Ryan two or three times and forced him out of the pocket several other times. And we stopped a couple of really great running backs in Leroy Kelly and Ernie Green. In fact, on our side of the line, Jethro (Pugh) and I, allowed the Browns only 1.2 yards per gain. The other side, Bob Lilly and George Andrie, allowed only 1.3. We really got after their offensive line (which, incidentally included current Cowboys scout John Wooten) that day. Hey, Kelly came into the game with 1,205 yards for the season and he never really even got untracked."

Following the game, for which he was among those receiving game balls, Townes remembers Landry telling the team that "there's no way we can lose when we play as a team the way we did against Cleveland."

RON WIDBY

Three-Sport Pro

The date stands out in Ron Widby's mind, not so much because of what happened but what it would trigger soon thereafter. It was November 3, 1968, late in a game with the New Orleans Saints when the then-Cowboys punter stood in his own end zone and boomed a punt 84 yards to help preserve a hard-fought 17-3 victory.

Today it still stands as the longest punt in Cowboys history. "It was one of those days," the San Antonio resident recalls, "when I was hitting the ball very well. Earlier in the game I had kicked a 54-yarder into the wind. But, yes, I was a little surprised when that particular punt sailed over the return man's head."

Perhaps overshadowing his surprise was his wife's reaction of unrestrained excitement. Pregnant at the time, she had watched the game at home on television. Two days later the couple's first son, Scott, was born. "I'm sure the excitement she experienced that day," Widby recalls, "hurried things along."

As the Dallas punter for four years (1968-71), the Tennessee-ex compiled a record which sees him still ranked as the third best punter in the club's history behind Sam Baker and Dave Sherer with a 41.8 career average. Oddly enough, in the same year he got off his record kick, he finished with the lowest average of his Cowboys tenure, a 40.9 reading. The following season, however, he would end the season with a 43.3 average which saw him ranked second in the NFL.

There was a time, however, when Ron wondered if he would survive to ever punt in the league.

After coming to the Cowboys in 1967 he was placed on the taxi squad while Danny Villanueva continued handling the punting responsibilities. It was, he recalls, a long year.

"I went to the Cowboys from the Saints," he remembers, "and was never activated. It was a frustrating time, really, working out every day but then having to sit in the stands and watch the games on Sunday."

Serving as a spectator, however, always seemed to come after a quick plane trip back to Dallas from Oklahoma City. "Back then," he explains, "the Cowboys had this program whereby several of us on the taxi squad would go to Oklahoma City and play Saturday games with a semi-pro team. The thinking was that. it would provide us the opportunity to get some game experience."

What Widby and friends got for their efforts was a free plane ride and a $50-per-game paycheck from the Oklahoma City Plainsmen. And more bumps and bruises than he cares to recall.

"I never really felt I got much out of it," he points out, "because of the way they played in the league. In the first place, you never knew who the center was going to be so you generally found yourself chasing the ball all over the place before you could get a punt off. And I've never had as many roughing the kicker penalties as I got up there. Finally, one night I came back with a deep cut on my leg and went to Landry and told him I thought it would be best for everyone if I didn't go back up there anymore. Fortunately, he agreed."

Despite the fact he was not active with the Cowboys that first year, the fourth round draft pick stayed busier than most professional athletes. In addition to trying to earn a place for himself with the Cowboys, he was also working as a forward for the old American Basketball Association New Orleans Buccaneers. He was a member of their roster for the last three-fourths of a season which saw the Bucs lose the ABA title to Pittsburgh in the seventh game of the championship playoffs.

In '68, however, his full concentration turned to punting as he assumed the job which Villanueva vacated that season.

While he modestly insists that there are few days in his punting career which he would label outstanding he does admit that he felt he was consistent. He survived the winds of New York and came away from San Francisco's Kezar Stadium, "the burial ground of a lot of good punters," in one piece.

"A punter will have a hot day, just like a golfer," he admits, "but what you have to shoot for is the solid effort week in and week out. While a punter doesn't have to be that physically tough, he has to be mentally prepared to get the job done. The toughest thing to deal with is the wind. A punter has a hard time putting it out of his mind. The wind can make you have a bad day even before the game starts. You can go out in pre-game and have troubles, and if you don't watch it, you're whipped before you get started. That was the kind of thing I tried to avoid."

Following the '71 campaign Widby was traded to the Green Bay Packers and worked there for two seasons. There he met with misfortune which would end his career. The Packers, having suffered a rash of injuries to their wide receivers, summoned Widby to fill in inasmuch as he had worked at the position as a collegian. In a practice he suffered a ruptured disc and nerve damage to his legs. So ended his NFL career, but not his athletic pursuits. An excellent golfer, he worked for a year as a club professional at Rancho Viejo in South Texas. Today he is a sales representative for a roofing manufacturer.

"Playing in Dallas," Widby says, "was a great experience. It's funny, but there aren't a lot of specific things I remember. There was my first punt in the NFL: I was in my own end zone and got it out beyond the 50. There was the 84-yarder. And, of course, there was the last minute against Baltimore in Super Bowl V, watching that field goal go through. I guess you have to remember the good and the bad."

BOBBY JOE CONRAD
★
String Ended, New Career Began

It was the fourth game of the 1968 season and All-Pro St. Louis Cardinals wide receiver Bobby Joe Conrad was on the verge of something special. He had caught passes in 94 consecutive games and, going into a meeting with Cleveland, needed but a single catch to equal the NFL record of the legendary Don Hutson.

Early in the game Cardinals quarterback Jim Hart threw in his direction but the pass was off target. There was no chance to make the catch.

It would be late in the game before the former Texas A&M standout would get another try. "It finally dawned on somebody that they hadn't thrown to me," Conrad recalls, "so late in the fourth quarter Hart called a pattern that had me as about the third receiver. I went downfield and, after bumping into (Browns defensive back) Erich Barnes, managed to get open and make the catch. But the official called me for shoving off and called the play back."

Thus he would go without a catch and a chance at the record that day. Monday morning found him in the office of owner Billy Bidwell to complain. It happened that a member of the St. Louis press was on hand, and an ear, sympathetic or not, was all the incentive Conrad required; he spoke his piece. Loudly and clearly. He was not exactly enchanted with the idea of playing for coach Charlie Winner. He wouldn't, he told the attentive neswpaperman, be back in St. Louis the following season.

He wasn't. Such, then, is the sequence of events which would bring Conrad, the Cardinals Most Valuable Player in '62, the man who caught a team record 73 passes in '63, and gained 5,828 yards in receptions in his career, to the Dallas Cowboys in 1969.

"I knew I was about at the end of my career anyway," recalls the Clifton, Texas, resident who now works as a manager of the Federal Land Bank Association of Waco, "so I told them I would only play for the Cowboys if I played the following year."

The Cardinals would eventually receive a fifth round draft pick for him and Dallas had a backup receiver. "I was actually nothing but an insurance policy for the Cowboys," Conrad admits. "At first they had me backing up Bob Hayes but when he got hurt they put Dennis Homan over there and moved me to backing up Lance Rentzel. What I did mostly, was sit on the bench for the first time in my life. It was frustrating, but I understood my role. I was there just in case injuries made it necessary for me to play."

Another of his roles, he says, was to push the fleet Hayes to a more maximum effort. "Coach Landry wasn't very pleased with the way Bob had been playing — feeling he wasn't working as hard as he should — so I got the starting nod in a couple of pre-season games, just so Landry could get Bob's attention. It worked, I think, but Hayes later injured a shoulder and I thought I would get a chance to play some. But Homan was a young player they were trying to develop so they moved him in ahead of me. I wasn't exactly happy about it, but I understood what was going on."

Toward season's end, in fact, the gifted receiver who had been fighting an uphill battle throughout his football career, was anxiously awaiting special team assignments just to get into some action.

"I never even started when I was at Texas A&M," he says. "I played backup at about three positions (including running back where starter John David Crow was playing at a level which would win him the Heisman Trophy) and actually was drafted by the Cardinals as a defensive back. It wasn't until the '62 season that I was moved to wide receiver and began to make a name for myself."

In four different seasons he averaged 60 or more receptions before his career with the Cardinals ended.

Ironically, it would be a Cowboys game against his old teammates which would be one of his best during his one-year stay. "I played most of the second half in that one and caught two or three balls," Conrad says. "But nothing spectacular. That, in fact, was the story of my career. Even when I was having good years with the Cardinals I was a first-down type receiver, not a big touchdown man. But, I like to think I'm looked upon as a good, steady ball player. Sitting on the bench in Dallas wasn't fun, don't get me wrong. But by the same token I'm not at all bitter about it. I knew going in what my function would be. The truth of the matter is I was treated most fairly. I got to know some really good people while I was there, people like Walt Garrison and Bob Lilly.

"It's just that I would like to have made more of a contribution."

While his playing time was limited and his contract was not renewed for the following year, it would later become obvious that Landry appreciated his football knowledge. "He called me later and told me he was going to hire a receiver coach and wanted me to come up and interview for it. It wasn't something I was really interested in, but I did. But being a football coach is like being a lawyer or a doctor; you're always on call. I was actually relieved when he called to tell me they had decided to give the job to Mike Ditka who had been working as a tight end in previous seasons."

When first invited to attend one of the annual Cowboys players reunions, Conrad did so reluctantly. "I had been there only that one season and hadn't really done anything, so I felt I was really an outsider. But I went and didn't feel that way at all. Now I wouldn't miss one for the world. I feel a little more a part every season."

MALCOLM WALKER
✪
The Frustrations of Injury

For a football player who had no previous acquaintance with serious injury of any sort throughout a brilliant high school and collegiate career, it was a frustrating time; a horror, an absurdity without rhyme, logic or reason.

Big Malcolm Walker, having completed a noteworthy career at Rice, had been the Dallas Cowboys' second round draft selection in 1965, picked immediately after a University of California quarterback named Craig Morton. Scouts throughout the NFL predicted an immediate and bright future for the linebacker the Cowboys planned to convert to an offensive lineman because of the quickness he had to go with his 6-4, 245 pound size.

But before he would begin his bid for professional stardom the youngster who grew up in Dallas — a gifted football and basketball player at South Oak Cliff High — would make an appearance in the annual College All-Star Game in Chicago.

That was the beginning of the troubles which would haunt Malcolm Walker until his playing days were over.

Working on the practice field at Northwestern, he stepped into a hole, badly twisting a knee. Thus instead of starting for the College All-Stars and then hurrying off to the Cowboys' training camp, he was rushed to Baylor Hospital for surgery. "It turned out," the current Dallas-based CPA remembers, "that there was torn cartilage and some messed up bones." The damage would force him to spend his entire rookie season waiting for the knee to mend.

"It was a bad time to be standing on the sidelines," he says, "because that was when the Cowboys really began to make their move. In 1965 people like Bob Hayes and Jethro Pugh and Ralph Neely came in. Hayes really became 'Mr. Excitement,' and Coach (Tom) Landry was finally in a position to open things up like I think he really wanted to. Attendance really jumped that year (from 38,000 to 58,000 in fact)."

In 1966 there were still fluid problems with the knee and the impatient Walker wasn't activated until late in the season. In his third year he served as something of a utility lineman, backing up center Mike Connelly and tackle Ralph Neely who was well on his way to All-Pro status.

"They kept saying that I had potential," Walker says, "but I wasn't getting much chance to show any of it. I was beginning to question a lot of things about myself. I felt I could perform, though, and I wanted badly to prove it to myself and to the team."

Thus in that off-season, (prior to the 1968 season) Malcolm Walker went through one of the most taxing, demanding programs any member of the Cowboys has ever undertaken. Following a program outlined by trainers Larry Gardner and Don Cochren to strengthen the upper part of his body and take weight off his massive legs, Walker worked harder in the off-season than most players do *during* the season.

"Not many people are capable of the kind of discipline Walker forced upon himself," recalls Gardner. "He literally worked twice as much as anyone that summer." The result was that Walker took two and one-eighths inches from his hips, two and five-eighths from his right thigh and three-fourths of an inch from his left thigh. "That may sound unbalanced," Malcolm notes, "but because of the surgery my thighs were different sizes. What I wound up with was two pretty good legs, finally."

It was the price he paid for a chance to play. "I figured I had to get myself totally ready. I wanted a chance to play on more than a spot duty basis."

In the season of 1968 — three years after his arrival with the Cowboys — Walker finally won (over also-returning Dave Manders) and earned the job as Dallas' starting center.

"It wasn't a cliché, cut-throat competition between Manders and myself," Walker recalls. "In fact, we did everything we could do to help each other, picking up keys, pointing out any little flaws we saw in each other's performance. At that point we both felt like we were going to be around so the main thing was to do whatever we could to help the team."

Magic moments for centers, Walker says, are few and far between. When you spend the entire game virtually standing on your head you aren't likely to be any part of a headline-making performance: "For that reason there aren't many games that come to mind as better or more important or more enjoyable than others. I think most centers look back on games in generalities, thinking more about who it was they had to go against."

There is, however, one incident which Walker has not been allowed to forget. Longtime fans of the Cowboys and writers who are wont to review the story on rainy days keep reminding him.

"I guess," he says, "I have the distinction of being a part of one of the most screwball plays in Cowboy history. It came in the Philadelphia game in 1968 (won by Dallas, 45-13).

"As I recall, (Don) Meredith threw a pass to Lance Rentzel. I was making my block and got hit in the stomach. The blow spun me around just as Lance was fumbling the ball. Somehow, I managed to get off this really great dropkick. Hey, the ball was spiraling and everything as it went on downfield. Everyone just stood and watched for a split second. Then Hayes and John Niland went after it. Bob got a hand on it downfield but he got hit and the ball flew one way and his helmet the other. Finally, Niland fell on it. It was, as I remember, one of our biggest gains of the day. The play covered 35 yards!"

Not exactly what Malcolm Walker had in mind when he went through that painful off-season to get himself ready to play, but at least he was on the field as a full-time performer at the time.

It was, however, in the '69 season that he again tore his knee up and underwent surgery. Before the 1970 season he was traded to Green Bay for cornerback Herb Adderley. At the end of his lone season with the Packers he found himself back in the operating room.

"I just told them to clean it up as best they could and I was going to forget it. Enough was enough."

CRAIG MORTON

⭐

Like Old Man River

Against Atlanta on that previous Sunday in October, 1969, he had suffered a separated right shoulder, and as the Dallas Cowboys prepared for their home date with the Philadelphia Eagles, there was serious doubt that Craig Morton

would play any role in the game. The 71,509 who turned out to the Cotton Bowl, in fact, had been made aware throughout the week that Morton would likely view the contest from a sideline vantage point.

He had not thrown at all during the week's practice and reportedly was still suffering considerable pain.

"The day of the game," recalls Morton, the man who spent 10 years in a Cowboys uniform before departing for New York and finally arriving in Denver, "was warm so I decided I'd give it a try in pre-game warmups and see if I could throw. I got a shot in the shoulder to numb the pain and started warming up. After a while Landry came over and asked what I thought and I told him I'd like to give it a try."

Suffice it to say it was not a totally confident Craig Morton who went onto the field for the first series of Dallas offensive downs. "Shoot, I was as much in the dark about how I would be able to perform as anyone," he says, "but Landry had told me he would leave the decision up to me, and I had made it, so I was determined to have a go at it. I remember being aware of the pain in the shoulder even though the medication I had taken was supposed to have taken care of it."

To avoid the suspense of an O. Henry ending to this story, be aware that on that sunny Sunday afternoon as Dallas defeated the Eagles 49-14, Morton hit on 13 of 19 passing attempts for 247 yards and five touchdowns. Three of his scoring shots went to Lance Rentzel, one to Bob Hayes and yet another to Pettis Norman. The five TD passes tied a club record set originally by Eddie LeBaron in 1962 and tied by Don Meredith on three occasions. (Morton would again throw for five the following season against Houston.)

"It was one of those days," the current Denver Broncos quarterback remembers, "when everything just seemed to go right. The blocking was great, the receivers were getting open, and I was on the money. The better things got, the better the shoulder felt. By the time the game was over I had completely forgotten about the pain.

"Everyone on the team was really giving me a hard time in the dressing room afterwards. Raymond Berry, our receiver coach, suggested that the whole team jump on me and beat me up real good so I would be in top form for the next game. Clint Murchison came up to me and said, 'Craig, I just have one request and I think it might make you an even more effective passer. Why don't you separate the other shoulder, too?' "

In time the pain of the shoulder separation was forgotten. The accomplishments of the day, however, would never be. "It was," he says, "a big thrill for me. I had a lot of thrills while I was in Dallas, as far as that goes. I remember, for instance, that the first pass I ever threw in a pro game — in 1965 — was for a touchdown to Bob Hayes. No matter how long you play, you don't forget things like that."

For that matter, Craig Morton has been making memories as a professional for 17 seasons. Traded to the New York Giants six games deep into the 1974 season, he was there for three years before moving to the AFC Denver Broncos in 1977. To many the third trade signaled the end of the rollercoaster career of the former University of California All-America. A gifted athlete, he had set college records, and had been a good enough baseball player to earn bonus offers from several clubs. Now, the man who had taken Dallas to a Super Bowl, had also, in the opinion of many, reached the end without having ever attained the greatness expected of him. Booed in Dallas, then New York, he would not likely see enough action in Mile High Stadium to generate any kind of fan reaction at all.

Those reporting his athletic demise, obviously, were quite premature in their judgements.

Moving in as the 26th quarterback to gain a starting job in the 18-year history of the Denver franchise, Morton proved dramatically he was far from over the hill. Despite immobility caused by long-standing knee problems, he led the Broncos to their first division title ever. When Denver made its first and only championship appearance in Super Bowl XII, there to face the Dallas Cowboys, it was Morton at the helm. And while his team would lose, the simple fact it had come that far was a credit to Craig Morton. So impressed were members of the media with his season that he was selected the AFC Player of the Year.

Again in 1981, however, it was assumed that his days in the spotlight were done. Quietly, most felt, he would move into a backup role for one more year, then host a retirement party at the urging of management. But former Cowboys teammate Danny Reeves suddenly appeared as the new Denver coach and made it clear immediately that Morton was his quarterback. Craig responded with yet another superlative season: finishing second to Cincinnati's Ken Anderson among AFC passers with 3,195 yards and 21 touchdowns.

In his 17 years, then, he's thrown for an amazing 27,715 yards and 183 touchdowns and is one of the few, if only quarterbacks, to take two different teams to the Super Bowl. There's been a lot of passing since that afternoon in 1965 when he threw that first completion to Hayes, and if Morton has his way, there'll be even more to come.

"I've always said I'd quit when it is no longer fun," he says. "That hasn't happened yet."

CALVIN HILL
★
A Fan Who Got to Play

Looking back on it with the advantage of hindsight, he says his recollection of the day is still the same. As an athlete, before or since, Calvin Hill has never known the kind of fear he felt that afternoon in 1969 when he began a long walk down a tunnel which led onto the playing field of Kezar Stadium in San Francisco.

"It was the first game of the pre-season in my rookie year," says the man who played running back for the Dallas Cowboys from 1969 to 1974, "and I was scared to death. In fact, walking down that tunnel was like walking through the valley of death.

"I was going to get the chance to start and I kept thinking about all the things that people were expecting of me. There I was, a number one draft choice out of Yale, out of the Ivy League. There were a lot of people who had made it clear that they didn't think I could make it; that I surely couldn't live up to being a number one draft pick. And, truthfully, I didn't know either.

"I kept thinking about all the great defensive people the 49ers had — Charles Kreuger, people like that. And, for a crazy reason I was worried about playing in Kezar. Being from Baltimore, I had always followed the Colts and I remembered how they had had so much trouble in Kezar.

"As it turned out, I had a pretty good afternoon, getting over 100 yards rushing. But, honestly, I never really knew what the heck was happening all day. I was really unconscious. And, no, the fear never went away. It felt good afterwards, though, when a couple of the veterans came up and shook my hand. That's when I began to feel that I was going to make it. That's when I first began to quit worrying over whether the Dallas Cowboys had made a mistake by drafting me in the first round."

Indeed, in that rookie season the 6-3, 230-pound Hill not only led the Cowboys rushers with 942 yards on 204 carries, but went on to earn Rookie of the Year honors. Before he would end his tenure with the Cowboys he would lead the team in rushing on three more occasions — 1972-73-74 — and was the top receiver in 1972-73. His name is still scattered through the Cowboys record book: most touchdowns in a single game (4), most points (24), most carries (32). His 5,009 yards on 1,166 carries ranks third behind Tony Dorsett (6,270) and Don Perkins (6,217) on the all-time Cowboys career rushing list.

Without question, the Cowboys had not made a mistake.

Still, Hill, now retired after 12 NFL seasons, recalls the rookie pressures of being a first round draft pick.

"Most of the pressure," he admits, "was self-inflicted, but it was there nonetheless. I'll say this for the Cowboys: they make every effort *not* to put pressure on a first round pick. But, you know people are watching you, expecting things of you. You get to a point where you feel you have to be better than anyone on the field just to show you deserve to be a first round pick. I remember we had the Landry endurance run when we got to camp. It was a mile and three-quarters, as I recall, and the longest distance I had ever run was a mile. I actually trained for that endurance run before I went to camp. I felt it was important that I not only complete it, but win it. I wanted to win it — because I knew people were going to be watching."

Calvin did not win, but he did perform well.

"Really, that's all you can do in this game, whether you're a rookie or a

veteran. You just go out and give it your best and try to keep your ego in check. If you put it (ego) on the line too much, it's going to get chopped down. There are just too many things you can't control, so you just work as hard as you can on those things you can handle."

Hill makes his point. There was a time when the man who went on to be an All-Pro and Pro Bowl running back wasn't sure he would ever get the opportunity to carry the ball for the Cowboys. When he first arrived in training camp in '69, he was tried first at tight end, then linebacker. "I think what they were doing," he reflects, "was checking my mettle.

"To this day I'm not sure I would have ever had the opportunity to play running back if Danny Reeves hadn't gotten hurt and Craig Baynham hadn't suffered some cracked ribs. I got the opportunity because of something I had absolutely no control over. But when it did come, I was ready to take advantage of it."

While the learning experience of his rookie campaign ranks as his most memorable time spent in a Dallas uniform, it was not the most satisfying.

"My third season in Dallas, I was hurt for most of the year. But looking back," he says, "it was the greatest season I ever went through from a contentment standpoint. That was the year (1971) that we beat Miami to win the Super Bowl. There was great satisfaction in being a part of that, of being on a team which finally made it all the way to the top."

In 1975 Hill moved to the World Football League, playing for Hawaii before the league folded. He returned to the NFL as a member of the Washington Redskins in '76, playing sparingly before closing out his career as a highly effective third-down back for the Cleveland Browns for four years.

"It was finally time to call it a career," Hill said after the '81 season. "I enjoyed every minute of it. I enjoyed playing, watching film; I even enjoyed training camp. I've always loved the game. I was a fan who was fortunate enough to get to play, too."

HERB ADDERLEY
⭐
A Cornerback From Green Bay

The football life of Herb Adderley was an unbroken succession of superlatives. It began at Northeast High in his hometown Philadelphia, where he was a much applauded running back. Then it continued on to Michigan State, All-America recognition, post-season all-star game invitations and the distinction of being the No. 1 draft pick of the Green Bay Packers in 1961.

163

He spent nine years helping make the Pack the dominant power of pro football. Five times he was cited as All-Pro. Teammate Bart Starr called him the greatest cornerback in the game. Traded to Dallas in 1970, he caught on for two more trips to the Super Bowl before retiring after the '72 season. In a dozen years in the game he earned a record $116,200 in the playoff appearances alone.

No wonder he always answered the telephone with "Peace, love and happiness."

Now an account executive working for a Milwaukee radio station owned by former Packers teammate Willie Davis, Adderley took time recently to reflect on his days in a Dallas Cowboys uniform. It was a time of highs and lows, comfort and discomfort.

"I had one of the highest and one of the lowest points of my career with Dallas," he says. "When we lost to Baltimore in Super Bowl V, it was the only Super Bowl I had ever lost and the only big game I had ever lost. That was a big disappointment. On the other hand, to come back and win it the next year against Miami was a great thrill. To have been a part of the first Super Bowl victory the Cowboys had was something special to me."

Getting to that point in his brief but outstanding career with Dallas was no easy task. Making the changeover from the Green Bay style of playing cornerback, one which allowed him great freedom and asked man-to-man coverage of him most of the time, to the controlled, zone defenses of Tom Landry was, Adderley freely admits, a problem. "In fact," he says, "I never felt comfortable playing the Dallas type defense. Even when I would make a big play or an interception it seemed I was out of position or something. I just never really got the feel for it.

"And I think Landry recognized the difficulty I was having, because on some occasions he would allow me to just go ahead and play man-to-man while we were actually supposed to be in some other kind of coverage."

Certainly Adderley was allowed no gradual working into the scheme of things. "I came to Dallas on a Wednesday before the final exhibition game of the season with the Jets," he remembers, "and I started that Saturday night in the Cotton Bowl. Joe Namath threw at me 14 times. He hit on four, maybe five, but I felt like I held my own. I was 31 years old then, trying to make an overnight adjustment to a new system. I knocked a few down and might have even picked a couple off if I hadn't been playing so cautiously."

Caution was a byword when he came to Dallas. "I was honestly concerned about how I would be accepted," he admits. "You'll remember that there was never any love lost between the Packers and the Cowboys. In fact, I can still remember an anti-Green Bay song that was on the bulletin board in the fieldhouse the day I arrived. My first thought was, 'Hey, I've got to watch out for some of these guys. They're liable to take out a lot of frustrations on me.' "

With the help of people like Mel Renfro, Rayfield Wright and Cornell Green, however, the concern passed quickly.

"Mel was a tremendous help for me; a great athlete and a great person. He

and I were roommates and we did a lot of talking. He recognized the problems I had with the system and did everything he could to make it easier for me. He taught me a great deal about the Dallas coverages and how Landry wanted the game played. And he would help me out with his knowledge of some of the receivers I hadn't faced that much while I was in Green Bay. He'd sit down with me before a game and say things like '(Washington's) Charley Taylor runs really outstanding short patterns,' or '(St. Louis') Mel Gray doesn't run the turn-in too well but he'll go by you in a hurry on the post if you aren't careful.' Little things like that help a great deal.

"Still, the truth is, the kind of defensive scheme Dallas used always went against my basic philosophy. In Green Bay we played about 90 per cent man-to-man. I had the freedom to line up where I wanted to — a freedom of expression, really. In Dallas, there was only one way to do things and after nine years of doing it a way you felt comfortable with, it (adapting) was hard. It caused some problems for me. I couldn't help but think man-to-man in certain situations and it obviously showed because the coaches would stay on me about it.

"But, don't get me wrong; I appreciated my days with the Cowboys. It isn't often that a player has the good fortune to be traded from one highly successful, class team to another that's also successful and has the kind of class the Cowboys have."

JOHN NILAND
✪
The Ring That Got Away

It was a day in which the Dallas Cowboys were, to coin a popular verse, "so close and yet so far away." Having finally advanced beyond the barriers of not winning the big ones, Dallas had come to Super Bowl V to do battle with the Baltimore Colts. And for most of the afternoon in Miami appeared ready to bring home its first championship ever.

They were leading 13-6 and Craig Morton had driven his team to the Baltimore one yard line. With only second down showing on the scoreboard there were many who felt Dallas would add to its lead, therefore, sealing the fate of the Colts and putting the Cowboys into such a commanding position that they could not be overtaken.

Morton sent running back Duane Thomas through the line — into a play that many former Cowboys players and longtime fans will recall as the most infamous in the club's history. Baltimore linebacker Mike Curtis, seeing no chance to stop the hard running Thomas, hooked the ball loose. An instant pileup covered the ball just inches away from the goal line. The next thing anyone on the field knew, Baltimore defender Billy Ray Smith was yelling

"Our ball!" and referee Jack Fette was signaling a Colts recovery. Meanwhile, Dallas' Dave Manders stood up, a puzzled look on his face, holding the ball which even today he insists he recovered.

"I know he recovered it," says former Cowboys All-Pro guard John Niland. "I was right there on the ground next to him. There was no way it should have been Baltimore's ball. Some official just came running in from out in left field and made the call. That was the turning point of the game. If we had made the touchdown we would have been up 20-6 and it would have been almost impossible for Baltimore to come back. I couldn't believe it when I heard the call. I still can't."

Indeed, it is a moment in his lengthy pro football career which isn't likely to ever be forgotten. A three-time All-Pro who performed for the Cowboys from 1966 to 1974 before finishing out his career with the Philadelphia Eagles, Niland was reminded of the episode just recently.

"I was in a restaurant in Dallas," he said, "and looked across the room and there was Billy Ray Smith having dinner. I yelled over to him, 'Hey, Billy Ray, you still wearing my ring?' He knew exactly what I was talking about. He raised his hand and showed me his Super Bowl ring."

"The following day," Niland remembers, "Bob Lilly, Mel Renfro and I climbed on a 747 to fly out to Los Angeles for the Pro Bowl. I sat down in my seat and hadn't even put my seat belt on before this guy sits down in the seat next to me. It was Norm Schecter, one of the game officials. He hadn't been the one who made the call, but I couldn't help but say something. I looked at him and said, 'Norm, you guys blew it yesterday.' He didn't even answer me. In fact, we made the four hour trip without exchanging so much as another word.

"Later, after we had been in Los Angeles for a couple of days, I got a call reminding me of the fact I had agreed to speak to a group at a local high school. Generally in things like that the principal of the school usually comes by and picks you up. Well, I was ready at the appointed time and this fella, a teacher, I think, showed up and said the principal was tied up and had sent him instead. He said the principal was really sorry he hadn't been able to make it.

"We got to the high school, and just before I got ready to make my talk I found out who the principal was: Norm Schecter. I began to think I was never going to get away from those officials."

DAN REEVES

★

He Learned His Lessons Well

He was first invited to the Dallas Cowboys training camp in the summer of 1965 as a free agent; he was in fact a long-shot country boy out of Americus, Georgia, who didn't even have a position to play. Beyond the boundries of South Carolina where he had played his college ball, the name Danny Reeves rang precious few bells.

As a quarterback, his passing abilities were shy of professional standards. As a runner he was a step slower than the scouts would have liked. What the young Reeves brought with him to camp that long ago July was the manner of hustle and determination that catches the eye of coaches. That, and the knack for being at the right place at the right time. He was making the plays most rookies aren't expected to make.

Thus it was that he earned work as a member of the Cowboys specialty teams in his rookie year while Tom Landry and his staff pondered the possibility of his ever being a productive member of the Dallas backfield.

It took the drawling Georgian but little time to answer that question for them. In the next two seasons, working as a running back in the Cowboys attack, he ran for 1,360 yards, caught 80 passes and even threw a couple of touchdown passes. The coaching staff had long since stopped concerning itself over Reeves' lack of speed and size and head-spinning moves and were satisfied just to marvel at his productivity. Dan Reeves, they collectively decided, was destined to be a bonafide NFL star. *Sports Illustrated* magazine, picking up on the cue, put him on its cover.

But then things began to turn sour. Reeves' knees betrayed him. Though he would remain with the Cowboys for eight seasons, much of his career was spent dealing with pain, rehabilitating from surgeries and making his yardage by outsmarting more agile defenders.

Before he would retire from active duty he ranked as the fifth most productive back in Dallas history, journeyed to two Super Bowls, gained a national reputation as a clutch performer, and saw a fantasy fulfilled when he spent a season listed as the Cowboys' No. 3 quarterback.

It was in the final period of a game with Philadelphia in 1971 that Landry sent him in to direct the offense. His first two passes gained 24 yards and he drove the team to the Eagles' 17-yard line before a 15-yard penalty killed the drive. "Looking back," Reeves says, "I wish I'd been able to get us in the end zone on that drive. Shoot, if I had people might never have heard of Roger Staubach."

With that he laughs. Dan Reeves, despite being one of the most serious students of the game ever to play for Landry, always laughs. For him, the game has always been fun. Even if it did require him to establish a club record for knee operations before his playing days were done.

Five times he underwent surgery — four as a pro — and with each operation his playing days were shortened. By 1970 it was apparent he could not withstand the demands of a complete season. Yet so valuable was his presence, Landry made him a player-coach.

"The things that made Reeves such a valuable player to us," says Landry, "were those intangibles that are so hard to describe. He had a knack that some people just seem to be born with. And he studied the game constantly. After just a couple of seasons with us he knew every offensive assignment in the playbook."

"That," says Reeves, "is just the way I went about learning a play. If you knew what everyone was supposed to do, it was a lot easier to figure out why something worked or went wrong."

Dan Reeves, the coach, was at work long before Dan Reeves, the player, was finished.

When the job of offensive backfield coach became open prior to the 1972 season, (after Landry assigned Ermal Allen the duties of special assistant) Reeves made application. Landry had already talked with one prospective coach and had the names of several others under consideration when Reeves came to his office to advise him he would like to be considered for the job.

Landry pondered the idea and hired him. And he provided Reeves the kind of departure from the playing field he had hoped for.

"You have to swallow a lot of pride to know when to quit playing," Reeves says. "I had always felt it was important to know when to quit, but as that time draws nearer it gets progressively more difficult. You keep thinking you can play just one more year."

The year before he had carried the ball only 17 times but still did his part to help Dallas to New Orleans where it had won Super Bowl VI over Miami. Earlier, when the Cowboys were trying desperately to hold to a 7-3 lead over San Francisco in the NFC Championship game, starter Calvin Hill had suffered a knee injury and Reeves was summoned to duty.

With time running out in the third quarter and momentum apparently turning in the 49ers' favor, Staubach rolled to his right on a third-and-seven from his own 23. He found Reeves open at the 40 for a first down on the scoring drive which iced the victory.

It is such heroics, Reeves says, which too often give a player a false sense of value. "To have been able to come up with a play like that was a great feeling. But when you step back and look at things, you realize it was a one-time thing — that you couldn't step out there and still do it every Sunday like maybe you had been able to do years earlier.

"Being a coach helped me deal with retirement," he says. "It kept me close to the people on the team and the game itself. I found that I was still involved, still contributing, even if it was from a sideline vantage point."

It also convinced him that he wanted to pursue coaching as a lifetime profession. Aside from a brief venture into private business in '73, Reeves served as Landry's assistant until the call came from the Denver Broncos before the 1981 season, seeking his services as a head coach.

It was a step he was eager to take.

"I guess I would have been happy to play forever," he says, "but I'm grateful that when the time did come that I couldn't play, Landry let me coach. I feel like I'm one of the luckiest guys in the world. I played eight years of pro ball when there weren't too many folks around who thought I'd play a minute in the NFL.

"I played with a great team and was in two Super Bowls. Then, the coaching experience I got in Dallas made it possible for me to realize my dream of becoming a head coach. You can't repay those kind of things. You just appreciate them and take advantage of them. You take the lessons you learned and use them to the best of your ability. That's what I'm trying to do now."

That's what he's been doing since that first day of training camp back in the summer of 1965.

THE
✶ CHAMPION ✶
YEARS

The decade of the '70s was one crammed with milestones for the Cowboys, a time in which a still relatively young franchise not only came of age but captured the imagination of an entire sports-minded nation as well. While the Pittsburgh Steelers were the first to win three Super Bowls in the '70s, the Cowboys, with five appearances in the NFL showcase game, became what general manager Tex Schramm privately dreamed they would be.

They came to be recognized as the New York Yankees of pro football, a team whose symbol and players were known coast to coast. They were applauded not only for their innovative play but for their progressive scouting department and business-like front office approach. They became the model after which other expansion teams were fashioned.

Over the course of the exciting '70s, the Dallas Cowboys broke virtually every televised sports record on the books. Of the most viewed sporting events of all time, three of the top four were Super Bowls in which the Cowboys participated. Their 1978 NFC title game against Los Angeles was the highest rated non-Super Bowl game ever. They hold records for Monday nights, Thursdays and if they ever decide to hold a league game in the wee morning hours some Tuesday . . . well, you get the idea.

Cowboys-related items were easily the top sellers among the myriad of NFL Properties souvenirs. Ex players went on to excel as actors, authors and on television commercials. And the aura which surrounded the organization prompted the producers of NFL Films to finally refer to them as "America's Team" as the decade came to a close.

Such things, of course, happened for a reason. And that reason was winning, something the Cowboys did more regularly than any other team in the league in the 1970s. In a ten-year span they won 105 games — edging the Miami Dolphins by a half game to finish the decade with the most regular season victories. Twenty-one times they appeared in playoff games, winning on 14 occasions.

During the decade they would win seven division titles (1970-71-73-76-77-78-79), five conference titles and twice would climb to the game's highest peak, winning Super Bowl VI over Miami, 24-3, and Super Bowl XII over Denver, 27-10.

And they would do it with flair. They would vacate the Cotton Bowl, their original home, for a stadium of their own in Irving. They would add a dash of color and excitement to the sidelines with a group of cheerleaders who would become almost as well known as the team they cheered for, starring in movies and on television specials and selling posters faster than Farrah Fawcett.

And Tom Landry, ever the innovator, would sophisticate the term Shotgun, molding a style of attack ideally suited for a quarterback who would, on four different occasions, capture the league passing title. The scouting department, in its never-ending effort to stay ahead of the rest of the world, would have its finest hour in 1975, picking a "Dirty Dozen" rookies who would provide Landry with an overnight rebuilding job.

From that group alone came such Pro Bowlers as Randy White, Pat Donovan, Herb Scott, Bob Breunig and Thomas (Hollywood) Henderson as well as people like Randy Hughes, Scott Laidlaw, Mike Hegman and Burton Lawless.

It was, for that matter, a decade of super stars: Bob Lilly, Chuck Howley, Mel Renfro, Rayfield Wright, Lee Roy Jordan, Duane Thomas, Calvin Hill, Blaine Nye, John Niland, Walt Garrison, Cliff Harris, Charlie Waters, Harvey Martin, Billy Joe DuPree, Roger Staubach. The list goes on.

And records fell. In 1972 Calvin Hill became the first 1,000-yard ground gainer in the franchise's history. By the end of the '79 season, Tony Dorsett had accomplished the feat three straight years.

And Staubach, before his retirement, had used the decade to erase every quarterbacking record in the club's books.

MIKE DITKA

★

A Ticket to the Super Bowl

He is a man who once caught 13 passes in a single game during the prime of his pro football life with the Chicago Bears. Mike Ditka can look back to an afternoon when he tucked no less than four touchdown passes under his arm. He doesn't remember the number of times he has been awarded the game ball after particularly impressive individual performances.

Yet now he talks about an afternoon in Kezar Stadium when he caught but one pass, one that did not win the game or bring the attending crowd of pro-San Francisco 49ers fans to its feet. It was just another reception. No more, no less. Yet the game, played in 1970, still remains vivid to the former Cowboys assistant who is now head coach of the Chicago Bears. It was a day, he recalls, when a lot of positive things happened to the Dallas Cowboys. It was the day they defeated the favored 49ers, 17-10, for the NFC Championship; the day the team which some had said couldn't win the big one, was issued its first ticket to the Super Bowl.

It was also, he remembers, the day when a collective team effort replaced individual heroics. "It was one of the best feelings I had as a member of the Cowboys organization," he says. "Sitting in the dressing room after winning that one, I had a very good feeling about what was taking place on our team. With that game I was convinced we were molding into a great team rather than a team with a lot of great players. There's a big difference."

A week earlier the Dallas defense had been forced to take command to get the Cowboys past Detroit by a 5-0 count while the 49ers were defeating the Minnesota Vikings convincingly. Dick Nolan, the former Dallas assistant who was then directing the 49ers, could point to his as the most productive offense in the entire NFL.

Most observers felt Dallas' defense would again have to shoulder the load if the Cowboys hoped to advance to Super Bowl V. And true to those feelings, the 49ers were held to just 61 yards rushing. Lee Roy Jordan intercepted one John Brodie pass and ran it four yards back to the San Francisco 13 to set up one touchdown. Cornerback Mel Renfro, dealing day-long misery to wide receiver Gene Washington, intercepted another that put the second Cowboys TD drive in motion. Still, it was far from an all-defensive show.

The Dallas offense, led by Duane Thomas' 143 yards, ended the day with 229 rushing yards against the stunned 49ers defense.

"What made it even greater," Ditka recalls, "was that San Francisco had the reputation of being very good against the rush in those days. Nolan had them playing a flex, similar to the one we use. All week, though, Coach Landry had said that the key to winning the game was the establishing of a solid running game. Duane had moved over to fullback and Calvin Hill was playing halfback because Walt Garrison was sidelined with an injury."

Landry's game plan was relatively simple, based on successfully executing the "GT" series, a collection of quick tosses to the running backs going wide on some plays, off tackle on the others. For them to work, a series of demanding angle blocks would be required of the tight ends. Which meant that Ditka and Pettis Norman, who had alternated at the spot all year, serving as Landry's "messenger" to quarterback Craig Morton, would play critical roles.

"It was," Ditka says, "the best blocking game I had ever had. It was one of those rewarding kind of performances that comes every now and then. Usually, you feel it when you've caught a lot of passes. This was different, though. It wasn't the kind of game that would get me a big writeup in the paper or anything like that. It was more a personal feeling of accomplishment in playing a part."

While the Cowboys runners and defensive standouts would share the headlines in the next morning's editions, Ditka's efforts would not go unnoticed in the viewing of the game films at team meetings. "That," Ditka remembers, "was one of the few times I went in to look at the film feeling pretty good about the job I had done. In fact, I don't recall that there were many on the team who didn't enjoy looking at that one. It was, as I said, a very good overall team performance; one in which everyone did his job well. The runners, the blockers, the defense."

Landry, recalling the game and particularly Ditka's efforts, points to it as one of the finest blocking days a Dallas tight end has ever had. "Duane and Calvin ran well that day," Landry says, "but what was being done up front made their jobs a little bit easier."

Still, there would be critics. Dallas' Morton had hit but seven of 22 passing attempts for just 99 yards.

It would be left to Dick Nolan, then, to put that aspect of the game into perspective. "With a running game like the one Dallas showed against us," he said, "who needs a passing game?"

BLAINE NYE

A Season Turned to Fun

It was the season of the Great Disaster, a 38-0 defeat suffered at the hands of the St. Louis Cardinals on national television. The Dallas Cowboys, having

fallen to 5-4 on that particular gloomy evening, were given up for dead so far as the 1970 season was concerned. The team which had never won the big one would have to wait for some future date to prove itself an NFL power.

Blaine Nye, an offensive guard starting for the first time in his career with the Cowboys, loved it. At least he loved what would eventually take place before the turnaround season had run its course.

"That year," he says, "was a lot of fun. In fact, I had more fun that season than in any I ever played football." Best he explain:

"After we lost that game to the Cardinals Tom (Landry) decided the season was over. He let go and started taking a lighter approach. We'd go out and play touch football or volleyball on Mondays, things like that. Suddenly, it got to be fun and the team began to do better. For a reason that I still can't explain, there was suddenly the feeling that you were a part of this unified effort, this thing every athlete in team sports looks for.

"No individual did anything out of the ordinary. There wasn't anything you could put your finger on. It was just that the feeling I had heard about for the eight or ten years I'd played the game finally came. Suddenly there was this great feeling of being a part of a good team."

Indeed it did turn out to be a good team, winning seven games in a row to get into the playoffs and eventually to their first Super Bowl Dallas appearance.

"We lost it (16-13 to Baltimore), but, really the Super Bowl was anticlimactic. What had taken place in that second half of the season was the really exciting thing. Oh, it would have been great to win the championship, but, still . . .

"I mean, Landry really got into the spirit of what was going on that year. It was like a free lunch. We had a good thing going and nobody, players or coaches, wanted to foul it up, Tom really laid off. He had been the hard taskmaster early in the year but, after easing up and seeing us begin to win, he didn't make the mistake of changing back again. Looking back, that feeling we were able to get was a combination of things. It was part the results of Tom's system, part the fact that we were able to get this feeling I'm talking about."

Though an admitted admirer of Landry, the outspoken Nye has never been hesitant to criticize when criticism, he feels, is justifiable. "I've often said Tom was the reason we were 10-4 so many years," Nye says, "and also the reason we weren't 14-0. But, you know, in recent years I've gained a better understanding of why he operates the way he does. I've coached a youth soccer team for the past couple of years. Coaching is a frustrating job. The way I see it, you have to get your team to a peak and, once you're there, ease off and let things come spontaneously. You build up the head of steam with the hard driving, then let it go from there."

In the time he spent with Dallas (1968-76), the former Stanford standout was a member of three Super Bowl teams. And he recalls a similarity to each of the three seasons leading to the championship game.

"In each of those three years, the season had been written off before we came back to get to the Super Bowl," he notes.

"The year after we lost to Baltimore we went through some of the same things we had experienced the season before. We were 4-3 and again I think Tom wrote the year off. Maybe not to the degree he had the year before, but again there was evidence that he figured it was all over and began to ease up. Once again things got better, and that feeling returned. Not to the degree it had the year before, but it was there.

"That year we not only got to the Super Bowl but when we did, we won it right, beating Miami 24-3. In the one before we had played poorly, but so had Baltimore. This time we won it in the true fashion of a Super Bowl championship."

Nye's third trip to the Super Bowl came in '75, in a rebuilding year for the Cowboys. "That year a lot of people felt Tom could just take the year off. Everyone was convinced we were down and were picking us as also-rans. Tom knew that and felt it, I think, so he took a loose approach." The Cowboys would go 10-4 and lose Super Bowl X to Pittsburgh, 21-17.

Nye's career would end in retirement before the 1977 season would get underway. Contract negotiations in training camp came to an impasse and he called it quits and returned home. "It was a funny feeling," he says. "I wasn't dying to leave and I wasn't dying to stay. I just developed an indifferent attitude. I could have played three, four more years probably."

There would, however, be times when he would occasionally feel the draw of the game pulling on him. A year after his retirement, for instance, he chanced to be in Thousand Oaks to visit relatives. Knowing the Cowboys were training on the Cal Lutheran campus, he drove out. In the back of his mind was the thought that he might play again. "Once you're away from the game you find yourself thinking back on just the pleasurable things. You forget about the pressures, things like that."

But as he neared the campus he stopped. After a few minutes he put the car back in gear, made a U-turn and decided ended careers are best left ended. "Besides," he says, "I got to thinking about the fact that since I had walked out they had been fining me $500 a day for not being with the team. That's $500-a-day for 365 days. It occurred to me I owed them $182,500. I'd have had to play forever just to get even again."

BOB HAYES

World's Fastest Human

Read closely; this story is going to have a familiar ring to it.

The year was 1970 and the Dallas Cowboys, having finally emerged as a legitimate championship contender, had entered the season picked by many to finally win the Big One. All the tools were there — an explosive offense, a solid, coordinated Doomsday defense. And the team limped out of the chute with a case of blind staggers which reminded many long-time followers of the early days of the franchise.

The team labeled for greatness arrived at the stretch of the season with a 5-4 record after hitting a new low by losing to St. Louis, 38-0. There were team meetings, re-evaluations by the coaching staff, alternations here, minor changes there, and finally, just in time, came the turnaround. The 1970 Cowboys began streaking and had the division title wrapped up before the regular season officially ended. Momentum became the word as they closed out the season against the Houston Oilers, and momentum it was as Dallas roared to a 52-10 victory.

That December 20th day was special to Bob Hayes, All-Pro wide receiver, Olympic 100-meter champion, World's Fastest Human and the biggest of the big play men ever to wear a Cowboys uniform. "It was my birthday," Hayes remembers, "and I caught four touchdown passes against the Oilers to set a new club record. That was a lot of fun — we wound up winning the game 52-10 — but even more important it convinced us we were ready to go into the playoffs on an upward swing."

Indeed, that birthday performance in which he caught six for 187 yards and his four TDs, was graphic evidence that the Cowboys of 1970 had completely redirected their course and were legitimate Super Bowl contenders.

It was a season, Hayes notes, that, in some respects, reminds him of the one the Cowboys are currently engaged in. "We were everyone's pick to win our division," he recalls, "and for some reason we seemed to get a little complacent. Everybody that came in to play us came after us with everything they had. Before we realized it we had our backs to the wall. When we lost to St. Louis the way we did, it finally worked a lot of people up.

"I remember that things started getting quiet around the practice field and we all started looking around at each other and saying, 'Hey, we can't afford to lose any more.' One of the things I remember best about that time was that instead of working us harder, Tom (Landry) eased up. What he was saying, I think, was for everyone to just relax a little, take a deep breath, and think about playing the kind of football we were capable of playing."

It worked. From the St. Louis disaster would be born a seven-game winning streak which would not end until the Cowboys lost a last minute heartbreaker to Baltimore, 16-13, in Super Bowl V in Miami.

"It's interesting," Hayes pointed out, "how once you get things going, once you win a couple in a row, everything starts falling into place for you. By the time we played Houston it didn't really mean anything but everyone knew that it was important not to let down, to maintain the intensity we had in recent weeks.

"And, Jerry Rhome was starting for the Oilers after having played with us for several years, so there was a little bit of a rivalry on that count. And, the state thing was still pretty big then.

"I was looking forward to it for the simple reason that the AFC teams were still using the bump-and-run that they had in the American Football League days. They were good at it and were still several years ahead of the NFC teams in that respect. But, the way they played it, if you could get past the cornerback's bump you would usually be one-on-one with the deep safety. Johnny Robinson was deep for the Oilers and I felt like I had a good chance of beating him."

He did, with embarrassing regularity. All four of his catches that went for touchdowns were from 40 yards or more away. Few people have had more noteworthy birthdays. But, then, few people have created the brand of excitement that the former Florida A&M sprint star brought to the NFL. Having 9.1 speed can turn a mortal receiver into a superman.

During his career with the Cowboys (1965-1974) Bob Hayes made bomb a familiar word to those who watched him create havoc with opposing secondaries. The Dallas club records are testimony to his worth.

He is, for instance, second on the all-time receiving list with 365 catches for 7,295 yards (a 20-yards-per-catch average) and 71 touchdown catches. He still tops the punt return leaders with 104 runbacks for 1,158 yards and three TDs. His 456 points on 76 career touchdowns is tops, as is his four scoring receptions against the Oilers in a single game. In 1966 he accounted for 1,232 receiving yards, a single season best.

In 1970 he averaged a season record 26.1 yards-per-catch on his 34 receptions, and his 246 yards in nine catches against Washington in 1966 tops the all-time single game list.

Bullet Bob was the man who made the big play a weekly expected part of the Cowboys' show. It didn't matter who was throwing to him; just as long as the ball got there. To wit: there was the 95-yard TD pass from Meredith in '66 against the Redskins. Craig Morton hit him on an 89-yard scoring heave against Kansas City in 1970. Roger Staubach got into the act in '71 with an 85-yard shot to Hayes for a touchdown against the Giants.

Punt returns? How about a 90-yarder against Pittsburgh in '68 or a 69-yarder against St. Louis in '67. Or a 68-yarder against Cleveland in the same year?

"It was," Hayes says, "a lot of fun. But that day in Houston was the best. It was a great way to celebrate a birthday."

RICHMOND FLOWERS

He Beat the Odds

He had come to the Dallas Cowboys as an All-American wide receiver, yet his greatest college acclaim had been as a hurdler for the University of Tennessee Volunteers. Richmond Flowers, a second round draft selection in 1969, had the kind of blazing speed the NFL has long coveted. He had won the NCAA 100-yard high hurdles title with a best clocking of 13.3, world class time. His running abilities had earned him competitive visits to track and field stadiums throughout the world.

"I ran track for the fun of it," he said recently from his Nashville home. "But I played football for the money *and* the fun of it. Unfortunately, my life story so far as being a professional football player was that I was pretty much a jack of all trades and master of none. But, I made it in the NFL, I played in a Super Bowl — that's something to look back on. I was reading, in fact, just the other day that the odds of a college player making it in the NFL are now something like one in 60,000. Goodness only knows what the odds of being on a Super Bowl team are."

During his three-year stay with the Cowboys (1969-71), Flowers served on every specialty team the Dallas team had and labored as a backup defensive back behind the likes of Mel Renfro, Charlie Waters and Cliff Harris. "It was Waters and Harris," he laughs, "who got me traded to the New York Giants, in fact. But, even that turned out okay, really. I went up there and played for three seasons and was able to realize my dream of being a starter, playing strong safety for the Giants. I hung around for five years, got my pension, a lot of stories and some great memories."

The greatest memory, however, came during his days as a Cowboys specialty team player. "Everyone who played, I suppose, has that one play, that one moment that stands out in his mind. Mine came against the Cleveland Browns in 1970.

"The year before they had really killed us (42-10) and when it came time to play them again it was a very critical game. It was a typical Cleveland day with about four inches of mud on the field and our offense was getting nowhere. We had them backed up inside their own five and they had to punt. For some reason D. D. Lewis wasn't in the lineup so I moved up from safety to his position. My job as I understood it was to just rush in and make sure the punter did punt, that he didn't escape and break away for a first down.

"I managed to get a really good start and got to him quickly — nobody touched me — and I blocked the punt and Steve Kiner recovered it on their three-yard line. The offense lost a lot of ground but we managed to get a field goal out of it and won the ball game 6-2. And went on to the Super Bowl from there for the first time. I think everyone agrees that that particular game was one of the biggest in the history of the club. It did a lot to rub out the 'can't win the big one' thinking that was going around. It was a key game and, looking back, I like to think I made a key play in it."

And, while the Cowboys lost in the Super Bowl, it was a memorable experience to have played in the game's premier attraction. "I did nothing outstanding that day," Flowers says, "but I did my job."

No one, however, is ever completely satisfied with the role of a backup player, so it was that the trade to the Giants allowed him to fit the final piece of his athletic career into place.

And now, years removed from his competitive days, he remains in touch with the game. Following his retirement he entered the University of Alabama law school and got his degree and worked on the staff of famed attorney Jim Neal, who was one of the Watergate prosecutors. Flowers recently took a position with E. F. Hutton and moved to Chicago to work in the company's national commodity office. And he serves as a player agent. "That's my way of staying in touch with the game," he says. "I enjoy it. I enjoy seeing the kids I work with play and I like going around talking to the general managers and player personnel directors."

Thus far in his relatively new career as an agent he is yet to sit down at the negotiating table with the Cowboys. "But I'm sure one day soon I will. And I'm looking forward to it. Gil Brandt has always gotten the best of me. I'm still looking for a chance to get even."

DAVE EDWARDS
★
A Win in Cleveland, Finally

It had, until that magic day in December, 1970, been a struggle; a constant, sometimes grueling, always pressurized drive to prove once and for all that the Dallas Cowboys, then 10 years of age, were a team of maturity.

"I had been with the team since 1963," says former linebacking standout Dave Edwards, "and even though we had become winners by the mid-60s and were getting into the playoffs on a pretty regular basis, it was still a struggle. There were plenty of people ready to admit we were a pretty good football team, but there were still reservations. We needed to win a big one — one we

weren't figured to win — to make believers out of some people."

There were many who believed that need also existed among the Cowboys squad.

It would come on the next to the last game of the 1970 regular season on a windy day in Cleveland as 75,458 turn out to cheer the Browns past the visiting Texans.

"Up until that day," Edwards recalls, "it seemed that every time we went up to Cleveland to play the Browns we could depend on two things. It would be cold and raining. And they would whip our tails.

"And frankly, there wasn't a lot of reason to believe that time was going to be any different. We were having some problems, then, you'll remember. It was a time of controversy on our team. The players were all given questionnaires about which coaches they liked and didn't like, things of that nature. Still, despite all that we seemed to be playing pretty good ball late in the year. We had that 38-0 embarrassment against St. Louis earlier in the year and then got on a winning streak. In fact, we won seven in a row after that."

Of those seven, though, none would be so big as the victory over arch-rival Cleveland. It would be a defensive masterpiece with Dallas scoring a 6-2 victory on two Mike Clark field goals. After the Browns had taken a 2-0 lead, Clark kicked a 39-yarder against the 15-mph wind and would come back with a 31-yarder later in the day.

It would, however, take an interception by Edwards in the final minute of the game when the Browns were deep in Cowboys territory to seal the victory.

"That," Edwards says, "was a big thrill for me. In fact, I got the game ball that day. I had intercepted another one earlier and had played pretty well all day. It was a kind of day that makes you probably think a little more highly of yourself than you should, but it felt good. But it was something more than personal accomplishment," he continues. "I honestly believe that that was the day that the Cowboys grew up. It put us over the hump and convinced us that we were the kind of team that could beat anyone. Once you get past that stage and believe that you are not only capable of winning that kind of game but, in fact, are supposed to win it, you have overcome a big hurdle.

"That year we went on into the Super Bowl, winning over Detroit (5-0) and San Francisco (17-10) in the playoffs before losing to Baltimore 16-13 in Super Bowl V in Miami. Of course it was disappointing to lose the Super Bowl but I don't think there was anyone on the team who didn't feel we would be back. The Cleveland game, again, had changed the whole attitude of the club."

Edwards and the famed Doomsday Defense played a big part in the redirection of the Dallas attitude. A month before the Cleveland game he had suffered cartilage damage in his knee yet had continued to play and be a major factor in the fact that by the time the Browns game was history, Dallas' defense had gone 13 quarters without having given up a single touchdown.

"Dave Edwards is a pro," Ernie Stautner would say after the Browns triumph. "He not only plays hurt, but he still does an outstanding job. That's the sign of a real pro." Which was the case throughout his blue ribbon career in a Cowboys uniform. "There were," he said, "some great days, some great times, but for sheer importance and a feeling that something special had been accomplished, the 1970 Cleveland game is one that still means a lot to me."

In retrospect, it meant a great deal to the entire Cowboys organization. After all, it isn't every day that a team finally comes of age.

BOB BELDEN

★

The Frustration of Being No. 3

It was still early in the 1970 season, a year which saw the Cowboys struggling to get untracked, and quarterbacks Roger Staubach and Craig Morton were both being listed as doubtful for an upcoming game against the Kansas City Chiefs. Morton was suffering with a hip and shoulder injury and Staubach's elbow was infected.

People in Dallas spent the week wondering how the Cowboys would fare with an inexperienced third team quarterback named Bob Belden, a twelfth round draft choice from the year before who had not played a single down in an NFL game. Throughout the week the young Notre Dame ex drew more attention than he had ever received at practices. Members of the media asked him to speculate about how it would be to suddenly emerge as the starting quarterback.

The atmosphere, the whole idea fascinated him. Yet when game day arrived, Staubach was pronounced fit enough to play. Again Belden watched and waited.

Such would be his fate for two long years. Like so many No. 3 quarterbacks on NFL rosters, he would eventually leave the game much as he had entered it, making no waves, no headlines. The story of Bob Belden is as familiar as that of the player who climbs to stardom in the NFL. It just doesn't gain the attention of the public. He was one of those who gave it a shot, came close, but never quite made it. His brief role as a professional was to remain in the background, to wait. And finally the waiting became too much, the chances too slim to invest in for another year, another season.

"The time came," he admits, "when I no longer had the proper mental attitude. I really hadn't expected to play in my rookie year, but after going through a second full season without ever getting in a game, I began to think. It finally occurred to me that I didn't want to sit around another five years to find the answer to whether I could play in the pros, so I decided it was time to retire. I think Coach Landry realized my feelings and understood. I had gone to the University of Michigan in the summer to do some graduate work and just called him to tell him I wasn't coming back. That was all there was to it. I think I made a clean break from the game — no regrets."

It might have been different, he says, had he been a second team quarterback instead of No. 3. "There's a wide gap between being No. 2 and No. 3," he points out. "The guy on the second unit knows there's a chance that he might play, that any number of circumstances might arise that would result in his being called on. So he stays ready, physically and mentally. The third guy knows that something is going to have to happen to two people before he is ever called on. When you think you might have an opportunity to play, the whole world turns around. If not, it begins to look like a dead-end road after a while."

Belden's role as a member of the Cowboys was far removed from the glamor of the game. During the week's practice sessions he spent most of his time not with the offensive unit, but instead running the opposition's plays for benefit of the defensive squad. Then on Sundays he sometimes was not even on the sidelines.

"Some of my time was spent on the taxi squad (not as a member of the actual roster) so I would sit in the booth in the pressbox with assistant coaches Jerry Tubbs and Ray Renfro, charting the defensive coverages. A couple of minutes before the half, Ray would get them from me and go down to the locker room and put them on the board so the coaches could go over them with the team. It's a way of making a contribution, I suppose, but nothing like being physically involved in the game."

Belden is one of those rare cases of a player who did not even know the thrill of collegiate stardom before his attempt to make it as a professional. At Notre Dame he also labored as a backup, first to Terry Hanratty, then Joe Theismann.

"But there was a difference," he says. "In college, I had other things in addition to football. Football wasn't the beginning and end of my day every day. When you're playing professionally, it is."

A number of people, quite obviously, were surprised when he was drafted. Even more that he earned a place on the Dallas roster.

"In one respect, I guess it has worked out well for me," Belden says. "If I had had the opportunity to play more, I'd probably still miss the game. As it is, I was ready to leave it and not look back. I still enjoy watching football, but I don't miss it. I learned a lot about the game from Landry. But there comes a time when the learning process really comes to a stop if you don't get some chance to play. I realize the Cowboys system is complex, but not that complex. By my second season I felt I was ready to play."

Unfortunately, it is something few third team quarterbacks ever get the opportunity to do.

MIKE CLARK

Big Kick in the Playoffs

It was not one of those games which gives NFL historians reason for pause nor can Mike Clark recall anyone writing too many poems about it, yet today, years removed from that long 1970 December afternoon in the Cotton Bowl, it remains vivid in his mind.

It was the day his 35-yard field goal and a late stage safety lifted the Dallas Cowboys to a 5-0 victory over the Detroit Lions in the first round of the playoffs and sculptured a return to the conference title picture after a two year absence.

"What made the game special," says Clark, now marketing director for Mid-America Airways, Inc., "was the fact that it was another step in a late surge we had made that season. We had won our last five games to finish 10-4 and get into the playoffs and eventually to the Super Bowl."

The Detroit game, played before 73,167, would evolve into a defensive struggle with only occasional offensive sparks. Cowboys quarterback Craig Morton, having been able to work very little in the preceding several weeks because of a montage of injuries, lacked consistency and, aside from rookie running back Duane Thomas' bursts, the Dallas offense spent most of the day struggling. But, then, so did the Lions' attack as Doomsday was having one of its finest hours.

Clark's moment of glory would come early — in the first quarter — after Reggie Rucker was unable to hang on to a Morton pass in the end zone. The conventional style kicker who would lead Dallas' scoring for four consecutive years (1968-69-70-71) came on to lift the Cowboys into a 3-0 advantage with a 36-yard field goal. "At that particular stage of the game," he recalls, "it wasn't that much of a pressure situation. It was early and there was no reason to believe that my kick would end the scoring."

For two quarters, however, the game settled into a punting duel and only in the waning stages would Dallas mount a drive which fed anticipation to the unusually calm crowd. "The offense did its part," Clark remembers, "with a long drive which went from our 25 to the Lions' one before we were stopped. It took something over seven minutes and, while we didn't score, it kept the ball away from Detroit and made the chances of the field goal standing up all the better."

Detroit had to take over on the one, and Dallas was able to salvage two points from the drive when Jethro Pugh and George Andrie combined for a tackle in the end zone. But then came the whirlwind finish. Subbing for an ineffective Greg Landry, Lions backup quarterback Bill Munson came on with a hot hand and was moving the visitors well as the clock ticked off the final minutes. Only when Mel Renfro picked off a pass intended for fleet Earl McCullough with 35 seconds remaining was the victory safe.

"That kick in the first quarter," Clark says, "was my only chance of the day. It wasn't anything spectacular, to be honest about it, but when all was said and done it was very satisfying to know that I had played a sizable part in a game as important as that one."

Today he still maintains a close watch on the progress of the Cowboys and has viewed with great interest as the kicking game has changed since his days in the NFL. He also feels that the NFL rule makers have allowed the long distance college kickers to steal some of the thunder from the pros of late.

"Back when I came into the league there were a lot of guys kicking 50 yarders but they decided to put in the rule which says that if you miss one from that range the ball is brought back to the line of scrimmage rather than the 20. Everyone immediately began being more conservative with their kicking games from then on. They went with the percentages, ignoring the long kick and settling for a punt that would put the other team in poor field position. So far as I'm concerned what they did was penalize the kickers for being proficient at their jobs."

JETHRO PUGH

A Champagne Pro

Cincy Powell, former professional basketball player now operating an Oak Cliff restaurant, provided the final touch of class to the luncheon at which 14-year Dallas Cowboys veteran Jethro Pugh announced his retirement to members of the media.

The announcement made, the last questions asked, the gathering adjourned to a table for lunch. Powell, a longtime friend of the man who was so long a fixture in the defensive line of the Cowboys, appeared with champagne. It was appropriate.

Pugh, a mainstay in the original Doomsday defense, was a champagne professional; a champange person. Never mind that in his lengthy career he was never All-Pro, not once selected to participate in the Pro Bowl. He was a performer highly respected by his peers, teammates and opponents alike. "You know," says Ernie Stautner, Cowboys defensive line coach and an unabashed admirer of Jethro's talents, "Jim Murray, the Los Angeles Times sportswriter hit the nail on the head so far as Jethro's ability is concerned. He wrote a column once, saying that Jethro Pugh was the greatest defensive lineman in the NFL never selected to the Pro Bowl. I agree with that. In a way, Jethro was unfortunate. He was playing some of his greatest football at a time when a guy named Bob Lilly was in his heyday. Lilly got a great deal of attention from the media and Jethro just kept on doing his steady, super job."

That, perhaps, best describes the contribution of the soft-spoken defensive tackle who came to the Cowboys as an 11th round draft pick out of Elizabeth City State in 1965. "I like to think," he says, "that I contributed in a small way. I was able to play consistently as a starter for 10 years. I had a good, clean, honest career. It was enjoyable but, as with everyone in this business, there comes a time to call it quits and do something else. That time finally came for me."

But not before he had lived through numerous glory days, days of near misses, of near dynasties, Super Bowls and super seasons. Those are the sweet memories Jethro Pugh will take with him, not the fact he was annually snubbed by those dealing out post-season honors. "I never thought much about that part of it," he insists. "I felt I was playing good football. The fans knew it, the coaches and my teammates knew it, and I knew it. That satisfied me.

"You know, the biggest surprise to me was the fact I made it 14 years (thus tying the club longevity record held by Mel Renfro, Lilly and Lee Roy Jordan). When I first came to the Cowboys all I thought about was making the team. Then, my goal was to be a starter. That first year was frightening, though. I went to training camp not having any idea what to expect. But once I got there and saw that I had as much ability as a lot of the others I made up my mind that I was going to stick around."

He did, of course, and earned himself a ringside seat from which he was able to watch the growth of the organization.

"In the late '60s it was still an inexperienced organization and team. We had some great individuals but we hadn't really come together as a team. That part of it first took place with the defense. During the 1968-69-70 seasons we had a good defense. When we went on the field we were completely confident. I went out there thinking I could make every play; so did the other guys. And those were the real pressure years, the late '60s. Everyone was getting impatient for us to win a championship.

"For that reason, I suppose, the year we first won the Super Bowl (1971 over Miami, 24-3) was one of the biggest games I ever played in. It was a great relief to get that one behind us. We had been trying so hard to win. Our first trip to the Super Bowl was very disappointing. We lost it to Baltimore (16-13), but I strongly felt we were the best team on the field."

Then, of course, there was the infamous Ice Bowl in Green Bay when Bart Starr quarterback-sneaked into the end zone for the winning touchdown in the 1967 championship game. It has become a part of pro football history now, helped along by Packer offensive lineman Jerry Kramer's best-selling book, *Instant Replay*. It is Kramer's block on Pugh which is credited for opening the slight hole through which Starr went to score.

"It was a good play on Starr's part," Jethro says. "He hadn't run a quarterback sneak all season. But to this day I still maintain that Kramer was offsides. As far as that goes, (center Ken) Bowman actually got better contact on me on the play.

"I saw Kramer several months after his book came out and had become a big seller," Pugh laughs, "and asked him if he had any plans to give me a percentage since I had helped to make him a star."

For Jethro Pugh, however, there is no bitterness, no evidence of lingering scars. There were too many highlights, too many other championship games to linger over one play on a bitter cold day in Green Bay.

He is, then, a man with few regrets.

"There was one thing I always wanted to do, though," he points out, "that I never managed to accomplish. I wanted to play the perfect game. I came close a few times but after a while I came to realize that it was impossible to do. Still, it was a good goal to shoot for for all those years."

Which tells you a great deal about the approach Jethro Pugh brought to the game. It was one worthy of a champagne toast.

TONY LISCIO

To the Rescue

It was the season of 1971 and former Dallas Cowboys offensive lineman Tony Liscio had put his football career behind him. Deeply involved in a real estate business, he could look back on eight years as a member of the Cowboys and an additional season with the San Diego Chargers prior to his official retirement after the '70 season. At 31, Liscio had tired of the game. Hamstring pulls in both legs had limited his playing time in San Diego and he was being traded to the Miami Dolphins. Liscio didn't have another move in him and thus retired.

The former University of Tulsa standout was ready to sit on the sidelines and cheer — and progress in his new career in real estate.

He was back in Dallas in a season of great expectation for his old teammates. A veteran team which had lost the Super Bowl by just three points (16-13) to Baltimore the year previous, the Cowboys were being touted as the next World Champions. As the season progressed, however, there would be reason for concern. Dallas lost three of its first seven and then as it began a stretch drive (which would eventually see it win seven in a row before getting into the playoffs) a disaster hit. Veteran tackle Ralph Neely broke his ankle in a motorcycle accident and was out for the year. Suddenly, a gaping hole had developed in the Cowboys' offensive line.

Tony takes the story from there:

"I remember reading about it when it happened," he recalls, "and thinking it was really a stroke of bad luck. It never occurred to me in the wildest of my imaginations that it might be me who would be called upon to plug that hole, though. I was through with football. My career was over and I was nothing more than a card-carrying fan."

Until Tom Landry placed a call to him at his office on the Monday morning prior to Dallas' tenth game of the season. "I was happy, doing fine, and not really even missing football when he called," Liscio remembers. "I had spent the previous season in San Diego (after having been part of a trade which brought Lance Alworth to the Cowboys) and it had been a bad one. I didn't play much at all because I pulled hamstrings in both legs during the season. When they told me they were going to trade me to Miami, I decided it was time to call it quits."

Landry, however, had an optional plan for Liscio to consider. If Dallas could reacquire him, would he be interested in coming back for the duration of the season? "My first reaction would have been to think it was a joke if it had been anyone but Coach Landry calling. He explained the situation, told me that he knew I was familiar with the system and that he felt I could do the job. He did add that they really wouldn't expect me to be able to go the distance in the first few games.

"I told him I would need some time to think about it."

"Fine," said Landry. "I'll call you back in 30 minutes."

In that brief time frame Liscio considered the fact that one of his hamstrings was still very tight. He thought back to a series of knee operations which had kept him out of the entire 1965 season. He considered the fact that he hadn't taken a running step since mid-summer when he had decided to retire. He thought about the fact he was a 31-year-old man trying to gain a foothold in a new career.

And he called Landry back to say he would give it a shot.

"I was honest with him," Liscio says. "I told him I really didn't think I would be able to do it. He said to come on and give it a try." It would be the following Wednesday before the Cowboys could officially gain his services. Liscio did a little running on his own Monday and Tuesday and reported to workouts Wednesday. The following Sunday he would start against the Washington Redskins.

"Really," he says, "all I could do was play it by ear. I really didn't have much work, since we started tapering off for the game the day after I reported to the team. Still, by the time we got to Washington the hamstring in one leg was really tight and I had a very sore shoulder from what little contact I had been able to do in practice. I was convinced I wasn't going to make it."

Nonetheless, he was listed among the starters. "As soon as the game got under way," he remembers, "I completely forgot that I had been out of it for so long. I was so excited that I went after it just as if I had been working since the first day of training camp. All things considered, I had a pretty good game."

So did the entire Cowboys squad as it defeated the troublesome Redskins in the crucial battle, 13-0.

Tony Liscio spent the next three days in the whirlpool. And on the fourth day he played again, this time in a Thanksgiving Day affair against Los Angeles. "Obviously," he laughs, "things didn't get any easier."

Most of his teammates were complaining about the fact they had had so short a recovery time between games. "Shoot," Liscio says, "when I lined up for the first offensive series against the Rams I was so sore I could hardly get into a stance. I felt like I had played a game the day before.

"The whole first quarter I was a physical wreck. I was so stiff I wasn't even moving well. But, after a while I began to limber up and things began getting better. By the end of the game I felt I was doing a pretty good job."

And the Cowboys had delighted a home crowd of 66,595 by defeating the Rams 28-21.

Following that brutal two-game re-entry into the NFL, Liscio welcomed a 10-day respite that would come before a game against the New York Jets. By the time the Cowboys had bombarded them 52-10, much of the soreness and stiffness was gone. By the time Dallas had ended the regular season with an 11-3 record, he was feeling almost as if he had never been gone. By the time it won the Super Bowl, defeating Miami, 24-3, in one of the most productive offensive shows in the game's six-year history, Tony Liscio was, needless to say, feeling very good about his 30-minute decision.

Following that comeback season he returned to his Dallas based real estate business — that time for good.

RALPH NEELY

★

Long Search for the High Spot

The Dallas Cowboys had reached the mid-point of the 1971 season, collectively disappointed at the 4-3 record it had managed in what many had promised would be a championship season. Having lost to Baltimore the previous January in Super Bowl V, it was to be the year they would return and take the final step.

But the Chicago Bears had just beaten them, 23-19, and veteran tackle Ralph Neely, wishing to put the frustration of the defeat behind him for a few hours, loaded his motorcycle into his camper and drove to Grapevine Lake for a day of hill climbing on his Monday off. It was, he had already in-

formed the Cowboys management, to be his final professional season and he was none too happy with the course it was taking.

"I wanted to be a part of a championship team before I retired," he says, "but a New York investment firm had offered me a position in its London branch. It was one of those opportunities I couldn't see myself letting get away."

Not in his master plan, however, was the manner in which that '71 season would end for him.

Walking his motorcycle up a hill, going no more than five or ten miles per hour, he caught his foot on the ground, tripped and fell. His ankle was dislocated and the fibula in his right leg shattered.

"I broke the bone in three places," he recalls, "but if that had been all there was to it I could have come back before the year was over. But the dislocated ankle and the torn ligaments put me out for the remainder of the season."

Depression set in and would build as the Cowboys, turning the corner, began heading in the direction he had hoped they would that year. Ralph Neely, the man who wanted a championship as badly as anyone on the roster, was forced to sit and watch Dallas destroy Miami in Super Bowl VI.

"I was happy to see us win the championship," he says, "but the fact was, I wasn't a part of it. For a while I had a sick, empty feeling about it. After all those years of coming so close and yet never making it, we'd finally made it and I wasn't able to share in the feeling of accomplishment. I began to think that it just wasn't to be for me; that I wasn't, for some reason, supposed to be a part of something like that."

There was, then, every indication that the career of the All-Pro offensive tackle was due to end on a down note. He had a Super Bowl ring, a half share of the championship payoff, but none of the satisfaction of having helped reach the goal he had set for himself when the controversy finally cleared from his signing.

An All-America pick at Oklahoma, Neely became the centerpiece of the NFL vs. AFL war in 1965. Signing an agreement with Houston Oilers owner Bud Adams before he and his Sooners played in the post-season Gator Bowl, Neely had, along with three teammates (including Lance Rentzel), been dismissed from the OU squad. In the meantime, Dallas had negotiated a trade with the Baltimore Colts, who had picked Neely in the second round of the draft, for rights to try and sign him should an Oklahoma City district judge rule the AFL contract void. The judge did and Neely became a Cowboy. But not until Dallas had properly compensated the Oilers. To satisfy Adams, Dallas had to give up a first, second and two fifth round draft choices — and agree to play the Oilers in an annual pre-season game in Houston.

High stakes, indeed, but Cowboys general manager Tex Schramm looked at it as a bargain. "With Neely at right tackle our offensive line is established," he said. "He's the man you build around. You put him there and forget about the position for the next ten years."

In short time he became a regular on All-Pro teams and in the annual Pro

Bowl. And as he solidified the offensive line, the Cowboys moved closer to a championship. As Dallas' championship season of '71 opened, he made what members of the coaching staff still refer to as one of the most unselfish moves in the club's history. When problems developed at left tackle, Ralph moved from the position he had been an All-Pro at, giving it up to promising Rayfield Wright.

The transition wasn't easy. "I was never as good a left tackle as I was a right tackle," he says, "but I was the best left tackle we had at the time. You do what you have to when you're trying to accomplish what we were after. Making a move like that is something like having written right-handed all your life and suddenly being asked to write left-handed. You have to react to everything in just the opposite manner you had been doing all your life."

Neely, history shows, learned to adjust quickly. "It didn't surprise any of us," says former teammate Bob Lilly. "He's the only player I've ever seen who was never a rookie. He stepped right in and started to play. When he made the switch from one side of the line to the other it was the same way."

It would be a nationwide economic freeze after that '71 season which would prolong Neely's learning experience on the left side of the line. With the job in London suddenly a gamble, and the broken bones healed, he opted to continue his career.

"Toward the end," he insists, "I wasn't playing for the money. It was something more personal. I wanted to show that I could come back. Over a five-year period I had three knee operations and a broken leg. There was one year when I was supposed to be really healthy — and I had my knee drained 21 times. Things like that begin to wear on you. I just determined that after all that I wanted to go out on an up note."

In '72 he played most of the season with a broken hand. "The guy showed a tremendous amount of courage by getting out there and trying to pass block with that hand the way it was," says line coach Jim Myers. "But that was the kind of player he was. There haven't been many like him to pass through this league."

The oft-postponed retirement would come finally following the 1977 season, after Dallas had soundly defeated Denver to win Super Bowl XII. It was the high spot Ralph Neely had so long searched for.

PAT TOOMAY

The Highs and Lows

For Pat Toomay, who retired from the Oakland Raiders just prior to what would have been his tenth year of professional football, it was, he says, an experience. He's seen the game's highest and lowest moments and in doing so has been able to put it into a manner of perspective which escapes many.

A member of the Dallas Cowboys from 1970 to '74, he played defensive end in two Super Bowls. As a member of the expansion Tampa Bay Buccaneers in 1977 he started on a team which lost all 14 of the games it played. Which is to say the career of the big Vanderbilt ex ran the gamut.

"That first Super Bowl victory was quite an experience," he says. "Especially when you compare it with the disappointment of losing to Baltimore in the one the year before. Beating Miami and becoming Super Bowl champions was nothing but unmitigated joy. It was a great feeling, a great accomplishment, but, you know, when you're really young you really don't grasp the full meaning of something like that.

"For me it took a passing of time to realize what being a part of all that meant."

It took some hard times. After spending two seasons in Buffalo following his tenure in Dallas, Toomay was to arrive in Tampa Bay as part of the league's newest expansion team. It was a team which would establish a new NFL low water mark, going through an entire season winless. "Over the course of that year," Pat says, "we had no less than 22 players injured. After about the third or fourth game it was obvious we were never going to win one. You fight that kind of thinking, but deep down, I suppose, you look at things realistically. In the last game of the season I looked around and was the only starter left who had opened the season. I had next to me, a 175-pound outside linebacker they had picked up off the streets of Tampa, and a tackle who had been a construction worker when the season began.

"That was the absolute bottom. Being there gives you a little better perspective on the top. I'll forever be grateful to (Oakland owner) Al Davis for getting me out of that situation."

For two years he was a member of the Raiders, playing sparingly because of knee problems. Then, it was over. "The knee just refused to function. I just couldn't go. If you're physically unable to play any longer it makes coping with retirement a great deal easier. It becomes a simple decision," he points out.

Toomay, author of a non-fiction football chronicle titled *"The Crunch"* in 1975, was throughout his career an athlete who marched to a different drummer. While he is quick to admit great respect for Dallas head coach Tom Landry, he is just as quick to point out that he never completely understood the system he worked in while a member of the Cowboys.

"For instance," he says, "the philosophies of Dallas and Oakland are 180 degrees apart. I'll have to say that after I left (Dallas) I was better able to look back and see what Tom was trying to do.

Another thing Toomay, who grew up in California, never was quite able to grasp was the fervor for the game of football in the South. "Even though I played four years at Vanderbilt, that doesn't count because we never had the players to compete there," he says. "Football in the South is a different game than it is anywhere else in the country. The coaches, the fans, and even the other players get so wrapped up in it. I hadn't had much experience with that sort of thing when I first came to Dallas. It was a whole new world to me.

"Even today I'm still a little puzzled by it all. All the hype and stuff that goes on."

Now, however, it is something Pat Toomay worries less and less about. Football is behind him, a closed chapter in his life. "For a long time," he admits, "I had a recurring fear of being out of the game before I was ready. I'm glad I was ready when the time came."

MARGENE ADKINS

⭐

Right Place, Wrong Time

He had come to the Cowboys as a second round selection in the 1970 draft, already wise in the ways of professional football. At age 23, wide receiver Margene Adkins had already spent three All-Pro seasons with the Ottawa Rough Riders of the Canadian Football League before his arrival in the Dallas camp.

For the 5-11, 185-pound speedster it would be a homecoming of sorts. A graduate of Fort Worth's Kirkpatrick High, he had been an All-State selection before signing with Henderson County Junior College where he would earn junior college All-America honors twice.

Eager to test his talent in the professional ranks, Adkins chose to ignore a steady flow of major college scholarship offers and headed to the Canadian League which had no rules which prohibited signing an athlete before his college class graduated. That, Adkins decided, was the ideal route to go. Experience in the CFL could do nothing but enhance his chances when he was eligible to take a crack at the NFL. That opportunity would, then, come with the Cowboys. And despite the fact it would allow him to return to familiar surroundings, Adkins had serious doubts about the turn his career took during that '70 draft which saw West Texas State's Duane Thomas picked first, Vanderbilt's Bob Asher second and him third.

"To be quite honest about it," he says, "I was concerned over the fact Dallas already had so many great receivers. I had confidence in my ability and felt I'd proven myself with Ottawa, but Dallas already had Bob Hayes, Lance Alworth and Lance Rentzel. So, I think it is pretty understandable why I wasn't all that crazy about being drafted by the Cowboys. Once I was, though, I made up my mind to see what kind of impression I could make."

He arrived in his first NFL training camp with the understanding that the receiver jobs were open to the athlete who had the best pre-season. For two years Margene felt his pre-season performances were ahead of his more established rivals, yet he spent most of his two-year Cowboys career returning kicks and punts.

"I was young and confident and felt I should have been given the opportunity to start," he says, "but I never really made any waves about it. I just kept trying to learn, hoping the chance would eventually come. When I got to Dallas I found out that I didn't know nearly as much about the passing game as I had thought. All through high school and junior college and while I was in the Canadian League I never really ran routes. I just outran the people on defense.

"Ray Renfro was the receiver coach for Dallas when I arrived and he began working with me right away. He was a tremendous help. He was the man who taught me how to read defenses — something you've got to be able to do to play in the NFL."

Still, despite his 4.4 40 speed and his tremendous jumping ability, Adkins was on the Cowboys taxi squad when the 1970 season opened. "I was disappointed," he says, "because, as I've said, I felt I had played well in pre-season. I didn't always do things by the book, but I got results. Like in a pre-season game against Los Angeles when Roger Staubach called an audible at the line of scrimmage. I didn't pick it up and ran a post pattern instead of a fly pattern. But Roger picked me up and hit me for an 80-yard touchdown."

Once the '70 season got under way, he was activated for occasional kick return duties but his year-end totals did not satisfy him: seven kickoff returns for a 21.3-yard average and four punt returns for an 11-yard average. He did not catch a single pass.

During the off-season he asked to be traded but the Cowboys saw in him a valuable special teams performer and had him return for the '71 campaign. In addition to his specialty teams chores he did manage to make his presence known as a wide receiver, catching four passes for 53 yards.

Over the course of his brief tenure, he made it clear he favored Staubach over quarterback Craig Morton. "The reason was pretty simple," Margene says. "Craig just never would throw the ball to me. Not even in practice. When I was up to run a play in pass drills, Craig would just look my way and throw to another receiver, one of the big names working on the other side. I never understood why he wouldn't throw to me. On the other hand, I always felt Roger had confidence in my ability and was always trying to help me show the coaches what I could do."

After two seasons he was traded to New Orleans where he immediately became a starting wide receiver. Later in that '72 season, however, an ankle injury slowed his progress. "I did manage to lead the NFL in total yardage for kickoff returns that year, though," he says. "I received every kickoff we saw that year and had over 1,000 yards." Adkins then spent two years with the New York Jets before closing out his career in 1975 with the Chicago Fire of the World Football League.

"Timing is an important thing in pro football," he says. "Being in the right place at the right time is the difference in a lot of careers. In Dallas back then I was in the right place. It was just the wrong time."

FORREST GREGG
★
Hall of Fame Student

He had been called by the late, legendary Vince Lombardi, "the finest player I ever coached," and the record he established during his lengthy tenure with the Green Bay Packers served as adequate qualification. Eight times Forrest Gregg was an All-Pro offensive tackle, played in seven Pro Bowls and was a member of two Super Bowl championship teams. In 1977 he was inducted into the Pro Football Hall of Fame.

A native Texan who began his football career in Sulphur Springs, (then starred at SMU before becoming a second round draft pick by the Packers in 1956) Gregg would return to his homeland to finish out his career, playing the 1971 season with the Dallas Cowboys. It was a classic case of good timing. In the one season he was in Dallas, the Cowboys won the Super Bowl, enabling him to add a third championship ring to his collection.

"That was nice, but it wasn't the most important thing I took away from my year with the Cowboys," says the Cincinnati Bengals' head coach. "It was a great learning experience for me. As a player who wanted to become a coach, it was invaluable for me to get the opportunity to work in and learn a system that was different from the one I had been involved with at Green Bay. Without question, the system in Dallas — technique-wise, blocking, the offensive scheme — was far more complicated than that we had at Green Bay. It was one of the best things that ever happened to me so far as my progress as a coach is concerned."

One of the innovations which Gregg encountered upon his arrival in Dallas was an extensive weight program. "I didn't get into any kind of weight work until toward the end of my career," he says. "For years, going back to my college days, there was a resistance on the part of football players to lift because it was felt you would get muscle-bound and less mobile. The Cowboys, however, had obviously done their homework well and knew what they were doing. By the time I got to Dallas guys were beginning to realize that weight work prolonged careers and prevented injuries.

"I learned a great deal about the value of lifting while I was with the Cowboys, and when I left the next year to become the line coach of the San Diego Chargers, I immediately put my linemen on a weight program. Then, later, when I went to Cleveland (1975) as head coach, one of the first things I did was see that a strong weight program was established."

Even today Gregg insists that the '71 Cowboys team he played on was physically, the strongest team with which he has ever been associated. And, he offers numerous comparisons of the Green Bay Super Bowl winners and the Cowboys champions. "Both teams," he says, "were very experienced, very dedicated. They were teams with strong belief in themselves and their ability to win. And, there were a lot of similarities in Tom Landry and Vince Lombardi. Both were very dedicated and highly intelligent men. Though they motivated in different ways, they got the same results. Vince motivated, to a great degree, through fear which eventually turned into respect once you had been exposed to him and his system, while Landry, on the other hand, motivated a great deal through peer pressure; he established an attitude on his team that had every player wanting the other guys to know that he was pulling his weight, doing his part."

His brief time with the Cowboys, Gregg insists, was a "very pleasant experience."

"When you get right down to it, they contributed to me more than I contributed to them. But it was great to associate with some fine people, some fine athletes. During my years at Green Bay I got to know some of them pretty well and our relationships got stronger once I was with the Cowboys. I had — and still have — a tremendous amount of respect for guys like Bob Lilly, Jethro Pugh, Larry Cole, George Andrie and Walt Garrison."

Gregg became the head coach of the Cleveland Browns in 1975, and was named the NFL's coach of the year in '76. In 1979 he moved to the Canadian League to coach the Toronto Argonauts before Paul Brown summoned him to Cincinnati in 1980.

In January of 1982, Forrest Gregg made yet another trip to the Super Bowl, facing the 49ers as the coach of the Cincinnati Bengals. And although his team lost, he remains confident in his players and his guidance.

"One of the things that has benefitted me as a coach," he says, "is the fact I was able to play the game for as long as I did. Every year was a new learning experience for me."

MEL RENFRO

Pro Bowl MVP

It would seem a difficult question to pose to a man who, over the course of a dynamic career, was five times named All-Pro, and played in 10 Pro Bowls and four Super Bowls. A player whose defensive efforts dominated historical playoff games, he established an arm-load of Dallas Cowboys records in his 14-year tenure with the NFL.

Yet former cornerback Mel Renfro is quick to answer. It is obvious that the task of selecting his most memorable game is not that difficult. His answer, while qualified a bit, is quick, precise — and his memory for details of the moment are such that one can't help but believe him.

"There are a lot of great victories that come to mind," he says. "There were the Super Bowls, several big playoff wins, some come-from-behind victories. All were satisfying and special for various reasons. And, yes, there were some big, big disappointments — the Ice Bowl in Green Bay and losing the first Super Bowl.

"But the individual performance I got the biggest kick out of? That's easy."

Bear in mind this is a man who did it all. Would he choose, for instance, the Washington game in 1964 when he set a club record for kickoff return yardage in a single game, carrying four back for 168 yards? Or maybe that 90 yard interception return against St. Louis in 1965 for a touchdown? The entire '69 season wasn't too shabby inasmuch as he set a club record with ten interceptions. Maybe the 100-yard kickoff return against San Francisco in '65?

No, says Mel. The single-game performance he picks from a career which ran from 1964 to 1977 was not even a regular season game. The fact of the matter is, it came in a game he would have given his eye teeth not to have had to play in at all.

It was the 1971 Pro Bowl in Los Angeles.

"It was just after we had lost to Baltimore (16-13) in the Super Bowl and the last thing in the world I wanted to do was play another football game. I was really down after that loss. In fact, it was six full months before I got to the point where I wasn't sick inside every time I thought about that game.

"But I had been selected to play in the Pro Bowl — and it is quite an honor — so I went out to LA. Generally, you take advantage of sight-seeing opportunities and go out to all the nice restaurants; sort of make a vacation out of it. But I was in no mood for that kind of thing and I just spent the week staying in my room when we weren't practicing. I knew that every time I went out people were going to ask me about our losing the Super Bowl. About that tipped pass that gave the Colts a freak touchdown and their late field goal to win it. I just wasn't up to it, so I stayed to myself.

"I was in good shape, but I never did get really excited about playing the game. The truth is, I really didn't want to be there. I just felt it was something I was obligated to do."

Obligation or no, he went out into the massive Coliseum and returned punts for 82 and 54 yards — both for touchdowns — and was as close to perfect defensively as a cornerback can ever hope to get. By the end of the afternoon quarterbacks like Daryl Lamonica had sent receivers like Paul Warfield and Warren Wells in Renfro's direction 14 times — and never was there a completion. The NFC won the game, 27-6, and Renfro was honored as the Most Valuable Player.

"That day," he says, "took some of the sting out of the disappointment of losing the Super Bowl. It got my chin up."

The fact of the matter is Renfro seemed always to perform well in the Pro Bowl, going back to his first appearance in his rookie year. "That was an exciting thing," he remembers, "because I was on the field with so many players I had heard so much about in high school and college. In fact, John Wooten (former Cleveland Browns lineman and current Cowboys scout) was in that one."

In that first Pro Bowl appearance Renfro intercepted a pass and returned it for a touchdown.

"There were a lot of good times," he says. "I had the good fortune to come to the Cowboys when they were developing into a solid football team that did nothing but get better as time went on. We had our hard times, of course, getting over that hump of winning the big one, but finally we passed that barrier and proved ourselves to the world by winning that first Super Bowl in '72. That, I'd have to say, was the greatest feeling I ever had as a member of the Cowboys. But that was a team thing, something we had all worked long and hard for.

"Being the MVP in the Pro Bowl that previous year was more of a personal thing."

DUANE THOMAS

★

A Change of Perspective

Time, it must be noted, drastically changes perspectives. The Dallas Cowboys' 1971 season, for instance, is best remembered by those who chronicle the history of the franchise as the year Tom Landry's forces first won the Super Bowl and the one in which a moody, puzzling young running back named Duane Thomas refused to talk.

Now, with the advantage of years of retrospect, Thomas, one of the key figures in that highly successful season, refers to it as the most exciting time of his all too brief tenure with the Cowboys.

"That was the year the Dallas Cowboys knew they were going to win," the former first round draft pick from West Texas State recalls. "All that was necessary was to correct a few errors we had been making in the past and to become a little more detail-oriented and eliminate the mental mistakes. Everyone on the team scrutinized himself and determined what it was he had to do to make sure we didn't miss our chance at winning it all.

"There was an interesting chemistry on that '71 team," he continues. "Everyone was a student of the game. And as the year progressed and the games became more and more important, you could see the light get brighter. There was a steadily building enthusiasm for what was taking shape."

That season — climaxed by a decisive 24-3 victory over Miami in Super Bowl VI, a game in which Thomas' running, Roger Staubach's passing and a defense that was indestructible stood out — was the beginning of a tradition, Duane says. "That started the Super Bowl tradition for the Cowboys," he points out. "By going back and winning it, we established believability in the system: everything from Tom Landry's coaching to Gil Brandt's scouting. From that point on, the Dallas Cowboys symbolized excellence in pro football. That has carried through, right up to now.

"It is very rewarding to me to know that I shared in the establishment of that tradition. In the two years I was with the Cowboys, a lot of great things happened. In my rookie year (1970), we got past the last real barrier; we proved that the Cowboys could win the big game. Then the next year we won it all. That's when it all started.

"I never really understood it, but up to that point Dallas was doing something else. I can remember watching them play when I was in college and wondering why they always seemed to miss out with just one more victory left to win."

The difference in that championship season, he says, was the fact that everyone on the team, himself included, knew they were going to win. "It was like a movement," he says. "It made no difference who we were playing. We knew we had the ability and we knew we could get up for it. And we had such unbelievable weapons. And not just on offense. On defense we had people like Bob Lilly and the greatest set of linebackers who ever played the game in Dave Edwards, Lee Roy Jordan and Chuck Howley. The coordination between the line and the linebackers was unbelievable. It was like a right and left arm working together. And on offense we knew that we had any number of ways of beating people — with the running game, the passing game and even the kick return teams."

That season, just as the one before, Thomas was the man who paced the Cowboys' rushing attack. As a rookie he had gained 803 yards on 151 carries (for a 5.3 yards-per-attempt average) and in '71 he ran for 793 yards on 175 carries (a 4.5 average).

"You know," he says, "people still talk about the fact I didn't talk but, hey, Bob Lilly, who was one of the greatest leaders we had, said more on his TV commercials than he said in his whole career with the Cowboys. He didn't have to say anything. In truth, I found his charisma rather quaint. But after I was around him for a little while I realized how effective he was.

"Really, though, we didn't have a lot of people who needed motivating. That team was self-motivated to do something really special, to be a part of the team's history. When you have an opportunity like that, you don't have to have someone help you get ready to do your job."

WALT GARRISON

Rise From the Ashes

It would be one of those milestone days in Dallas Cowboys history, a time when yet another breakthrough was finally accomplished. As 59,625 looked on in Kezar Stadium, most expecting to see John Brodie lead his 49ers into the Super Bowl, the Cowboys made their rise from the ashes complete.

Five-Four at one point in the season, Dallas came together to win five in a row and on January 3, 1971 squared off against the 49ers for the NFC Championship and won, 17-10. The Cowboys conquered with the style of play Walt Garrison says, he has always felt wins the big games.

"When you get into the playoffs, you have to be prepared to control the ball offensively. That day against San Francisco we did that when we had to." Which is the reason the game remains today one of the favored memories for the former standout Cowboys fullback.

"It was a big game for a number of reasons," the rodeoing Cowboy remembers. "We had gotten off to a really shaky start that season so we needed to do something that would disprove a lot of negative thinking about us. Then, it was our first NFC championship and, of course, it was the game that got us into our first Super Bowl.

"But the most enjoyable thing I remember about it was the fact that in the fourth quarter it was imperative that we control the ball. The 49ers had the kind of offense that could get six against you in a hurry so we couldn't afford to let them have the opportunity. In the last quarter we had the ball for almost 10 minutes." (9:30 to be exact.)

Two of the big factors in that afternoon of ball control were Duane Thomas who ran for 143 yards in 27 carries and Garrison who managed 71 yards on 17 trips.

Garrison's accomplishment becomes even more impressive when one recalls that early in the game he was helped off with a cracked ankle yet returned to action in a brief period of time.

"Any other back," remembers coach Tom Landry, "would have stayed out for the rest of the day. I remember going over to Walt and asking if he thought he could go and he said yes, that he was going to be okay. Actually, it was obvious that he was just about to die. But he was that determined to play." Determination, in fact, was the keynote of Dallas' performance that day.

"The defense was unreal all afternoon," Garrison remembers. "Lee Roy Jordan picked off a Brodie pass early in the second half that gave us posses-

sion inside the 49ers 20 and Duane made an incredible run for a 13-yard touchdown. It was one of those plays where he did a lot of it on his own after seeing that the hole he was supposed to hit was closed off."

That touchdown scamper, coupled with an earlier 21-yard field goal by Mike Clark put the Cowboys into the lead.

Later Mel Renfro picked off another Brodie pass to set up one of Dallas' most impressive drives of the day. When Garrison and Thomas didn't get tough yardage through the San Francisco defense, quarterback Craig Morton came up with some key passes. Facing a critical second and 23 at the Dallas 27, he hit Garrison on a screen pass which was good for the needed 23 yards. Later an interference call on a Morton-to-Bob Hayes pass moved the Cowboys to the SF five. With the 49er defense blitzing, Morton dropped a short pass off to the slightly limping Garrison who scored with 4:35 left in the game.

"Catching the passes, particularly the one for the touchdown, was exciting," Garrison says, "but when all was said and done it was the short yardage plays, the ones that picked up first downs and kept drives going, that were most satisfying."

For the afternoon the Dallas rushing attack accounted for 229 yards while Morton's passing added only 90 to the total. The 49ers rushed for just 61 yards against the Cowboys defense. And although a majority of the near-capacity crowd might have been disappointed, it was — with Walt Garrison's assistance — a game played in championship style.

IKE THOMAS
★
He Ran to Daylight

He had arrived as a second round draft choice from across town, the highest picked Bishop College player in the school's history. And yet the rookie found conditions crowded at the position to which he aspired. The prospects of the young defensive back unseating the likes of Mel Renfro, Herb Adderley, Cornell Green, Cliff Harris or Mark Washington were slim.

Thus it was that Ike Thomas spent the first part of the 1971 season as a member of the taxi squad. Only when the veteran Adderley collided with a television camera and was injured did the Hot Springs, Ark., native with 4.5 speed get a chance to work at cornerback. He started against St. Louis and drew more than his share of attention. He knocked down a couple, had a goal-line interception in his hands only to drop it, and drew a costly interference call. "I did some good things and some bad things," Thomas remembers of his defensive debut. "About what you could expect from a rookie."

On the other hand Thomas later did some things far from expected. For instance: The first time he received a kickoff he returned it 89 yards for a Thanksgiving Day touchdown against the Los Angeles Rams. A week later, against the Jets, he scored again on the opening kickoff, returning it 101 yards.

Which wasn't bad for a youngster who had never returned kicks as a member of the Bishop Tigers.

"Coach Landry asked me if I thought it might be something I would like to do," Thomas recalls, "and I told him I'd give it a try. I honestly had no idea what to expect when I lined up to receive that first one. Man, I just took off running, looking for some daylight." He found 89 yards of it.

"What I eventually learned about returning kicks," he says, "is that the faster you can get to the wedge, the better off you are. There's no time for a lot of dancing around. You just take off and go as fast as you can and if an opening appears, go after it." That was what he did that December day against the Jets when he went 101 to tie the club record set in 1962 by Amos Marsh. To this day they share the mark.

Going into the final three games of the '71 season, Thomas needed seven returns to have enough to qualify for the NFL title. He would fall three returns shy — with a 47 yards-per-return average.

"I had some enjoyable experiences in my pro career," the recently retired Thomas says, "but going all the way with that kickoff on my first try has to be up there at the top."

The congestion in the secondary, however, did not clear the following summer as he reported to camp and he was eventually traded to Green Bay along with punter Ron Widby. He was with the Packers for three seasons before moving to the Charlotte Hornets of the World Football League. There his long range return heroics continued. "After a game against Jacksonville," he says, "I was named Player of the Week. I had returned a kickoff 96 yards, recovered a fumble and intercepted a pass (from his strong safety position). My award was to have been a color television set but when I went down to pick it up they wouldn't give it to me. It just so happened that that was the same week the league folded."

Thomas thus spent the final six games of the season as a member of the Buffalo Bills before going to the Canadian League where he played key roles on two Toronto playoff teams and then finished out his career with the Hamilton Tiger-Cats.

BILLY TRUAX

An Unselfish Act

The Dallas Cowboys, in the playoffs for the sixth straight time, had, on that cold, blustery day in Minnesota, scored a 20-12 victory over the Vikings in the opening round. It was the beginning of the post-season campaign that later saw San Francisco fall in the NFC title game, and Dallas reign as Super Bowl champions, following the defeat of the Miami Dolphins, 24-3.

For tight end Billy Truax, a gifted athlete who had labored successfully for seven years as a member of the Los Angeles Rams, earning a Super Bowl ring in his first season with the Cowboys was a treasured milestone. But on that day against the Vikings, he remembers, Dallas finally stepped over a barrier which had long been a part of the team; they had come away from the initial playoff game with a victory. It would be the launching pad for the most memorable experience of his professional career.

"George Allen's first year with the Rams," Truax remembers, "we went 8-6, and after that we regularly went into the playoffs, but always lost in the opening round. While I think Allen had a little bit of a coaching edge on everyone back then — maybe even intimidated a lot of people — we always seemed to have spent ourselves by the time the playoffs arrived. It would all end and you were left with an empty feeling."

Then came a call from Dallas Coach Tom Landry, informing him that the Cowboys had traded Pettis Norman for Truax. It would be the first step toward fulfilling that empty spot in Truax's career. "I realized it was a great opportunity for me," the successful Dallas realtor says today. "When Coach Landry called, I told him I would do everything I could to help the Cowboys to win the Super Bowl."

Even if it included shuttling plays from the bench with fellow tight end Mike Ditka. "The Staubach-Morton quarterback shuttle was still in use when I first arrived, so I naturally assumed it would just boil down to a competitive situation between Ditka and myself to see who started at tight end. I had spent my entire football career in systems where there were 11 starters and a quarterback who called the plays in the huddle."

When Landry finally announced that the starting quarterback duties would be carried out by Staubach, Truax and Ditka were selected as the play messengers. It took some getting used to. "But," Truax states, "it's hard to raise much fuss when you're successful."

By the time Dallas had moved past the opening round of the playoffs, Truax had no reason for discontentment. The very real possibility of owning a Super Bowl ring existed. An example of how much that eventual victory over the Dolphins in Miami would mean to him is mirrored in the fact that in his desk drawer at work Truax keeps a column written by Joan Ryan, wife of former Cleveland quarterback Frank Ryan. "She wrote, 'Stakes are high in the Super Bowl. Winning it means more than money and fame. It eliminates all the what-ifs. With no what-ifs after the Super Bowl, the winner is a contented man who can tell everyone, I was there, I won, and I am . . .' She really touched on it. To have reached that point, to have been a part of that team was a rare opportunity. My time had come."

It was an achievement, however, triggered by that initial playoff success in Minnesota. "We had an outstanding offense that day. Duane (Thomas) ran well and Walt (Garrison) was super. I don't recall catching even one pass, but I blocked well. After it was over, I had a great feeling of accomplishment.

"I doubt that there was anyone on the team who realized better than I did how important that victory was. It had been a very intense situation for us — just like all playoff games are. Suddenly you are the focus of national attention and aware that there is no tomorrow, no next week to come back. How well I knew it all could come to an end that day. I had been there too often before. Once we got the game behind us, though, I was confident that we would keep winning. By the time we were getting ready to play Miami I was convinced the game would be a rout."

Everyone who has ever been there, Truax says, will tell you that the playoffs are a totally different ball game. Suddenly, after months of hard work, you find yourself in a single elimination tournament. "You stand to lose so much," he points out. "What you do once you manage to get into the playoffs is begin a day-to-day existence until it's finally over."

The game of professional football, he says, is one of graduating stages: "You have different mental plateaus, beginning with a realization of the need for a good off-season training program. Then, there's training camp where you simply survive, hoping to get it behind you and to have gained something from it. You then spend the entire season just trying to get into the playoffs. Once that is accomplished, it all begins coming together; the pressure, the attention of the media, the realization that there is a great deal of money on the line. Once in the playoffs, every single play is a big play. Lose, and you find yourself thinking back to a block you should have made, a ball you should have caught, things like that."

All of which makes the memories of that '71 season all the sweeter. Even the fact that a damaged knee may have reduced Truax's effectiveness in the Super Bowl has failed to dim the memory. "My knee was in pretty bad shape by then (it would require post-season surgery) but I tried to just put it out of my mind. A writer who was aware of the fact that it was bothering me a great deal asked why I was playing on it. I told him that I was a part of the greatest team ever assembled and there was no way I was going to miss any of it — not a minute."

Still, it would have been nice, he admits, had he been at full speed for the Super Bowl. "Coach Landry had put in a tight end reverse for the game and when I tried to run it in practice, the knee just buckled. It was obvious, then, that the play would have to be run with Ditka. Somehow, though, during the game our shuttling got mixed up and the play was called as I went in. I ran about halfway out on the field and met Mike coming off. It suddenly dawned on me again what was at stake. I stopped Mike and told him the reverse had been called so for him to stay in. He nearly scored; went down to the five or so on it."

At that stage, with pro football's greatest accomplishment within grasp, personal achievements were secondary to Billy Truax. He had passed the barrier in that first game of the playoffs and wanted nothing to block the final mile on the road to being a part of the best team in the game.

His time, he well knew, had come.

LANCE ALWORTH

✦

An Honest-To-Goodness Miracle

Speaking from Canton, Ohio where he was awaiting ceremonies which would officially induct him into the Professional Football Hall of Fame, Lance Alworth was talking of another highlight in a career filled with highlights. It was not his All-America career at the University of Arkansas nor his glory days as a member of the San Diego Chargers he was reflecting on. Rather, it was a zany afternoon in 1972 when, as a member of the Dallas Cowboys, he witnessed his first honest-to-goodness miracle.

"Never before or after was I ever involved in a game like that one," he says. "Even after we had the chance to watch it on film and see how it all happened, it was hard to believe."

His reference was to the Cowboys' 30-28 victory over San Francisco in the Division playoffs in '72; the game in which Dallas scored two touchdowns in the last minute and a half to clinch the victory. And while it was not a game in which his performance would demand the spotlight — though he did catch a Craig Morton pass for a 28-yard touchdown just before intermission — Alworth looks back on it as one of the most memorable games in his storied career.

"I've never seen such an emotional display by a team after a game," he says. "We all went a little crazy, hugging each other, rolling around on the ground out there in front of 60,000 (61,214 to be exact). It was all so unbelievable. I mean, can you imagine Larry Cole turning cartwheels? That's the kind of emotion there was."

Indeed, it was one of those happenings hard for even those who served as eyewitnesses to believe. And, there were any number of people who were at the game who didn't see it. Many of the writers, resigned to a 49ers victory,

were already crammed into elevators enroute to the field and missed both of Dallas' comeback touchdowns. The San Francisco assistant coaches who had been calling the plays from the pressbox had deserted their post and were on their way to join the celebration. Many people were already well on their way to their cars in the parking lot.

"That was when there was still some question about who the No. 1 quarterback was," Alworth remembers. "Craig had started and had us on the board a couple of times in the first half (it was 21-13 at halftime), but the 49ers came out and got another one in the third. We could have gotten back into it earlier when a long bomb got away from Bob Hayes — it was one of those near misses that can really break your heart. So close. At any rate, with just a minute or so left in the third period, Coach Landry put Staubach in. (It had been a dismal year for Staubach who had suffered a serious shoulder injury against Los Angeles during the exhibition season.)"

Late in the game, Roger began connecting with Billy Parks. With time ticking away he hit on three straight to move the ball to the 49ers 20-yard line, then fired a touchdown pass to Parks. The clock showed 1:10 to play and the score stood at 28-23.

It is safe to say there was not a knowledgeable football fan in attendance who did not anticipate Toni Fritsch's off-side kick. San Francisco's Preston Riley certainly was ready for it. Still, the ball hit him in the chest and bounced away into the arms of Dallas' Mel Renfro.

"Even at that it seemed like a long shot," Alworth remembers, "but you could feel the tensiison building. Suddenly the snide remarks the 49ers defensive players had been making were replaced by serious expressions. You could almost feel that they were wondering how in the world they had allowed themselves to get in a position like this, to be in a fight for their lives in a game which they had had such control over just a few minutes earlier. On the other hand, we were really pumped up. We saw that we had a chance."

And Staubach went to work. With 1:03 left he again went to Parks, the hottest receiver on the squad that day, hitting him on a corner route at the San Francisco 10. Suddenly a hush fell over the crowd which had been a chorus of premature celebration just minutes earlier. All hopes of a local celebration died on the next play when Staubach fired a perfect shot over the middle to Ron Sellers for the final yards and the winning touchdown.

Sellers' end zone dance would initiate the celebration of the comeback Cowboys. "Even Coach Landry was running around hugging people," Alworth recalls.

214

CHUCK HOWLEY

★

A Confident Feeling

It was, he remembers, a time of great confidence. And embarrassment. And, ultimately, overwhelming satisfaction. Chuck Howley, now sheltered from the violent world of professional football, a successful Dallas businessman, was reflecting on Super Bowl VI, January 1972.

Howley, the man Cowboy outside linebackers are now measured against, spoke in a savoring voice about that day — when the Cowboys demolished Miami, 24-3.

"You know, confidence is a funny thing," he pointed out. "It isn't something you can talk yourself into on the day of a game. It's something that builds, grows. With maturity. So, when I say we went into that game confident that we were going to win it, I don't mean to imply that we simply woke up that morning and said, 'Hey, we can win this thing.' It was something we had known, had felt for quite some time. Through most of the season, in fact. And it wasn't just a few of the guys on the team. It was a feeling shared by everyone, I know even Coach Landry has said he felt sure we were going to win."

And win they did, in one of the most decisive Super Bowl victories ever achieved.

While the defense was shutting down the Dolphins' attack, (powerful Bob Lilly once dropping Miami quarterback Bob Griese for a 30-yard loss) the offense, led by quarterback Roger Staubach, the game's Most Valuable Player, and running back Duane Thomas, Walt Garrison and Calvin Hill, set a Super Bowl rushing mark of 252 yards.

Kicker Mike Clark got Dallas on the board first with a 9-yard field goal. Then followed a brilliant 76-yard drive capped by a 7-yard Staubach-to-Lance Alworth scoring pass. The Dallas offense later upped the margin with a 71-yard, 8-play drive which saw the controversial Thomas sweep into the end zone from three yards out.

Early in the fourth period Miami faced a third-and-four situation at its own 49 and Griese dropped back to pass to running back Jim Kiick. Howley, a thorn in the Dolphins' side all afternoon, was knocked down, then bounced up to step in front of the intended receiver and intercept the ball. All that remained between him and a sure touchdown was a caravan of Dallas blockers. He began his run toward the goal, six points a certainty. But at about the 15 he began to stumble. At the nine, with no Dolphin player near him, he slipped, lost his footing, and fell.

"Imagine," Howley laughs. "Nobody around me, blockers everywhere, and I just crash. Needless to say it was a little embarrassing. Lilly and (George) Andrie looked back and couldn't believe it. At that particular moment I was wishing it had been a very deep hole I had fallen into."

No damage was done, however, as Staubach later hit Mike Ditka with a seven-yard scoring toss to ice the victory.

A moment of embarrassment aside, however, it would ultimately rank as the most satisfying victory of Howley's career. It would even rank above the unprecedented achievement of having been cited as the MVP in the previous Super Bowl when a last second Baltimore field goal defeated Dallas, 16-13. "That was a nice feeling," he admits, "but the ball just didn't bounce right for us that day against the Colts. I thought we played well enough to win it, but it just wasn't to be."

"I think maybe we got a little caught up in all the hoopla of the game that year and weren't totally concentrating on what we had to do. The next year we did. We knew what Miami was going to do. Maybe against Baltimore there was some doubt that we could win. Maybe we were a little too nervous. None of those things got in our way as we prepared for the Dolphins. We were a mature team which went down there to get a job done. And we did."

By knowing that they were going to do so.

CLINT LONGLEY

⭐

The Mad Bomber

He was then, as now, a free spirit. A happy-go-lucky kid rolling with the flow and enjoying the good life. When he wasn't off somewhere in West Texas hunting rattlesnakes or partying with old Abilene Christian college buddies, he would turn his attention to becoming a professional quarterback. And on occasion Clint Longley gave indication that he would one day mature into one of the NFL's finest.

For two seasons with the Dallas Cowboys he labored as Roger Staubach's understudy, coming off the bench in his rookie season of 1974 to engineer a Thanksgiving Day comeback against Washington which still stands as an important part of pro football's folklore. The following year he got a starting chance against the New York Jets while Roger rested for the playoffs and rang up yet another victory.

Then in the training camp prior to his third season there was the infamous altercation with Staubach. Punches were thrown, angry words were exchanged, and Longley hit the road. In a manner of speaking he's been on it ever since.

216

His career with the Cowboys, once so promising, ended in a puzzling sequence of events. Some insist the arrival of a new quarterback threat on the scene, a youngster named Danny White who had played well in the World Football League before it folded, caused the easy-going Longley to withdraw. Others suggest he came to resent the suggestions Staubach made to him during practices. Longley will no longer discuss the matter, considering it closed and private.

Whatever the cause, things began to come apart in Thousand Oaks in 1976. Twice in the final week of training camp Longley and Staubach were involved in fisticuffs, the last encounter coming on the final day of camp. Longley, having been summoned to Landry's office for a meeting, chose to ignore the invitation and instead reported to the training room. There, he waited for Staubach's arrival and got in one final round-house punch before bumming a ride from a Dallas radio announcer to Los Angeles International.

The strange, confusing scene, played out by an angry young man, was far removed from that heroic day two years earlier when the entire nation watched him defeat the Redskins.

Coming into that Texas Stadium date with Washington, the Cowboys were struggling along with a 6-5 record and spent the first half doing little more than going through the motions. By intermission the Redskins led 9-3 as nothing but field goals had gone on the scoreboard.

Then in the third period a name from the past came back to haunt the Cowboys defense as Duane Thomas took a pass from Washington quarterback Billy Kilmer for the day's first touchdown. And shortly thereafter Staubach was helped from the field, dazed. Enter Longley, a rookie who had not set foot on the field for a single regular season down. Trailing by nine and with a rookie at the helm, the Cowboys' chances were a long shot.

Still, Longley had success with his first offensive drive, moving the Cowboys downfield before hitting tight end Billy Joe DuPree with a 35-yard touchdown pass. Then he moved Dallas into the lead with a drive culminated by a one-yard touchdown dive by fullback Walt Garrison. No sooner had Texas Stadium hope risen, however, than Thomas broke on a 19-yard scoring run that put the Redskins back on top with just 45 seconds left to play. The stands began to empty even as Longley prepared for his last chance.

With 35 seconds remaining he had moved the Cowboys to midfield, but the chances of connecting on the long bomb were reduced when Washington sent seven defensive backs onto the field. Choosing to ignore the odds the prevent defense presented him with, Longley sent wide receiver Drew Pearson sprinting down the sidelines and lofted a high, arching spiral toward the goal line. Pearson took the ball at the four and danced into the end zone to tie things at 23-all. Efren Herrera's extra point gave Dallas the win and Longley hero status.

"It was," one veteran member of the Cowboys team would later point out, "a victory of the uncluttered mind." His reference was, of course, to the fact Longley had gone into the critical situation with little knowledge of what was possible and impossible. The following year he directed that 31-21 victory over the Jets for his finale.

Longley tried to recapture the position that was lost in that final week at Thousand Oaks in '76, but never did. There were stops in San Diego and St. Louis and eventually Hamilton of the Canadian League. He didn't stay long anywhere. On occasion there would be slight mention of him in the press, but before other reporters could find him he was gone, destination unknown. Clint Longley became, in a sense, a ghost personality.

For a while he played with and helped coach the Shreveport (La.) Steamers of the American Football Association.

"It was fun," he says, "and provided me an opportunity to stay around the game. I'm not your typical frustrated jock, mind you, but it was fun." It was not, he insists, a road he hoped would lead him back into the big time.

"No, I don't aspire to get back into the NFL," he says. "The truth is, I don't do much aspiring at all. Oh, if someone called and asked me to come to camp, I'd probably do it. But I don't expect that to happen." The fact of the matter is he is quite happy with his current lifestyle, living in Rockwall near Dallas, writing sports for the weekly Lakeside News.

No, he says, he is not sure why he failed to earn a spot for himself elsewhere in the NFL after leaving Dallas. "Football is a fickle business. In the NFL your ability and your longevity are not really that related. A lot depends on circumstances."

Longley does not agree with those who insist his clash with Staubach turned his promising career to a downhill slide. "I can't really say that," he says. "I had plenty of opportunities. There are a lot of things that enter into how things work out. What happened between Roger and me is something I don't think about. That was a long time ago. And it isn't as if I didn't make it. I played in the NFL with one of the top teams ever to play the game. I went to a Super Bowl and, while I didn't get to play in the game, I had the opportunity of being a part of it. That's what every player in pro ball wants to do. It was a great thrill, something I'll never forget."

On the other hand, it is not something he dwells on. Now 30, he still plays life loose.

DUANE CARRELL

★

The Passing Punter

It will be remembered as the day Clint Longley saved. On that 1974 Thanksgiving afternoon, with starting quarterback Roger Staubach on the sidelines, the young Abilene Christian rookie came in shooting from the hip in the middle of the third quarter and, with a bomb to Drew Pearson in the final seconds, lifted the Cowboys to a 24-23 victory over the Washington Redskins.

There was, however, yet another passer involved in a bit of razzle-dazzle that afternoon. Duane Carrell doesn't like to brag, but he can point to a 1.000 record as a passer. Which isn't bad for a guy who makes his living punting.

"It was early in the game," the 29 year-old Lake Highlands resident recalled recently. "Back then, Washington's punt rush was considered the very best in the league. They came at you strong, trying to block everything. Because they were so aggressive, we had put in a pass play to use if the opportunity arose."

Said opportunity came to be the very first time the Cowboys were faced with a punting situation. With the ball near midfield, Landry sent Carrell in to attempt his first pass as a professional.

It worked like a dream.

With Benny Barnes in to serve as a blocking back, Carrell took the snap and, much to the surprise of the Redskins, flipped a quick pass to the man who normally would have been trying to lend protection. Barnes took it 35 critical yards, setting up a field goal. "It was an exciting thing for me," Carrell says. "Even when we worked on it during the week I was a little doubtful that Coach Landry would use it because it was such a high risk kind of play. But our position on the field happened to be just right, so we went with it."

Carrell had never thrown a pass in a game before. Nor has he thrown one since. "Which is fine with me," he grins. "I'll just let the perfect record stand and not mess with it."

He originally came to the Cowboys at mid-season in '74 after the World Football League and the Jacksonville Sharks, whom he had been punting for, had given up the ghost. The Cowboys punting game was a problem spot at about the same time and a call for help went out. Before the season would end Carrell would have punted 40 times for a respectable 39.8 average, booming one 59 yards.

Still, the following year he was traded to Los Angeles. Then in '76 to the Jets. The next year he opened with the Jets and closed with the St. Louis Cardinals. Being a professional football player, he admits, was fast becoming a king-sized hassle. He decided to retire and went to work in the food brokerage business in Dallas, content to limit his athletic endeavors to a two-or three-mile jog a few times a week.

Then came a call from Tampa Bay. The Bucs, head coach John McKay admitted, were having punting troubles. It was suggested that Carrell see if he could get into kicking shape, and upon doing so, give Tampa Bay a call. "I can honestly say that it never occurred to me that I would actually make a trip to Florida. But, the idea of going out and doing some punting excited me. I was getting a little tired of just running and thought maybe that would break up the routine some and still offer me some exercise. So I started kicking the ball around."

And, whether he admits it or not, he again toyed with the idea of returning to pro ball. "My thinking later was that if Tampa Bay were to offer me a really exceptional salary, something more than I probably was actually worth, I would consider it strongly. I was relatively sure, though, that the kind of offer I'm talking about would never be forthcoming."

Neither did he have reason to think that he might hear from Cowboys player personnel director Gil Brandt in the summer of 1979. The thought didn't even occur to him when he heard that Dallas punter Danny White had broken a thumb.

And when the call did come he was rather tied up . . . in traffic on the LBJ Freeway. He had, in fact, just been involved in a three-car fender bender and was waiting for the investigating officers to arrive on the scene when he called home from a nearby phone booth and his wife relayed the message that the Cowboys had called.

So, depositing his change, he immediately placed a long distance call to Brandt, heard the proposition, spoke briefly with Landry, and agreed to take an evening flight to Thousand Oaks.

In less than a week he would go from food broker to the Cowboys kicker against the Seattle Seahawks. All without having to pack anything more than a suitcase.

"That was the great thing about it," he points out. "It didn't disrupt our family life a bit. In fact, it was something that had everyone kind of excited. My boss granted me a leave of absence on the spot and wished me luck."

"And it felt comfortable being back with a team whose system I already was familiar with."

Carrell harbored no illusions about the duration of his last stay. "I'd been around football long enough to know not to look past tomorrow," he says. "They told me that Danny would be out for maybe as long as six weeks, and when he got well, the job was his again."

PERCY HOWARD

★

One Catch, One Touchdown

He came to the Dallas Cowboys as a free agent, a standout collegiate basketball player who the scouting department and computers felt might be able to make the changeover to the National Football League.

And though his NFL career was brief, Percy Howard, wide receiver, left his mark in the memorable 1975 season. He has, in fact, become the subject of a trivia question referring to that day in Miami when he came in for injured Golden Richards and caught a 34-yard touchdown pass from Roger Staubach. It was the only time he touched the ball all day. One-for-one and a TD in the biggest game in town: Super Bowl X.

Needless to say, it is a moment the Dallas resident still remembers vividly.

"A few series earlier I had run a similar pattern," he recalls, "and got past (Pittsburgh defender) Mel Blount, but Roger went to the other side of the field. I was trying to play a little psyche game with Mel, so I made a big show of disappointment over the fact Roger hadn't thrown to me.

"Mel laughed and said, 'Hey, if you really think you were open why don't you get Roger to call the pattern again?' I told him I definitely would. Sure enough, a little later (Tom) Landry sent the play in and I got past Blount. He knew I had him whipped even before I caught the ball. I'll never forget how big his eyes got when I did catch it."

It was a catch which narrowed the Steelers' margin to 21-17. But, says Howard, there is a later pass, one he never got a hand on, that stays with him to this day. It was in the game's fading moments and Staubach fired a desperation alley-oop pass into the end zone. Howard went up along with Steelers defenders Glenn Edwards, Andy Russell and J. T. Thomas. The ball was batted away by one of the Pittsburgh Steelers before Howard had a chance at it.

"That's one I wish I had back," he says. "After looking at films of the play from various angles, I think if I had jumped earlier I might have had a chance at it. But, I was hit before I had the opportunity."

There were, in fact, a lot of things which happened to the 6-4, 215-pound Howard before he really had an opportunity. His was a one-year career that ended in the pre-season of 1976, when he damaged a knee on a reverse against the Denver Broncos. Three times he had the knee operated on before it was properly mended. And when it was, football was out. "After Super Bowl X," he says, "I think I was ready to make a place for myself in the NFL. But the injury put an end to that idea. I just had some bad breaks."

The first of which came in his first professional game.

"I was running back the kickoff in the first exhibition game of the year against Los Angeles and had my cheekbone fractured. I spent the rest of the summer in Dallas, getting well, and rejoined the team after it came back home from camp." He mended in time to be active on the kicking teams. And the following summer, against Denver, he saw action when a rookie quarterback named Danny White came on in relief. "I caught three that day, one post pattern for about 40 yards," Howard remembers. (But his TD catch against Pittsburgh remains his one and only official catch in the NFL.)

"I was a Danny White fan back then and still am. I always felt he would do well when he got his chance."

Though his tenure in the league was brief, Howard looks back on it as a time in which the pluses outweighed the minuses. "It was a great experience for me," he says. "The Super Bowl, of course, was the high point. But there were other good times, too, like my first rookie scrimmage we had against the San Diego rookies. I caught four and scored two touchdowns that day."

Which was a different sensation than averaging 17 points-per-game and hauling down eight rebounds as an Austin Peay forward with leg springs enough to jump center.

"I had never really thought much about playing football until I began to get a few letters from some pro teams. The Steelers, Giants and Falcons all contacted me in addition to Dallas. I remember Cornell Green (who had also been a basketball player-turned-pro football player) came down to try me out. There was never any question what team I would go with. I had always been a Dallas Cowboys fan and was a big admirer of Bob Hayes.

"Having been a part of it, even for just a year, is a nice memory," he says. Even if the knee aches now and then and the desire to have one more shot at that last reception comes to mind now and again.

JIM JENSEN

★

The Idle Ball-Carrier

He had come to the Cowboys as one of college football's premier running backs, a 6-3, 235-pounder who had not only started as a key member of the University of Iowa football team, but had also displayed his unique combination of strength and agility by earning track letters as a shot putter and hurdler.

Obviously, Jim Jensen promised to be something special, and the Dallas Cowboys made him the second player selected in their 1976 draft. They then spent the better part of a year and a training camp trying to figure out what to do with his particular skills. What they settled on, really, was the fact he was a big plus on specialty teams, particularly when teamed with Butch Johnson as a deep back on kickoff returns. Those moments aside, however, Jim Jensen spent an entire season watching other people do the thing he felt he could do the best.

"I spent an entire season never carrying the football," he says, "and it was a frustrating experience. I tried to tell myself to just watch the older backs and learn as much as I could, and I did that. Still, to go a full year without carrying the ball got to me. In fact, by the time I was traded to Denver I'd have to say I was a little scared that I might not be able to get the job done."

The fact that he was Denver's second leading ground gainer in 1979 with a 3.8 yards-per-carry average is testimony to the fact he could.

When he arrived in camp at Thousand Oaks in his rookie season it was quickly apparent to him that the Cowboys weren't sure where his talents fit into their offensive plans. "They started working me at halfback, then moved me to fullback, then to tight end, and finally back to halfback again. I was afraid by then that I was going to have to go through the entire cycle again."

With the likes of Robert Newhouse, Scott Laidlaw, Doug Dennison, Preston Pearson and Charlie Young on hand, it was difficult to get noticed as a back. In fact, the only offensive play Jensen ran in 1976 was as a tight end. "And that didn't work out too well, either," he says. "I was the primary receiver on a short yardage pass and wound up getting all tangled up with the linebacker and wasn't even close to getting open."

His situation with the Cowboys got no better in 1977 as Dallas drafted an exciting young running back named Tony Dorsett. On the Monday before the regular season was to open, he was called to Tom Landry's office.

"That's a hard time for anybody," Jim points out. "I had played quite a bit during the pre-season and suddenly I was being told there was no place for

me on the team. Shoot, yes, it's a discouraging thing to deal with. But it was much nicer to hear the word 'trade' rather than 'waived.' I remember when Landry said I had been traded that I immediately began thinking, 'Oh, no. Detroit, Buffalo, Kansas City.' When he said Denver, my spirits lifted. I said, 'Hey, that's not too bad.' A lot of guys I've known since I've been in the league have said if they were traded they would like for it to be to Denver. It's a great team and in an absolutely fantastic area.

"I had gone up there to ski a couple of times while living in Dallas, so I was actually excited about the move."

And obviously it worked well. After four seasons, he felt more comfortable about his status as an athlete. Jim Jensen proved he could make it in the NFL. "The first year I was with Denver," he says, "I began to play immediately. That was a big boost for me. I missed the entire '78 season with a bad knee, but when I came back the next season there was no doubt in my mind. Nothing like the doubts I dealt with after that first season in Dallas. But I learned a lot there, really. I gained valuable knowledge about pro football and the way it works."

Any particularly memorable Dallas incident? "Naw, not really. The thing I most remember is that one play as a tight end and the fact that just about every time I got to work in the backfield in practice I wound up either running into Robert Newhouse or bumping into Roger Staubach."

Obviously, times finally changed for the young running back for whom they couldn't find a spot.

DOUG DENNISON

☆

He Understood His Role

He had turned down scholarship offers to attend such recognized universities as Pitt and Brown to go to tiny Kutztown State, a school light years removed from ever being branded a football factory.

Even then Doug Dennison, a running back of no small ability, was a man of unique priorities. Football, for him, was enjoyable, something in which he performed well. Yet it was not the end-all. Education, Christian values and family held priority over athletics. It would be the same after he had made the free agent transition into the NFL, earning a place on the Cowboys roster in the summer of 1974.

That Dallas ever found him remains something of a mystery to the former back, still referred to as the best goal-line runner in Cowboys history. "I knew when I decided to go to a small school that my chances of getting the kind of recognition that might earn me the attention of pro scouts would be lessened," he says, "but by the time I was ready to go to college I had reached a point in my life where I realized athletics were not the highlight. I was already looking ahead to the future, a career. I guess I was what is best described as serious-minded."

Add to that the fact he spent half of his senior year on the sidelines, suffering from a knee injury, and it is no small wonder that his was not one of the names called during the annual college draft. "It was really funny how things worked out; I didn't pick the Cowboys, they picked me. In my senior year I got something in the mail from them just about every week, telling me they had their eye on me and were interested. They were the only team that contacted me."

Call it, then, another victory for the touted Cowboys scouting system. Signed to a free agent contract, he made the team in 1974 and would remain for four seasons, once leading the team in rushing.

"I'll never forget the pressure I felt during training camp my rookie year," he says. "Pro football was a great opportunity for me, and I was determined to take advantage of it. I really had no idea of how good I was, but I knew that if I did everything in my power to make the team I would get a fair chance. So I just kept my head down and worked, hoping I wouldn't be the next guy released. I had a pretty good pre-season game against Houston and I think that earned me a spot on the team."

Certainly, he insists, it wasn't his "vast knowledge" of the game. "Coming from a small school to the Dallas Cowboys was a big transition for me," he admits. "When I was in college I never bothered with learning to read defenses. They just handed me the ball and told me to run. One of the first things I had to learn when I got to Dallas was to read defenses and figure out how to react to different situations."

Former Cowboys defensive great Mel Renfro adds another reason for Dennison's making it in the NFL: "We've never had anyone who ran harder than Doug did. He ran every play as if his life depended on his gaining three yards." Tom Landry agrees. "Doug always had tremendous explosion and you knew he was going to hit the right hole. You could always count on his giving 100 percent."

Indication of the power with which he assaulted the line of scrimmage is mirrored in the fact that as a rookie he carried the ball only 16 times yet scored four touchdowns out of the Power I formation. Thus he established himself as a promising back in a time when those vying for backfield jobs included Ron Johnson, Duane Thomas, Charles Young, Preston Pearson, Robert Newhouse, Scott Laidlaw and Jim Jensen. His most productive season would come in 1976 when, in a year the Cowboys had great difficulty with their running game, he led the team with 542 yards in 153 carries and scored six touchdowns. Hardly Pro Bowl statistics, but a personally satisfying accomplishment for the Kutztown ex.

His primary role throughout his career, however, would be that of a specialty back, the man Dallas went to in short-yardage situations.

"I understood my role with the Cowboys," he says, "and was happy to have the chance to play as long as I did. For me to even make the team was something divine, something I prayed would happen to me.

"I was a team player and was ready to do whatever I could to contribute. Like most, I would have liked to have been able to do more. But, then, as I said, just getting a chance to be there for four years — that was something special."

LEE ROY JORDAN

⭐

Doomsday Mainstay to Fan

He was for years a mainstay in Dallas' famed Doomsday Defense. It was a comforting sight to loyal followers of the Cowboys to see Number 55, Lee Roy Jordan, stationed at middle linebacker, ever ready to deal destruction to enemy offenses.

That now is but a part of the colorful Cowboys history. Happy and at peace in retirement from professional football, Jordan today is just another face in the stands on Sundays at Texas Stadium. Well, maybe something more than just another face, but a fan just the same. It is doubtful, for instance, that there is a paying customer in the house more knowledgeable about what is taking place on the field than the former Alabama standout.

"It's been a real experience to sit in the stands, watching what's going on down on the field and hearing the comments of people around me. I tried watching a couple of games from one of the boxes," he says, "but soon realized that just wouldn't do. For me, that's too far removed from what's going on. I found myself doing too much visiting and not keeping up with the game. It didn't take me long to decide to get out in the stands.

"I suppose I respond to the game differently than most people watching because I've got a first hand knowledge of what the team is attempting to do. I find myself sitting there trying to analyze what players are doing strategically and what they're going through emotionally. And, yes, I'm just like everyone else, getting caught-up and yelling my head off at times."

While he makes it clear that he has no regrets over his decision to end his career, he is equally quick to admit that there is still a bit of the old firehorse in Lee Roy Jordan. "I find myself thinking ahead to who they are going to be playing and I get really charged up if it is a particularly tough opponent or a critical game. We went to St. Louis with some friends for the first Cardinals game and as I was sitting there waiting for the kickoff my stomach began to churn. I knew it was an important game and I found myself reacting much as if I was going to be playing in it.

"I'm glad I retired when I did," he says. "It was the right time; I had resolved that in my own mind before I ever got to the point of calling it quits. I was certain it was the right thing for me to do and the right time to do it. I didn't have to deal with what some guys go through — thinking back that maybe they should have stayed around another year and tried to make one more trip to the Super Bowl or anything like that. Nothing in the world would please me more than to see Dallas win another Super Bowl, but I know that I wouldn't regret not being part of it."

While comfortable in his knowledge that his playing days are behind him, Jordan still maintains close ties to the team for which he labored so long. "I'm still close enough to it," he says, "that I can feel what it is this team is trying to do. Knowing some of the players and the system like I do I don't feel any need to go around wringing my hands — when something goes wrong."

Which sets him apart from many of his cohorts in the stands. "What goes on among the fans," he says, "is really amusing at times. I'm amazed at how hostile some people get when they really don't know what's going on out on the field. Your average fan really knows very little about the technical side of football. So, yes, I get a little frustrated with some people at times, but I try not to let it bother me.

"I really had a pretty good idea of what to expect. Our bench, you know, is pretty close to the stands so for years I've had a pretty good idea of how the fans in the first 25 or 30 rows feel about things. We (the defense) were always able to hear what the fans' reaction to our offense was. It's not much different now except for the fact I'm sitting up there with them. But I'm too busy keeping up with what's going on in the game to concern myself too much about what other people are yelling. I figure they're going to do their thing no matter what I might say to them, and, besides, I'm out there to enjoy myself and to see the game."

As he speaks, his voice is that of a man who has successfully made the transition from the playing field to the stands. Time was when three days after a game Lee Roy Jordan still felt lingering soreness in his muscles. Now, the only tell-tale sign of his Sunday trips to the stadium is a slight case of hoarseness. He's that kind of fan.

CLIFF HARRIS
★
No More Nightmares

It was one of those situations he would find himself in often during the nine years he labored in the Dallas Cowboys' defensive backfield: a berth in the playoffs was again on the line, his team was holding grimly to a five-point lead, and the opposition was mounting an attack.

Cliff Harris' voice takes on a tone of the dramatic as he recreates that afternoon in Texas Stadium late in the 1976 season. "We were playing St. Louis," he recalls, "and (quarterback) Jim Hart and (wide receiver) Mel Gray were at their peaks. We had led them all day, but now it was late in the fourth quarter and they were driving. Gray had really given us trouble earlier in the year when we played them in St. Louis, but hadn't done a lot of damage on this particular afternoon, until Hart sent him down the sidelines on a pattern that I always seemed to have trouble with. It was one of those 25-30 yard passes and Gray caught it just before I hit him and knocked him out of bounds at our 12-yard line. He jumped up and held the ball in my face as if to say, 'We've got you now.' "

Indeed, Gray had apparent good reason for his positive stance. The Cardinals, with one of the most inventive quarterbacks in the game calling the shots, had a first down just 12 yards shy of the winning touchdown.

"At that point," Harris continues, "Hart decided to really test me. He threw four straight times from the 12, each pass at me, and didn't complete any of them."

The Cowboys would thus hold on for a 19-14 victory which Harris, a man who has been to five Super Bowls, four Pro Bowls and a party to more dramatic victories than he can recall, remembers as his shining moment.

"There were bigger games, more important victories," he says, "but from an individual standpoint, that's the one I like to let myself think back on now and then. Gray was always tough to cover — he and I had a running verbal battle from the first game we played against each other — and Hart was one of the quarterbacks I least enjoyed facing. So to be able to keep them out of the end zone at a time they were, in effect, challenging me personally, was something special."

"Something special" ideally describes the free safety career of the gifted athlete who came to the Cowboys as an overlooked free agent out of Ouachita Baptist to start as a rookie in 1970. Before he abruptly announced his retirement after the 1979 season, he had been named All-Pro four times, had participated in six Pro Bowls, and was generally regarded throughout the NFL as the standard for measuring all other free safeties.

Still fifth on the club's all-time interception list with 29, his trademark was aggressive play in a system which actually limited his style. Cliff Harris never cared for the boundaries the sophistication of the Dallas defense imposed, preferring a more free-wheeling approach. "The longer I played," he says, "the thicker the game plan got, the bigger the computer printouts were. The game became less personalized. For me that was a problem because, as a player, I was always so involved in the emotion of the game." Yet he adjusted, rarely voicing his concern. "I was never one to complain too loudly about a loss, to say, 'hey, we should have won that game' if I honestly didn't think we should have."

However, the Super Bowl XIII loss to Pittsburgh in Miami haunts him. That is one he feels the Cowboys should have won. "We really could have beaten them that year," he says. "It was the only game we ever lost that I felt we should have won. In our preparation for that one we became too obsessed with the printouts. Too much attention was paid to what the computer told us we could and should do against particular plays. We were trying to beat (Steelers quarterback) Terry Bradshaw before he called his plays.

"Terry and I have talked a lot about that game since. I would ask him why he didn't key on this or that and his answer would be something like, 'Well, the plan was if Lynn Swann wasn't open, I'd try to throw to John Stallworth. If neither of them were open, I'd dump it off to a back.' It was that simple. They were just playing basic football."

The kind Cliff Harris always preferred.

"Pro football was a tremendous experience for me," he says. "I got to start in my rookie year, was in a winning Super Bowl in my second year, and was comfortable with what I was doing by my fourth year. Cornell Green always said it would take six years, so maybe I was a fast learner. One of the things that really helped in the early part of my career was being involved in so many aspects of the game. I was on all the kicking teams (he still ranks second in career kickoff returns with 25.7 yards per carry) as well as playing defense. Because of that I was able to learn a great deal about the game.

"In time, as I became more confident, I was able to develop my own style of play, to slip away from what the playbook said now and then. It is a rule that if you're to make it early, you have to play it their way to the letter. But once you've established yourself you can experiment a little. I enjoyed that part of it; the experimenting. Particularly when it was successful."

Harris began to contemplate retirement during the 1977 season. Injuries were slowing him from time to time and the roster was being filled by new, younger faces. "When you're young and the people around you are too, you're full of energy. But eventually you see people get older, slow down a step. You've got to be really dumb not to think about the whole process. Lee Roy Jordan sat me down and talked to me about it my first year in the league. Pat Toomay, who was my roommate in the early years, did too. That helped prepare me. Finally, I got to a point where I was tired of certain parts of the game. I knew then it was time to call it a career and go on to something else."

"You know," he says, "since I've retired I haven't had a single nightmare about Mel Gray. That's just one of the nice parts about it."

ROGER STAUBACH

⭐

King of the Comebacks

For thirty years he played the game, establishing milestones the way some people put up fence posts. For Roger Staubach, the highlights were not so much measured by games, even seasons, but decades. Even as his final year of play wound down in that winter of 1979 he was hard pressed to point to that single moment of glory he would carry as a touchstone with him into retirement. There simply were too many from which to choose.

His involvement began with then-overwhelming excitement as he made the cut on a Cincinnati pee-wee team at age seven, and continued into all-star years as a schoolboy at Percell High School when winning a city co-championship was something special. Eventually there was the Naval Academy and All-America honors, the Heisman Trophy, the cover of Time magazine, and the memorable Army-Navy games. And on to the professional ranks where, as a Cowboys quarterback for 10 years, the glories were numerous: Super Bowls, MVP honors, Pro Bowls, playoff victories, and an almost unbelievable record of having directed Dallas to come-from-behind wins on 23 different occasions.

As his career developed, so did a country's awareness of this athlete who came to be recognized not only for his uncanny abilities on the field, but his personal dedication to his Christian beliefs, his family and American values. He disliked the fact some members of the nation's press referred to him as "Captain America," but the moniker fit. In an era of disappearing heroes, Roger Staubach stood firm as an example to young and old alike.

When he made final his intention to retire after the '79 season, his press conference attracted more members of the media than the governor of Texas had ever gathered. Local radio and television stations broadcast the announcement live. The networks would bid him farewell not on that segment of the evening news reserved for sports, but in that time slot used for things more vital, more important. A Dallas newspaper distributed a special retirement section, NFL Films hurried into production a documentary biography and a song titled "Goodbye Roger" immediately climbed on the local charts.

"It was unbelievable," Staubach says in retrospect. "For a few days after announcing that I was retiring, I thought maybe I had died. The reaction was far more than I expected it to be."

It would, then, seem an unfair request to ask that he isolate a moment, a single game, from such a career and call it the most memorable, the high time of high times. Yet Staubach, true to his form as an athlete, did not even hesitate: "December 16, 1979," he says. "Dallas 35, Washington 34. Up to that point I felt sure the high point had already been reached somewhere in my career. But that one was like no other game I've ever been a part of. It was, to put it simply, the most thrilling 60 minutes I ever spent on the football field."

That it was a game matching the Cowboys and Redskins was enough, blood being bad between the two Eastern Division rivals, but on that particular chilly Sunday a great deal was at stake. Both teams came into the game with 10-5 records and a chance to claim the division title. In an unusual twist of the NFL tie-breaking system, however, the Redskins stood the most to lose from defeat. Win it, and they were the champions of the East. Lose, and they were completely out of the playoffs. Dallas, on the other hand, would earn a wild card berth regardless.

"But it was important for us to win the division and get that first round bye in the playoffs," Roger says. "And there was the matter of making up for what had happened in Washington earlier in the year."

In the first meeting of the two teams the Redskins had soundly defeated Dallas, adding insult to injury by calling time out in the final seconds of play to kick a cinch field goal which upped the margin to 34-20. It was not a tactic easily dismissed. Thus despite the fact running back Tony Dorsett would sit the game out with a bruised shoulder and wide receiver Drew Pearson would be limited in his contribution due to a strained knee, enthusiasm was high.

It was difficult to detect in the early going, however, as the Cowboys offense went nowhere and gave up two fumbles which helped Washington jump out to a 17-0 advantage early in the second quarter.

"I've never been in a game with a stranger scoring pattern," Staubach says. "They scored the first 17, then we scored the next 21. Then they scored 17 more and we finally got the last 14. We finally got something going in the second quarter, moving 70 yards for a touchdown and then, with just nine seconds left before the half I threw a touchdown pass to Preston Pearson. We weren't in the greatest of positions at the time, either. We were facing third-and-20 at the Washington 26 when that one finally came.

"In the dressing room Coach Landry was calm, telling us that we now had some momentum. He also said that the results of the third quarter would determine who would eventually win the game. Which goes to prove that even Tom Landry isn't right all of the time. We did win the third quarter, 7-0, thanks to a Robert Newhouse touchdown. And we still led 21-20 into the fourth before things really got crazy.

"We were at midfield and moving pretty well when I tried to force a pass to (tight end) Jay Saldi. It was a bad decision on my part. Washington intercepted it and scored two plays later to regain the lead at 27-21. I remember going to the sidelines after the pass and telling Tom, 'I blew it.' He gave me one of those 'truer words were never spoken' looks and then turned his attention to the defense."

Once again Washington was the team with momentum. On its next posses-
sion John Riggins broke for a 66-yard touchdown run that caused some
Dallas fans to begin heading for the exits. With 6:54 left, the Redskins owned
a 34-21 advantage.

It would be defensive tackle Randy White who came up with a play that
would breathe some hope into the fading Dallas cause. He recovered a
Clarence Harmon fumble and Staubach would quickly pass his team
downfield, hitting Ron Springs, who was subbing for the injured Dorsett, for
a 26-yard touchdown with 2:20 left to play. Then it would be Larry Cole's
chance to step into the spotlight. Washington, needing only one more first
down to all but assure itself the victory, faced a third-and-two situation at its
own 33 when the two-minute warning was delivered. The Redskins opted to
try and pick up that needed two yards with the same play Riggins had scored
on earlier, but as it developed Cole burst through to drop the Redskins running back for a two-yard loss and forced a punt.

With 1:46 remaining Dallas got one more chance, taking over at its own
25-yard-line.

Staubach best describes what took place from that point in his own book,
"Time Enough to Win." A very appropriate title.

"I'll remember the first play of that series almost as long as the last
because I sort of made it up. Instead of having (Tony) Hill run an inside route
. . . I told him, 'Act like you're going to break inside, then go to the outside,
. . . I threw the pass that somehow sailed between two defenders. How it did
I'm still not sure because the ball wobbled all the way. It became a great pass
only because it reached Hill who helped by making a great adjustment to be
in the right place.

"The fact was we free-lanced our way 20 yards upfield with that one. Then
Preston worked free for completions of 22 and 25 to put us on Washington's
eight-yard line . . . In the huddle I told Hill, 'Be alert, because if they blitz
I'm coming to you.' I think if I hadn't mentioned that to him he wouldn't have
been looking for the ball because tight end Billy Joe DuPree was the hot
receiver. The Redskins did blitz and frankly I never looked for DuPree. Instead I lobbed a semi-Alley Oop pass toward the end zone corner where Hill
had gotten behind cornerback Lemar Parrish. Tony ran under it to make a
touchdown catch with 39 seconds left.

"What had happened was so unbelievable I ran around jumping in the air.
According to a picture in the paper the next day I jumped into the arms of
Springs. In all the excitement, I don't even remember doing it."

For the day Staubach would complete 24 of 42 passing attempts for 336
yards, his second highest total as a pro. But on that day it was not the yardage
which was important.

Days later a disappointed Washington coach Jack Pardee would offer the
best summary of what had taken place that day: "I went through that film
trying to find out what we did wrong so it would never happen again. My
final conclusion was that Roger pulled off two or three plays that made the
difference — with sheer athletic ability."

PRESTON PEARSON

✮

Super Bowl Expert

The subject was the Super Bowl and he was an obvious choice to speak on the matter. Preston Pearson, an NFL running back for 14 seasons, five of those (1975-1980) in a Dallas Cowboys uniform, was there on five occasions; the only man in the game's history to play in Super Bowls as a member of three different teams. He was there with the Baltimore Colts, the Pittsburgh Steelers, and finally with the Cowboys.

Now retired and pursuing various business interests in Dallas, the man judged by many to be the finest third down back in NFL annals, Pearson saw, during his career, the atmosphere of the championship game go from outright insanity to more controlled mayhem. He was there in Super Bowl III when New York Jets quarterback Joe Namath courted the press with his famous guarantee of victory. He was there again in Super Bowl IX when the Pittsburgh Steelers dynasty was on the rise. And on three occasions he was there as a member of the Dallas Cowboys.

At that time, he admits, the pre-game celebration of the event was, in fact, a problem. But as years passed and better organization came to the game, he realized that it was impossible to isolate the game itself from all the hype that surrounded it.

"Back in 1969," he says, "the league was just beginning to realize what it had created and still had a lot to learn. Over the years they have been able to put a pretty good game plan together, to a point where the teams are able to properly prepare without having the distractions that once were such a focus of concern. In fact, the thing that I learned after the first couple of times I was there is that the Super Bowl is supposed to be fun, a rewarding experience. That's the underlying thing about football that too many people forget; that it is supposed to be enjoyable."

He can, however, well remember when being a participant in pro football's biggest game was more hassle than high time.

"The '69 Super Bowl, we (Baltimore) played against the Jets," he says, "was the first one that caused everyone to really go crazy. It was Broadway Joe Namath and the New York media, and people everywhere. The league simply wasn't prepared for it. The players had no privacy whatsoever. There were no restrictions on times for interviews, no security in hotels. You could be in your room, getting ready for bed, and a reporter would drop in for another interview. Or maybe a couple of fans would knock on the door. It made concentration almost impossible. And, as everyone knows, concentration is the key to proper preparation for a game, particularly if it is one as important as a Super Bowl. There simply were no controls."

But things have changed. Specific times are set aside for interviewers and players are isolated from much of the hoopla. Which, in Pearson's view, is good — and bad.

"I really think the players ought to be allowed to feel some of the excitement of the game, to get more involved in what's happening on the outside. The player misses a lot that he could look back on years later. Part of it, of course, is because of the strict rules set down by the respective teams. I know with the Cowboys and Pittsburgh everything was very carefully planned out, down to the minute. The teams provided their own security. Coupled with the security and regulations the league itself set up, there was a feeling of almost being held prisoner at times."

Which, he admits, is why curfews are occasionally broken, even at the risk of sizable fines. "There comes a point," Pearson says, "when you have to do something crazy like that to keep from going crazy. The pressure and intensity gets to you after a while. Sure, I violated curfew, but not just for the hell of it. Going out didn't affect my performance. In fact, it helped to relax me, got me ready to play in a sense."

The extremes players will go to in order to escape for a few hours of late night fun and frolic are as ingenious as they are juvenile. Preston explains:

"Okay, if you see a player walking around a hotel lobby during the day, collecting books of matches, you are not to assume he is either a heavy smoker or a matchbook cover collector. What he's doing is collecting them to use as wedges in the side door exits. Of course, the doors are all supposed to self-lock at night, so you have to spend a great deal of time during the day planning your get-away. I remember a guy who wedged matchbooks into doors for eighteen floors so that he could get away via the fire exit stairs. Then, you have to stash a change of clothes somewhere on the first floor. See, what you have to do is sneak out in your underwear so if you're caught on the way down you can just explain to a coach that you're looking for ol' so-and-so's room. He's not going to think you're trying to sneak out when you're running around in nothing but your shorts."

Pearson recognizes the difficulty of policing an event the magnitude of the Super Bowl and also supports the protection provided the players. On the other hand, he wonders if perhaps there isn't some way it can be less restrictive.

"Security is so tight," he says, "that it is all but impossible for even a member of your own family to get in touch with you. On the other hand, it is easy to see why such care is necessary."

He recalls Super Bowl XII when a death threat was called in to the Cowboys' headquarters at New Orleans' Airport Hilton. Teammate Tony Dorsett, the caller had said, would not live to finish his first Super Bowl.

"There are always going to be kooks running around and it is great to know

there is someone watching for them and keeping them away. When Tony's threat came, he was quietly moved to another room at the hotel just to be safe. Most of the players on the team didn't even know about it until the game was over and we were headed back to Dallas."

Pearson is not among those who would suggest that the teams involved in the game be allowed to conduct practices at home, arriving at the game site just 24 hours in advance. "Ideally, it would probably allow both teams to better prepare for the game since they would be in familiar, more comfortable surroundings, but I think it would take something away from the game to do it that way. As I've said, the Super Bowl has become more than just a game. It is a week-long holiday celebration which happens to end with a football game. That, as much as anything else, makes it as unique as it has become.

"All I can say, really, is that it is a rare experience that you carry with you for the rest of your life. I was fortunate enough to go five times in a nine-year period. I saw the game grow into the greatest single-day sporting event in history. I'm glad to have been a part of it."

LARRY COLE

Captain Zero

People should realize, Larry Cole says, that had it not been for an unfortunate turn of events years ago, it might well have been him they were calling "Captain America" instead of Roger Staubach. The legendary Cowboys quarterback would not have been the only player on the team with the colorful military academy background for the sportswriters to build their stories around.

As easily as not, it could have been Air Force Academy grad Larry Cole. "Of course," he adds, "if I'd ever become an officer I probably would never have considered pro football."

Which, in retrospect, would have been the Air Force's gain and the NFL's loss for 13 seasons.

It was 16 years ago that Cole, then a junior at the Air Force Academy, learned that a fellow cadet, a member of the football team, had received illegal help on an exam. "According to the Academy code," he explains, "anyone with any knowledge of cheating is supposed to report what he knows. I had heard about it from two of my friends and wasn't about to turn them in."

Eventually, though, it became known that Cole and his friends had knowledge of the incident. What ultimately resulted was their expulsion along with the guilty party.

Far from bitter, Cole does not look back on it as a time of misfortune. Had he not been expelled, he might never have enjoyed the distinguished career he had with the Cowboys before his retirement after the 1980 season.

What he did was take his act to the University of Hawaii where he captained the Rainbows' first winning team since 1920 and became a 16th round draft pick of the Cowboys in 1968.

"You know," he says, "if I had stayed at the Academy through graduation I would have never made it through my first training camp. Camp was too much like being at the Academy. It's a good thing I had a break from it before I went out to Thousand Oaks for the first time."

The annual six weeks exile, in time, became something Cole not only endured but looked forward to. In his later years with the Cowboys, it provided a vacation from overseeing the operation of his successful home-building business. "I got to the point where I enjoyed going to camp, which should tell you right there that I wasn't any ordinary football player."

Certainly he wasn't. Before his retirement, Larry (Bubba) Cole had fashioned a list of accomplishments unprecedented in Cowboys history. He participated in a league record 26 playoff games, was in five Super Bowls, scored four touchdowns, amazingly never endured any manner of knee surgery, and made the Zero Club a household word. He was low-key, yet seemed always to come up with the spectacular play in the big games; never an All-Pro, but the kind of steady, reliable performer Tom Landry insists help form the foundation of championship teams. The record will show that at one time or another during his career he played every position in the defensive line. He seldom smiled, but was full of more good humor than you could say grace over. The favorite target of Larry Cole's jokes was always Larry Cole.

"The only thing I hated about retiring," he says, "was that I had become something of a symbol to the middle-aged man. I was living proof that a 36-year-old with not much ability could somehow still play a kid's game."

And while teammates viewed his year-to-year performance with something akin to awe, they did their best to convince the rest of the world that they did not take the awkward-looking guy who once played high school ball for something called the Granite Falls (Minn.) High School Kilowatts too seriously. To wit:

"Larry's the only guy in the league who once got faked out by O.J. Simpson so badly," says former linebacker D.D. Lewis, "that he got a 15-yard penalty for grabbing his own facemask."

"If people were cars," says former teammate Pat Toomay, "Larry would be a four-wheel drive International travel-haul. Or maybe some kind of farm implement. Maybe a plow. Who else do you know who has a tattoo on his arm, reading 'Born to Raise Wheat'?"

When word reached the West Coast that Cole was retiring, another former teammate, Blaine Nye, sent a telegram to the Cowboys office which read: "I guess you could say Larry was my best friend for ten years. But when I think about our relationship today, I'd rather have had a dog."

It was Nye, Toomay and Cole who formed the now famous Zero Club, an organization which, by careful design, was nonfunctional. Its primary purpose was to avoid attention. Apathy was its byword. It is the only club which met for the primary purpose of doing absolutely nothing. If anyone so much as suggested interest in joining they were vetoed simply for having shown the interest.

Cole spent the last couple of years of his Cowboys career on probation handed down by Nye and Toomay. In those final seasons, in fact, he earned more publicity than in all his previous years combined. He became the club's elder statesman, the man reporters consulted with to gauge the team's attitude. While the Cowboys continued to go through their regular "transitions," Cole remained a permanent fixture. When younger players seemed to lack the proper attitude, it was Cole who did the lecturing.

In 1979, just after the Washington Redskins had soundly defeated the Cowboys, Cole spent time on the team flight back to Dallas making a list of ten things he felt wrong with the team. At the practice field the following Tuesday during a meeting, he asked that he might have the floor. Never a cheerleader type, Cole carefully listed the shortcomings he felt most glaring.

In days to come, they would be known as Cole's Ten Commandments.

The next time Dallas faced Washington, the Cowboys won on a heroic last-minute touchdown pass from Staubach to wide receiver Tony Hill which climaxed a 35-32 come-from-behind victory. Many, however, point to a tackle Cole made on Redskins running back John Riggins on a critical third down which gave the Cowboys offense one last shot at earning the victory.

When Ed (Too Tall) Jones took leave of the Cowboys to pursue a boxing career, Cole's career was given new life. Having resigned himself to life as a backup defensive tackle still effective on the pass rush, he made yet another move and became a starter at left defensive end. Gradually, newcomer John Dutton would take over at end, allowing Cole to move back to left tackle. There he would remain at the position he was best suited for, not as a reserve but a starter, until announcing his retirement. "He was," Landry would repeatedly say in those final two seasons, "the miracle of the defensive line. Really, he became kind of indispensable."

The Washington Redskins, no doubt, would review his career in less glowing terms. What Larry Cole was to them, from start to finish, was a classic pain.

His four touchdowns, which tied Bob Lilly as the all-time most productive scorer of all Dallas defensive linemen, were all against the Redskins. The last came in his final season on a 43-yard gallop with an interception of a Mike Kruczek pass. It was also the only one punctuated by a left-handed spike.

"All I could think when I got my hands on the ball (after it had bounced crazily off his helmet) was, 'Hey, I'm gonna do it again.' I wonder what the Las Vegas odds are on something like that — four against the same team?"

he says.

When a reporter pointed out that almost ten years had elapsed between his third and fourth trips into the endzone, Cole stretched to his full six feet, five inches and sniffed, "Anyone can have an off-decade."

Cole historically used his wit to downplay his personal accomplishments. Individual high moments rate little mention over those things he was a part of as a member of the team. In an era when it is viewed as a tired cliché, Larry Cole, Dallas Cowboy from 1968 to '80, was the prototype of what the "team player" was supposed to be. "I always saw myself as a guy who was a cog in the machine who didn't let his ego get in the way. I like to think that I did my part."

That, he did.

CHARLIE WATERS

Comeback Champion

The knee brace was bulky, awkward and slowed his movement considerably. It was, in a sense, his crutch during that 1980 season. Charlie Waters, All-Pro strong safety, did not like playing on it. But without it, participation would have been impossible. Given that kind of option, Waters chose to wear it.

There is, perhaps, no player in Dallas Cowboys history who has, during the course of a career, endured more highs and lows than Waters did in his eleven years in the game.

"I always had great admiration for athletes who were able to make comebacks," he said following his retirement after the 1981 season. "To me it was a measure of one's competitiveness. I wanted to be able to do it myself, to prove that I was capable of doing it."

He proved his point repeatedly, most recently in the final years of his career when courage was the most noteworthy tool he carried to work with him. After starting 128 consecutive games for the Cowboys and reaching All-Pro status, he missed the entire 1979 season with a damaged knee suffered in a pre-season game against Seattle. He underwent surgery and began rehabilitation as soon as the doctor gave approval. He returned in 1980 to share the club interception lead with teammate Dennis Thurman. He would wait until the season's end to admit that the heavily braced knee had gone out on him no less than eight times during the year.

"Looking back," says Tom Landry, "I'm not sure how he played as well as he did. Yet he played very well under the circumstances. He played much of

the year on courage alone."

Additional surgery was performed during the off-season and Waters came back for one final year. "I wanted to go out as a champion," he says. "I felt we had a Super Bowl caliber team and I wanted to be a part of that. We missed it by one game, but it wasn't a disappointing year in a lot of respects. Football is a team game, but there are individual goals, too. I wanted to show I could take that brace off and play well again. I like to think I made my point."

He did so in several ways. Working in a secondary that included free agent rookies Everson Walls and Michael Downs, Waters became a coach on the field, directing traffic, lending advice and suggestion. It was as impressive a performance as he ever gave, right up there with his playoff record three interceptions against Chicago in 1977, his two interceptions and a fumble recovery which sparked Dallas' '78 win over Los Angeles in the NFC Championship game, his three Pro Bowl appearances, his twice being named All-Pro. Or his 41 career interceptions.

And along the way there seemed always the need to come back from some manner of adversity. For instance:

There was a compound left arm fracture in 1972, requiring four operations and the implant of a steel rod before he would mend and be allowed to return. But come back he did.

And the nationally televised humiliation in Los Angeles that following year when Waters, playing cornerback, was soundly beaten by wide receiver Harold Jackson who caught four touchdown passes over him in the first half alone, ending the afternoon with seven receptions and 238 yards.

It was at cornerback, a position he lacked proper speed to play, that Waters endured the most misery. His play at the position against the Washington Redskins was a study in frustration. In six games at left cornerback against them, Waters allowed 16 completions and four touchdowns to Charley Taylor. "He would tell me," Waters remembers, "I could never cover him. I tried to put it all behind me, but, yes, I still remember those days. You don't forget things like that."

Even in those trying times, as he played at the corner from mid-'72 through the '74 season, there were positives, however. A high percentage of his fan mail was encouraging, some quick to point out the good games he had enjoyed.

"I remember our comeback win in San Francisco in '72, I had two interceptions. And in '73 we lost the NFC Championship game in Minnesota but I intercepted a pass and recovered a fumble."

Still, he never lost any love on the cornerback job. "I guess some people will say my whole life changed when I changed positions, moving to safety. I know my entire attitude toward the game changed dramatically. Suddenly I felt I was playing from my strengths and not trying to overcome my weaknesses. That makes a great deal of difference. As I got comfortable with the position, the game took on a whole new meaning. Cliff Harris and I became a team and we worked well together. We thought alike, we studied together, and complimented each other. I think probably we helped each other be a little better than we would have ever been alone.

"Interceptions and big plays were always nice, but the real thrill of the game for me in the later years was the strategy of it. The mental part of the game was always the most exciting part for me. I think I finally reached a point where I was able to make a complete mental commitment to my job. And that part was satisfying."

That and the fact he proved, one last time, that he could come back.

SCOTT LAIDLAW
⭐
Big Game, Big Results

It was one of those afternoons when the frustrations were forgotten, the injuries set aside, and promise was finally realized, if only for a brief period of time. It was 1978 and the Cowboys were making a drive toward Super Bowl XIII despite troubles at the fullback position.

With starter Robert Newhouse sidelined, veteran backup Scott Laidlaw got his first starting call in two years. And he responded with the finest game of his five-year Cowboys career. Before the Washington Redskins were set aside that afternoon in Texas Stadium, Laidlaw's celebration had accounted for 122 yards rushing and two touchdowns. Along the way there was a 59-yard burst which brought the capacity crowd to its feet.

That day there was little cause for doubt that the former fourteenth round draft-pick from Stanford was a legitimate candidate for stardom.

"The reason that day sticks in my mind," he recalls, "is that it came after I hadn't played for quite some time, and it was a big game. I didn't feel any pressure despite the fact a lot of people assumed I would. And I can understand that. Generally, there's a lot of pressure on a backup player because he's got to be able to keep himself mentally and physically ready to play even when he knows the chances are he won't. It gets easy when you know you're going to start."

Which he did in each of the final four games of that '78 season and then in the first two playoff victories. In the divisional playoff against Atlanta he rushed for 66 yards and two touchdowns, then caught a four-yard scoring pass in the NFC Championship game against Los Angeles.

In the Super Bowl in Miami, however, Landry returned Newhouse to the starting job.

And while Laidlaw made no secret of his disappointment in not playing a role in the title game, he admits the drive to get there was the most enjoyable time of his professional career. "The lead-up to the Super Bowl was great," he says, "because it was just at that time that we had really begun to kick into high gear offensively. You could just feel the way we were getting wound up, that the second half of the season had arrived and it was time to grab the tiger by the tail and get after it. And being able to play a lot really made me feel a part of it all. It really got my motor running."

Then, however, came the disappointment in Miami when Landry informed him Newhouse would start against Pittsburgh. "When he told me that," Laidlaw says, "it destroyed a lot of things for me. It just didn't sit right. But, there was nothing I could do but sit and be ready in case I was needed.

"I remember when Tom told me of his decision he added that I'd done a really good job as a starter and that if I tried hard I had a good chance of getting what I wanted (to become the fulltime starter) the next year."

The 1979 season would be yet another disappointment, however, as a thigh injury in training camp ended his chances of battling Newhouse for the starting job. It was a scene he had played too often during his professional career.

"Every other year, it seemed," he says, "I would be healthy and think I had things going, that I was moving ahead. Then, I'd pull a hamstring and that would be it for a season. Looking back, I'd have to say one of my problems was that I was always trying to rush to get well, pushing too hard after being so frustrated at being injured. And there were some communication problems about my injuries. There were times when I wasn't hurt nearly as badly as people were led to believe. I could have played and I wanted to play, but the decision wasn't mine to make. Dallas has always had a philosophy of letting an injury heal properly before letting a player go back into action — which is good — but there were times when I felt maybe the wait was a little too long in my case."

When healthy, he made his mark. As a rookie in 1975 he established himself as a solid receiver, catching 11 passes for 100 yards coming out of the backfield. Then with Newhouse injured as the '76 season opened, Laidlaw was brilliant against Philadelphia, rushing for 104 yards on 19 carries and catching seven passes for an additional 66 yards.

"I was coming off knee surgery that year," he says, "and we really caught the Eagles off guard, running four or five draw plays in the early stages of the game. Each time I got 10 to 20 yards. It was great fun. But it was so hot that day that I simply ran out of gas and had to leave the game in the third quarter."

The following year there were no highlights as hamstring problems again developed. For the season Scott carried the ball only nine times, gaining just 15 yards.

That Super Bowl XIII season was, in effect, Laidlaw's last chance at the brass ring. Before the 1980 season got underway he was traded to the New York Giants where he spent half a season in what he describes as "a bad situation." It was time, he decided, to give it up.

In something of an odd twist, he chose to walk away from his pro football career the morning of a scheduled Giants-Cowboys game. "I didn't consider the irony of it at the time," he says. "It just seemed as good a time as any."

JACKIE SMITH

The Last Hurrah

He found himself awakening each morning promptly at six, something he'd never been in the habit of doing before. "I would get up, put the coffee on," he remembers, "and sit there at the kitchen table before anyone else in the house was up and just think about the situation I was in."

The situation Jackie Smith refers to is that which, in 1978, found him preparing to play in a Super Bowl after 15 exceptional seasons of professional football. "My wife would join me after the coffee was made," he says, "and we would just sit and talk. It was a chance I had thought about for years and years. We would get downright emotional just talking about it."

After 15 years and 482 receptions as an All-Pro performer for the St. Louis Cardinals, the 38-year-old Smith was certain his playing days were over following the '77 campaign. When Dallas player personnel director Gil Brandt called to explain that backup tight end Jay Saldi had been lost for the year with a broken forearm and that his services were badly needed, Jackie was certain it was a practical joke. Only after Tom Landry spoke to him on the phone did he realize the offer was for real.

Even after agreeing to come out of his brief retirement for a one-year stay in Dallas he had reservations. In due time, however, he ceased to doubt his decision. Soon he became enthusiastic and excited. After spending the first few months of his brief career in a Dallas uniform referring to the Cowboys as "they" instead of "we," he came to feel comfortable, at home.

Twice as an All-Pro member of the Cardinals, Smith had participated in playoffs and twice St. Louis was eliminated in the opening round, first by Minnesota, then Los Angeles. "Both times," he remembers, "we knew we had to be lucky to go any farther. We knew we had good teams, but not great teams. You think Super Bowl but you can't help but look at things objectively and deep down you know — whether you admit it or not — that you weren't as good as the other teams in the playoffs."

It was not a feeling he had that year in Dallas.

"I'm just an old redneck football player," he says, "and I don't always put my feelings and thoughts into words all that well, but that year what I wanted to do more than anything in the world was sit down with some of the guys on that team and tell them how really fortunate they were. Oh, I'm sure they realized it to a degree, but on the other hand, I wonder if they'll ever know. So many of them were never on the other side of the fence. They've never known how hard it is to begin a new season, trying to regroup one more time, not really having any better prospects of success than the year before. You have to have been there to really understand it."

The thought of making it to the Super Bowl, Smith notes, is something that spurs all professional teams on. "But for the Cardinals when I was there," he says, "it wasn't a realistic thing. We would never admit it to ourselves, but that's the way it was. In Dallas, the idea of getting to the top starts with the front office, the management, and works down to the players. In St. Louis, the players started the idea and tried to get it worked up to the front office. It never worked.

"I saw so many little things while I was with the Cowboys; little things that explained to me why they're such a class team. It was obvious to me right away that everything was done to make things go as smoothly as possible for the players. Things like being able to buy extra tickets without a lot of hassle. More accommodating air travel, everything. They eliminate all the distractions. I was even impressed at the fact they sent out Christmas cards. In the grand scheme of things it was no big deal. But all the little things add up. There was also a more serious attitude on the part of the players. I saw more studying, more communicating with each other about game plans. And almost everyone on the Cowboys was team oriented; team members first, individual performers second.

"Once I'd been there for a few weeks I couldn't believe I'd had reservations about signing. It became a personal challenge to play one more year. It was the kind of challenge few ever get the opportunity to accept. It meant a lot to me to have accepted it and responded to it.

"And finally getting to the Super Bowl, well . . . ."

Therein is another story. Jackie Smith's fondest dream produced something of a nightmare.

Roger Staubach's pass was low and behind him as he circled into the endzone, skidding off-balance. For a split second receiver and ball were one, but then the ball dropped away, incomplete. No touchdown for Jackie. The picture of his frustration would appear in newspapers nationwide the following day.

After 16 seasons it was not supposed to end that way.

Dallas went on to salvage a field goal from the drive but the final score, Pittsburgh, 35-31, might have been different if . . . Jackie Smith can count as well as anyone. Despite efforts of his new teammates to cheer him up, to convince him that the loss of Super Bowl XIII was not his responsibility, the frozen moment haunted him. Almost 500 catches in his career, and he would be remembered for that one he didn't make.

"That play," he says, "was the beginning of one of the most gratifying things that ever happened to me in my career, though. It's one of the most unusual things that ever happened to me. Afterwards for weeks I got a warm, compassionate reaction from people. Most of them I didn't even know, hadn't ever met. They'd just pat me on the back. I got hundreds of letters from people that said, 'I love you.' It was incredible.

"It's hard for ol' Jackie, as strong as I thought I was, to justify and forget what happened. You can say that it just wasn't meant to be ... that it wasn't fair ... that sort of thing. But it made me more aware of the basic principles and people. That would never have happened had that pass been completed."

Today Jackie Smith wears no Super Bowl ring to remind him of his season as a Dallas Cowboy. His stay, he says, earned him something far more valuable — the affection of his fellow man.

JOHN FITZGERALD

★

The Final Season

Throughout that final off-season he was, without fail, always the first to arrive at the Cowboys practice field. The sign on the door indicated that the facility would be open daily at 7 a.m. But by 6:30 John Fitzgerald, preparing for his eleventh season, would be on hand, ready to drink coffee with equipment manager Buck Buchannan before beginning his Spartan routine of running and lifting weights.

As he worked his body into condition a scenario would run through his mind, blanking out the aches and pains of the practice. He would report to training camp in top condition, would fight off the challenge of backup center Robert Shaw, would play out the 1981 season injury-free, then call a press conference to announce his retirement from the game. By his own estimation it would be a fitting end to a career which had been filled with ups and downs.

A fourth round draft pick in 1970, he had come to the Cowboys as a defensive tackle out of Boston College. The move to offense had not been easy. He was tried at tackle, then guard, and finally center in his rookie year. The latter was determined to be his best position but in order to prepare for it he spent his first year with the Cowboys on the taxi squad.

It would be three years before he would move into the starting job which had been vacated by a retiring John Manders. But once established at the position it was his. And while his talents would earn him no All-Pro mentions, his peers marveled at what he did. For years he was the only center in the NFL who had to center the ball to a quarterback working out of the spread formation.

"That would have ended the career of a lot of centers," John admits. "I don't want to make it sound tougher than it was, but there are some guys who

249

just don't believe they could do it. The snapping of the ball isn't the really difficult part. It's what happens afterwards. When you have to spirial the ball eight yards back, you've got your head down. And that puts you at a considerable disadvantage when you've got some mad defensive lineman coming after you. Sometimes I found myself wondering if it was a fair fight."

The most unfair thing about Fitzgerald's career was the injury factor which seemed always to haunt him. As early as 1975 he considered retirement following knee and elbow surgery. But he decided to come back. In the '78 season he was hospitalized with severe back spasms, unable even to walk for a time, yet he returned to work. Then, in 1980 foot trouble developed during the midpoint of the season and he went to the sidelines. In his place came former No. 1 draft selection Robert Shaw, the heir apparent. Fitz, in fact, had been helping groom Shaw for the job.

"I had hoped it would be a situation like I had with Manders when I was younger," he says. "When he was getting close to retiring he told me to watch, ask questions, and get myself ready. He was a tremendous help to me. It was as if he was helping me to take his job away. But he didn't really want me to have it until he was ready. I felt the same way about Shaw. It was obvious he was the guy who was going to wind up with my job, but I wanted to be the one to decide when."

The change-over would come sooner than John had hoped. Late in the 1980 season he developed a foot problem and Shaw moved in. By season's end Fitzgerald was again fit, but his replacement finished the year. The battle lines, then, were drawn for John's final campaign.

"I had felt we would probably go to camp even," he says. "One of us would have to win the job. I wanted it badly, maybe more badly than ever before, because I knew it was going to be my last year. It's only natural to want to go out on top. So I worked hard at getting ready for camp."

It was not to be for the man who served as the starting center for Dallas for longer than any other. During an intrasquad scrimmage he suffered a bruised thigh. "That," he says, "was a break I didn't need." Any manner of injury, any absence from the two-a-day workout grind, he knew, would lessen his chances.

Then, in an exhibition game against Los Angeles, he hobbled to the sidelines with another knee injury. That was it.

For a while he hoped to be able to return and at least assume a backup role in his swansong season but doctors advised against it. He was resigned to the injured reserve list. Yet he was at the practice field daily, helping where he could. He assisted line coach Jim Myers on the field, he studied film, offered suggestions, and traveled with the team to games.

"It was a frustrating way to end it," he says, "but it wouldn't have felt right to just walk away. My contributions in 1981 were very small."

That is but one man's opinion. "John was one of the most unselfish football players I've ever been around," says D.D. Lewis. "He could have just taken it easy that last year, but he wanted to help wherever he could. And he did, just by being there."

D.D. LEWIS

★

He Made Others Look Good

He sat in front of his locker, removing his uniform for the final time, still feeling the sting of a 28-27 loss just suffered at the hands of the San Francisco 49ers in the NFC Championship game. He had missed a chance to participate in a record-setting sixth Super Bowl by inches, seconds, and Dallas linebacker D.D. Lewis made no attempt to mask his disappointment, and the confusion he was feeling.

Having already made public the fact that the 1981 season, his thirteenth with the Cowboys, would be his last, he felt a rush of conflicting emotions. "My first inclination," he said, "was to say something like we would be back next year. But then it occurred to me that I wouldn't, that that was it for me. It was a kind of helpless feeling. The Cowboys will be back, but I won't be with them. Sure, I wish we could have won that one. I would have liked to go to another Super Bowl. But, hey, it wasn't bad while it lasted."

Indeed, for Dwight Douglas Lewis, professional football represented the Good Life, far removed from the hardscrabble poverty of his childhood days. Football got him out of the going-nowhere lifestyle he knew back home in Knoxville, Tennessee. It got him to a station in life most can only imagine.

"Damn right I'm going to miss it," he says. "I loved every minute of it. But there comes a time to move on, to do something else. That last season was important to me, though. I wanted to give it one last shot, to go out with my head up, having people feel I did my job."

He clearly accomplished that. As the starting outside linebacker for the Cowboys, he was not only a physical mainstay but an inspiration who contributed immeasurably. A quiet leader, Lewis served as a guiding force to younger players who would one day assume his role, his job. Once labeled too small to be an NFL linebacker, never recognized as All-Pro or invited to a Pro Bowl, a man who had to wait until his fourth year to move from specialty teams to a starting role, Lewis' career was indeed something special. It would have been so even without the two Super Bowl rings he owns, without all the playoff money he earned, the interceptions he made, and the fumbles he recovered.

In and out of trouble as a youngster, jailed at age 13 for stealing a car, washing dishes as a ninth grader to help support the family, his life took positive direction only after he discovered football. By the end of his senior year in high school, an assistant coach from Mississippi State was on his doorstep, offering him a full scholarship.

It would be his escape route. "I know this sounds a little dramatic," Lewis says, "but if it hadn't been for football I'd probably be in jail somewhere right now."

Despite his size, he twice earned All-Southeastern Conference honors, was cited as the league's top player in 1967 and earned one All-America plaque. He had a reputation for hardhitting football, the kind the professional scouts were looking for.

The Dallas Cowboys, calling him the best player in the country, pound for pound, selected him in the sixth round of the 1968 draft. The kid from Knoxville, quite clearly, was on the move. At age 23 and with things looking up, he reported to his first training camp with the promise of making $15,500 a year for three years — if he made the club. All but $500 of his $7,000 signing bonus had already been spent to clear up long overdue family bills.

"Looking back," he says, "it wasn't the best deal any pro player ever made, but it was the best one I'd ever seen at the time."

Earning a spot on the Cowboys' roster, however, was no easy task. There were, in fact, times when his chances did not look good at all. From a group of 80 rookies in camp that summer, only six would make it. It was a sudden trip to the College All-Star game in Chicago which provided Lewis with some needed insight to the pro game. A player originally selected to participate was injured and Lewis was called in as a last minute replacement.

"We were playing the Green Bay Packers," he remembers, "and I had the opportunity to talk with Ray Nitschke. I told him that I was surprised that there were so few team drills in training camp, that almost everything we had been doing was individual, one-on-one sort of things. He told me that it was going to be the same when I got back to camp, that those were the kind of drills you had to prove yourself at. He told me that he made the Packers by knocking people around and then excelling on the specialty teams once the exhibition games began.

"Man, I went back to Thousand Oaks and went nuts. I played like a wild man, doing everything I could think of to gain the coaches' attention."

It worked. He made the team.

But for five years he wondered if he was, in fact, good enough to be playing in the NFL. His service was limited to specialty teams. Missing his third season while serving in the Army didn't help. His confidence began to diminish. "It got frustrating, sitting on the bench, watching everyone else playing, contributing. I found myself becoming a very bitter, negative person."

That changed in the 1973 season when he finally became the Cowboys' starting weakside linebacker. "Once I became a starter," he says, "the maturing process began. I quit being bitter and began concerning myself with being a good, solid football player." Such would be the case for the duration of his career. Though never a flashy performer, Lewis was called by Landry Dallas' most underrated player. Twice, the head coach says, D.D. should have been selected to participate in the Pro Bowl (after the 1977 and '78

252

seasons).

That he was never picked was one of Lewis' few unfulfilled dreams which he carried with him throughout his career.

"If he had been a flamboyant-type player," suggested former teammate Charlie Waters, himself an All-Pro, "he might have received more honors. If he had gone for the interception more, gambled to make the big play more . . . but that was never his style. He was always the one who would turn the run in so the great play could be made by someone else. He was always the consistent, dependable kind of player you had to have to win championships.

"D.D. Lewis' whole career was spent making other people look good."

It isn't a bad legacy to have left.

RANDY HUGHES

★

Of Promises Never Delivered

A wake-like quiet had fallen over the Cowboys 1981 training camp on that mid-August Sunday. Two ragged pre-season defeats had obviously come home to haunt coaches and players alike, but for the moment missed signals, poor pass rushes and wayward offensive plans remained things that could still be corrected.

The dislocated shoulder of seven-year veteran safety Randy Hughes obviously couldn't.

With just over a minute remaining in the previous evening's 33-21 loss to the Los Angeles Rams, Hughes tried to arm tackle an obscure rookie running back named Jairo Penaranda and dislocated his right shoulder — again. He failed to make the tackle on what would be his final play in football.

Walking to the sidelines under his own power, Hughes threw his helmet to the ground, gave team doctor Pat Evans an affirmative nod, and headed toward the dressing room. He would need no doctor to tell him the extent of the damage. "I knew immediately," he remembers. "By that time I had gotten to know the ropes of that sort of thing pretty well."

Indeed, he would find himself discussing surgery on the shoulder for the third time in just over 12 months.

Thus ended a career which always held great promise that was, in the mind of Hughes, never fully delivered. Most of his days as a pro were spent in the shadow of Cowboys safeties Cliff Harris and Charlie Waters. Throughout the NFL, Hughes was judged "the best backup safety" playing. For the athlete who was once named the Most Outstanding Prep Player in Oklahoma, who earned consensus All-America honors while playing on two unbeaten Univer-

sity of Oklahoma teams, it was never enough.

He was forced from the game before his goals were ever reached.

"All in all," he says, "pro football was pretty frustrating for me. I didn't accomplish the things I had hoped to. I did everything I could to prepare myself for the opportunity that was there, but things never really worked out. I've always been a goal-oriented person and hoped to achieve certain honors, to play in the Pro Bowl, for instance, but things didn't happen that way.

"There comes a point when you have to accept some things. I thought I could get that shoulder well and make a run at some of my goals. Cliff had retired and the free safety job was mine. I was looking forward to that last season, but the shoulder didn't hold up. It was that simple. As soon as I hurt it that last time I knew that it was time to begin focusing my thoughts and energies on something else. It's been a change, but I think I've adjusted pretty well. It's never easy to quit something after you've been doing it for 20 years."

Perhaps the most frustrating part of looking back is in the knowledge that he came so close. So often.

In his second year in the league he started eight straight games — six exhibitions and two in regular season — while Cliff Harris was sidelined with an injury. He strongly felt he had performed well enough to hold the job once Harris returned to good health. But when Cliff became available, Hughes returned to the bench.

"That really hurt," he says, "because I didn't feel I'd played myself out of the position. I just didn't understand how they could do that to me. It was very depressing.

"About my third year in the league my attitude got really bad. Oh, I worked hard, probably harder than anyone on the team, and kept up with what was going on. But I had no real goals, no real purpose. It was an empty feeling."

Even in his finest moment there would be a measure of disappointment. As Dallas dominated the Denver Broncos in Super Bowl XII, Hughes, playing only when the Cowboys went into their 4-0 defense, picked off a pass and recovered two fumbles in the first half of play. By game's end he felt strongly about his chances of being named the game's Most Valuable Player. The award, instead, was shared by teammates Harvey Martin and Randy White.

"To be very honest," he says, "that kind of dampened the victory for me. During the game I remember thinking I might have a shot at the award. I had three turnovers, six or seven tackles, and broke up a couple of passes. At the time, I really couldn't think of anyone who had had a really great game the way quarterbacks or running backs usually do. I made the mistake of letting my hopes get too high. That's not to take anything away from Harvey or Randy, mind you. They were outstanding that day. And it was a great thrill just to be a part of the team that won the Super Bowl. But the MVP award is quite an honor and I felt sick having missed out on it."

In 1979 Hughes finally got his long-awaited chance to be a part of the starting lineup when strong safety Charlie Waters was injured during the pre-season. Though he was, in a sense, winning the position by default, Hughes made the most of the opportunity.

"It was great to be so involved in what was going on," he says. "That year I really felt a part of the team and felt more accepted by the other players because I was contributing. I even began to feel that I was moving into something of a leadership position. I felt I played well that year, well enough to have been in the Pro Bowl. But that didn't work out, either.

"Looking back, I'd have to say the whole experience of pro football helped me as a person. It taught me a lot about life. I'm a Christian and I guess it was God's way of teaching me how to accept things. That's not a cop-out; it's the way I feel."

Still, even as he enjoys success as a Dallas-based home builder, there are times when Randy Hughes must wonder what might have been.

⭐ EPILOGUE ⭐

This collection of reflections has provided you with a different view of the colorful history of the Dallas Cowboys. Tracing the team's conquest through the years, it is history as told from the viewpoint of those who played roles — some major, others less so — in its making.

Throughout the story, however, there has clearly been a central figure, often praised, occasionally criticized, and more than once misunderstood. The man most immediately identified with the growth and success of the franchise is Thomas Wade Landry. It has become one of sport's worn clichés to identify him as "the only coach the Cowboys have ever had." Cliché or not, it is a distinction which makes him one of the most unique figures in the game today.

His revolutionary contributions to the game have been duly recorded and his successes properly charted. Yet in the discussion of his achievements as a coach, another side of his athletic history is often overlooked. You see, Tom Landry was making his imprint on the game long before Dallas was ever awarded an NFL franchise, long before there were Super Bowl championships to celebrate.

Tom Landry, the player, also made his mark . . .

The All-America Conference, wearied on its getting-nowhere battle with the more established National Football League, had finally thrown in the towel, agreeing to a merger which allowed teams in Cleveland, San Francisco and Baltimore to continue as a part of the NFL family.

The fate of the New York Yankees, however, was not as happy. Following that 1949 campaign, the team disbanded and six of their players were picked up by their struggling neighbor, the New York Giants. Among those whose professional football careers continued in the NFL was a lanky all-purpose youngster from the University of Texas. As a rookie with the Yankees in '49, Tom Landry had been more useful as a punter but had seen some action as an offensive halfback and defensive safety.

"I have to believe the main reason the Giants picked me up," he reflects, "was because of my punting. With the Yanks I had hardly distinguished myself in any other area. But, when I got to the Giants they began to look at me as a defensive back. Actually, I was more like what we call a cornerback today."

After establishing himself as a regular member of the Giants secondary in 1950, he went on to earn All-Pro recognition in 1954, played in the Pro Bowl the following year and served as a player-coach and then full-time assistant

during some of the greatest moments in the team's history.

He also played an important part in helping New York prepare for the 1958 sudden death championship battle with the Baltimore Colts, the game still referred to by many as the greatest game ever played and the single contest which brought the game of pro football to the nation's attention. "I'll never forget that one," Landry says. "I don't think anyone who was involved in it will."

But he was a non-playing coach by then. What of the days when he was still an active player?

There is little hesitation. Landry's memory is as sharp and crisp as his play selections: October 22, 1950. New York versus Cleveland. "The Browns were an outstanding team in the All-America Conference," Landry recalls, "and were obviously going to be an immediate powerhouse in the NFL with people like Otto Graham, Marion Motley and Lou Groza. We played them early in the season and defeated them, 6-0."

It was noteworthy enough that it had marked the first time in 62 games that the Browns had been held scoreless. The big news, however, was the unique defensive alignment the Giants had used to accomplish the stunning upset. On that day the famed "umbrella defense" was born.

Steve Owen, the fabled Giants coach, and his chief scout, Jack Lavelle, had watched the Browns defeat Philadelphia a week earlier and set to work constructing a defense which might slow the powerful, lethal offense of coach Paul Brown's club. What they came up with was a 6-1-2-2 alignment which had the defensive ends dropping off for pass coverage rather than rush the passer. It gave the Giants, then, seven defenders with which to cover the speed-blessed Browns receivers. Cleveland was baffled. By halftime, quarterback Graham had yet to complete his first pass.

Meanwhile, the Giants had driven 52 yards in the opening quarter to score with fullback Eddie Price doing the honors from two yards out. The extra point try failed, but the Giants had all the points they would need.

Following some intermission adjustments, Cleveland was able to move the ball in the second half as Graham solved the "umbrella" well enough to complete 12 passes. The Browns, in fact, threatened to score, advancing to the New York 10-yard line. But on a second down trap play Motley collided with Graham and fumbled the ball away to the Giants. And by day's end, New York's Otto Schnellbacher had set a club record, picking off three Cleveland passes (his record would later be equalled by Landry in a 1954 game against Philadelphia). In a bit of irony which neither Paul Brown nor Graham could fully appreciate, the three new members of the New York secondary — Landry, Schnellbacher and Harmon Rowe — had come to the Giants from the old Yankees.

"I think," Landry says, "that the manner in which we prepared for that game, putting in the new defense, is a good indication of how things have changed over the years. Coach Owen got up at our weekly team meeting and simply told us we were going to run a six-man line against the Browns. 'What we're going to do,' he said, 'is drop the ends into the flat on one play, drop them into the hook zone on the next, and rush them the next. That will give us better pass protection and also confuse the Cleveland offense.'

"That was it. No elaborate diagramming, no lengthy discussion of situations and tactics. It was, to Coach Owen, a very simple plan designed to confuse Paul Brown and the Cleveland offense. And it worked."

Both ways. "We," says Landry, "were every bit as confused as the Browns. It was obvious that Otto couldn't figure out what was going on. But, neither could I. We were just having to kind of play it by ear and make whatever adjustments we thought were necessary as the game went along. We would huddle before each play and talk about what the ends should do next — and what kind of coverage the secondary should be in. Looking back, I guess that might be the day my coaching career began because, as I recall, I was making quite a few suggestions during the time between plays.

"That's not to say, however, that I had any kind of commanding knowledge of what we were doing. Truthfully, I was just looking for some way to get through the next play without some disaster taking place. In fact, in the second half when Otto did finally begin completing some of his passes, several of them were in my area of responsibility. But when it was all over and we had been successful it was a great feeling."

The Giants defeated Cleveland again later in the year, 17-13, and went on to share the conference title with a 10-2 record, forcing a playoff. In a game played in 10-degree weather, the Browns won a berth in the world championship game in their first year in the league, defeating the defensive-minded Giants, 8-3.

"It was difficult to get so close, to get into that playoff with the championship game up for grabs, and then lose," he reflects. "But, in this game, you learn to deal with things like that; to just go back to work and try to do better the next time you get the opportunity."

It is a philosophy he carried with him into his coaching career, one which fueled his own journey to triumph.